By Reason of Insanity

Essays on Psychiatry and the Law

By Reason of Insanity
Essays on Psychiatry and the Law

Edited by
Lawrence Zelic Freedman

SR *Scholarly Resources Inc.*
Wilmington, Delaware

PUBLISHER'S NOTE

Extensive research has been done regarding the proper spelling of Daniel McNaughtan. The issue has received considerable attention, and more than ten different variations of his last name have appeared over time. Richard Moran in his book *Knowing Right from Wrong: The Insanity Defense of Daniel McNaughtan* (Free Press, 1981) has supplied conclusive evidence of the actual spelling, "McNaughtan," which we have adopted for our use in this volume.

© 1983 by Lawrence Zelic Freedman
All rights reserved
First published 1983
Printed and bound in the United States of America

Scholarly Resources Inc.
104 Greenhill Avenue
Wilmington, Delaware 19805

Library of Congress Cataloging in Publication Data
Main entry under title:

By reason of insanity.

   Includes bibliographical references and index.
   1. Insanity—Jurisprudence—United States—Addresses,
essays, lectures. 2. Forensic psychiatry—United States—
Addresses, essays, lectures. I. Freedman, Lawrence Zelic.
1919–   [DNLM: 1. Forensic psychiatry. W 740
B993]
KF9242.A5.B9   1983   345.73'04   83-3314
ISBN 0-8420-2203-1   347.3054

CONTENTS

CONTRIBUTORS

GEORGE ANASTAPLO is a visiting professor of law at Loyola University in Chicago. His publications include *The Constitutionalist: Notes on the First Amendment* (1971), *Human Being and Citizen: Essays on Virtue, Freedom and the Common Good* (1975), and *The Artist as Thinker: From Shakespeare to Joyce* (forthcoming).

RICHARD ARENS is professor of law at the University of Bridgeport Law School. Included among his works are the publications *In Defense of Public Order* (1961), *Insanity Defense* (1974), and as editor/contributor, *Genocide in Paraguay* (1976). He is currently president of Survival International.

WILLIAM K. CARROLL is a lawyer and psychologist. He received the J.D. degree from Northwestern University School of Law and his Ph.D. from the University of Strasbourg, France. Presently he is professor of law at the John Marshall Law School in Chicago and serves as legal reporter and draftsman for the American Bar Association Task Force on Standards for the Criminal Responsibility of the Mentally Disabled. As a trial lawyer in the federal court system, he has had substantial experience representing mentally disturbed defendants.

GEORGE H. DESSION was a Lines Professor of Criminal Law at Yale University, a cofounder of the Yale Study Unit on Psychiatry and Law, and a member of the Criminal Law Advisory Committee of the American Law Institute in the making of the Model Penal Code. Dession was a permanent delegate to the United Nations and a consultant to the U.N. Economic and Social Council. He was the author of classical texts in criminal law.

SIMON DINITZ is professor of sociology at Ohio State University and senior fellow at the Academy for Contemporary Problems. He is a former president of the American Society of Criminology, former editor of its journal, and a recipient of the society's Edwin Sutherland Award.

LAWRENCE ZELIC FREEDMAN is chairman of the Institute of Social and Behavioral Pathology and Foundations' Fund Research Professor of Psychiatry at the University of Chicago. He was a consultant to the American Law Institute in the making of the Model Penal Code, a permanent delegate to the United Nations, and a consultant to the U.N. Economic and Social Council. Dr. Freedman has researched extensively and has published widely in the fields of aggression and political violence.

vii

MANFRED GUTTMACHER was the chief medical officer of the Supreme Bench of Baltimore. He was one of the Isaac Ray lecturers and a distinguished pioneer in the field of psychiatry and law. The American Psychiatric Association has established a Manfred Guttmacher Award in his honor.

JOEL F. HENNING is a lawyer and writer. He consults with major law firms and corporate legal departments on lawyer training and publishes the *CLE Reporter*. He is president of EnDispute of Chicago, an alternative dispute resolution service, and a trustee of the ACLU of Illinois and of Columbia College of Chicago.

HAROLD D. LASSWELL was Ford Foundation Professor Emeritus of the Political Sciences, Yale University. His concern for the integration of knowledge with action led to the coinage of the term, "policy sciences." He performed research and analysis in such fields as political science (particularly law and jurisprudence), philosophy, psychiatry, psychology, sociology, anthropology, economics, and communication. He was the president of the American Political Science Association, and cofounder and cochairman of the Institute of Social and Behavioral Pathology.

NORVAL MORRIS is the Julius Kreeger Professor of Law and Criminology at the University of Chicago. His most recent book is *Madness and the Criminal Law* (University of Chicago Press, 1982).

WINFRED OVERHOLSER was the superintendent at St. Elizabeth's Hospital in Washington, DC, and former president of the American Psychiatric Association. Dr. Overholser was a consultant to the American Law Institute in the making of the Model Penal Code and received the Isaac Ray Award from the American Psychiatric Association. He was the author of major textbooks in psychiatry.

JACQUES M. QUEN is clinical professor of psychiatry and associate director of the Section on the History of Psychiatry and the Behavioral Sciences, Department of Psychiatry, New York Hospital, Cornell Medical Center.

ALAN A. STONE is the Touroff-Glueck Professor of Law and Psychiatry in the Faculty of Law and the Faculty of Medicine at Harvard University. He is also past president of the American Psychiatric Association, past chair of the American Psychiatric Association's Commission on Judicial Action, and present chair of the American Psychiatric Association's Council on Governmental Policy and Law. Dr. Stone has received both the Manfred Guttmacher and the Isaac Ray awards.

INTRODUCTION

President Ronald Reagan was shot and wounded by John W. Hinckley, Jr., on 30 March 1981. Press Secretary James Brady, a Secret Service guard, and a District of Columbia policeman were also wounded. Within moments the radio broadcast the news to the nation, and television reenacted the terrible scene. Magazines, newspapers, radio, and television reflected the nation's mood: Are we a sick people? Are we a violent society? For many, the answer emerged from the ever-rising crime of the cities, the after-dark fears of most Americans in their own neighborhoods, and from this assault on the president.

The four presidential assassins have been men whose personalities, motives, and attacks have frightened and angered the citizens of this country because of the symbolic nature of the presidency, a cynosure in a democratic society. The anxiety engendered by widespread assaultive and predatory crimes against persons has become fused, in fear, with attacks on the president, but such assaults differ significantly from predatory crime.

Presidential assassins are not common criminals. John Wilkes Booth, a southern sympathizer, assassinated Abraham Lincoln in 1865. A moderately successful actor, Booth was a psychologically marginal man. He was born a bastard; his father, a talented English immigrant actor, suffered from intermittent attacks of insane impulsivity. Booth was also the younger brother of Edwin Booth, hailed as the leading actor of his time. In 1881, James A. Garfield was killed by Charles Guiteau, an itinerant lawyer and evangelist, a scion from a "good family," who had lived six years in the Christian-communitarian society of Oneida. He was as miserable there as he had been in the larger world and later injected himself into politics, unjustifiably seeking a consular post. In 1901, Leon Czolgosz killed William McKinley. Czolgosz, a laborer who, in the last three years of his life, had become a paranoid recluse, killed for his faith in anarchism, but the anarchists of his time not only refused to accept him but also warned against him as an *agent provocateur*. The last presidential assassination was in 1962, when Lee Harvey Oswald shot John F. Kennedy. Oswald, born two months after the death of his father, had grown up uncertain, truculent, and despairing. Living in the Soviet Union, Oswald, like Guiteau, had experimented with another system of social and political organization. He, too, found that his private miseries persisted there as well and returned to the United States.[1]

Each American presidential assassin politicized his private misery. Each

---

[1]Guiteau and Czolgosz were tried under the McNaughtan formula, as Oswald would have been in Texas had he lived to stand trial and had he pleaded not guilty by reason of insanity.

appears to have had a combination of personality traits that distinguished him not only from the law-abiding but also from murderers whose motives were personal or predatory. In awesome confrontations, four anonymous, powerless, unhappy men struck down the most powerful political figure in the United States in an attempt to meet their personal needs.[2]

Hinckley appears to have a similar personality, and during his trial, the jury had to determine his mental state at the time of the assault. The jury, instructed by the judge, had to decide whether Hinckley was guilty of assault with intent to murder or not guilty by reason of insanity. If it concluded that, as "the result of mental disease or defect" Hinckley had "either lacked substantial capacity to conform his conduct to the requirements of the law, or . . . to appreciate the wrongfulness of his conduct," he would have to be held neither culpable nor punishable.[3]

The prosecution psychiatrist testified that Hinckley could conform his behavior to the law and appreciate the wrongfulness of his actions. Defense psychiatrists expressed a contrary view. The twelve members of the jury and concerned millions were puzzled and skeptical. Prestigious experts responded to the legal questions with answers that contradicted each other. How scientific could the mental health field be if its clinicians arrived at opposite conclusions from the same set of facts?

The concern over the differences in response by mental health experts to legally phrased questions reflects popular misunderstanding of psychiatric expertise. The study of human behavior, intelligence, feelings, and perceptions is in an earlier stage of development than many other sciences and clinical specialties. The issues are complex; certainty is difficult to attain. Determining Hinckley's mental condition during his attack on the president required the assessment of the signs and symptoms of his mental state and of their intensity as well. Direct examinations were conducted after the event. These were supplemented by the evaluation of writings such as letters and diaries and by hearing and reading descriptions made by other people. With such serious constraints, even conscientious experts differed.

---

[2]See Lawrence Zelic Freedman, "Assassins of the Presidents of the United States: Their Motives and Personality Traits," *Assassination and Political Violence: Report to the National Commission on the Causes and Prevention of Violence*, J. F. Kirkham, S. G. Levy, and W. J. Crotty, eds. (Washington: Government Printing Office, 1969), pp. 49–73; "Assassination: Psychopathology and Social Pathology," *Postgraduate Medicine* 37, no. 6 (June 1965): 650–58; "Profile of an Assassin," *Police* 10, no. 4 (March–April 1966): 26–30; "Psychopathology of the Assassin," in *Assassinations and the Political Order*, ed. W. Crotty (New York: Harper & Row, 1972), pp. 143–60; "Assassination: Psychopathology and Social Pathology," in *Social Structure and Assassination Behavior*, ed. D. W. Wilkinson (Cambridge, MA: Schenkman Publishing, 1976), pp. 96–107; "Assassins and Terrorists," *Today in Psychiatry* 5, no. 1 (January 1979): 1–4; "Are We a Sick People?" *New York Times*, 1 April 1981, p. 29; "Presidential Assassins Strike Out More at the Symbol than the Man," *Boston Sunday Globe*, 5 April 1981, p. A3; "The Assassination Syndrome," *Saturday Evening Post* 253, no. 5 (July–August 1981): 66–67, 114.

[3]The federal code for criminal responsibility.

A courtroom decision is a legal and not a clinical one. The mental health professionals are participants in a legal process. They must present their observations in language that the lay jury can understand. They are subjected to cross-examination intended to discredit their testimony and, at times, their competence and integrity. The legal formula for responsibility reflects the threshold of tolerance by the community for harmful or threatening behavior. Judicial decisions and community values that have gained the social weight of common law, and statutes, are the bases for the legal formulas for non-responsibility. They are not psychiatric in origin, function, or language. The American Law Institute formula for criminal responsibility, for example, reflected legal assessments and social judgment.[4] It was not intended to replace the decisions of judges and juries with the diagnoses of psychiatrists. This misunderstanding and the outrage aroused by Hinckley's insanity defense sprang from the requirement that the experts answer to a *legal* question, which mental health professionals are not competent to answer. When they try to do so, their social and political values must influence their responses.

The function of the jury is to try the facts of the case. The legal requirements for determining responsibility are based on the facts that are derived from evidence presented during a trial according to established legal procedure. In Hinckley's trial, the facts that the jury was instructed to determine concerned his mental state when he attacked the president. The jurors had to choose, or to discriminate between what was often conflicting testimony. This evidence led to their decision concerning Hinckley's responsibility. Psychiatrists, psychologists, and others can contribute to the jury's decision only within the limits of their competency. They can diagnose a person's state at the time of their examinations. They attempt to diagnose the defendant's state at the time of the alleged harmful act that preceded the examination. The judge instructs the jury to distinguish between these clinical opinions and the legal requirements for determining whether the defendant is responsible or not.

On 21 June 1982, Hinckley was found "not guilty by reason of insanity" of the crimes of shooting the president and three other men. The verdict indicated that the government had failed to prove to the jury, beyond a reasonable doubt, that Hinckley was sane when he had attacked the president. Almost immediately there were public protests, and popular confidence in the potential contributions of psychology and psychiatry to the criminal justice process reached a low point. As a consequence of the contradictory opinions voiced by the mental health experts for the defense and the prosecution, the insanity defense was called "insane" and the Hinckley verdict declared to be "mad."[5] The fields of psychology and psychiatry seemingly were without

---

[4]Lawrence Zelic Freedman, "A Psychosocial Analysis of the Making of the Model Penal Code," in *Crime, Law and Corrections*, ed. Ralph Slovenko (Springfield, IL: Charles C. Thomas, 1966), pp. 213–31.

[5]See, for example, "It's a Mad, Mad Verdict," *The New Republic* 187, no. 2 (12 July 1982): 13–16.

standards or a unified body of knowledge, a condition that allowed their practitioners the widest range of arbitrary opinions; they were useless in the serious and responsible business of conducting the criminal justice system.

Following the Hinckley verdict, twenty-four bills to abolish or amend the insanity plea in federal cases were brought before the U.S. Congress.[6] Powerfully supported senatorial initiatives suggested an additional verdict in criminal cases of "guilty but mentally ill," which three states (Illinois, Indiana, and Michigan) already had adopted. State legislatures also moved swiftly toward substantial modifications. The American Bar Association, which had adopted the criteria of nonresponsibility of the Model Penal Code of the American Law Institute, began reconsidering its position after the assassination attempt and Hinckley's trial.[7] The alternatives that it considered ranged from the abolition of the insanity defense to sharp limitations of exculpatory criteria.

In order to understand the origins of this debate, it is necessary to go back to the middle of the last century. The McNaughtan case of 1843 and the resulting legal formula for legal responsibility has dominated English and American criminal trials. Daniel McNaughtan killed Edward Drummond, the private secretary to Prime Minister Robert Peel, under the delusion that Peel's party, the Tories, had been persecuting him. McNaughtan was found "not guilty by reason of insanity." There had been several previous attacks on Queen Victoria as well as on her prime ministers, and assaults not resulting in death or injury of the intended victim were likely to effect a verdict of "not guilty by reason of insanity." Successful assassins, however, had been found guilty and executed.[8] The outrage of the public, Queen Victoria, and her prince consort after the McNaughtan verdict led to the request that the insanity defense be clarified by the law lords. The lords replied:

> To establish a defense of insanity, it must be proved that at the time of committing the act the party accused was laboring under such a defect of reason from disease of the mind, as not to know the nature and quality of the act he was doing, or if he did know it, that he did not know that he was doing what was wrong.[9]

The McNaughtan rule became the judicial precedent for statutory law of

---

[6]Richard P. Lynch, American Bar Association Standing Committee on Association Standards for Criminal Justice, *Memo to Members, Task Force on Nonresponsibility for Crime*, 28 September 1982, p. 2.

[7]*Model Penal Code*, American Law Institute (Philadelphia, 1962), p. 401.

[8]For example, John Bellingham, who shot and killed Prime Minister Sir Spencer Percival on 11 May 1812, was tried and executed within one week, but James Hadfield, who attacked George III in 1800, and Edward Oxford, who attempted to assassinate Queen Victoria and Prince Albert in 1840, were both acquitted by reason of insanity. Similarly in the United States, Guiteau and Czolgosz were executed, but Richard Lawrence, who attacked Andrew Jackson in 1835, and John Schrank, who attacked Theodore Roosevelt in 1912, were found not guilty by reason of insanity.

[9]Daniel M'Naghten's Case, 8 Eng. Rep. 721 (1843).

twenty-nine states and of all federal jurisdictions, and it served as the basis of numerous judicial decisions.

————

Beginning in the mid-twentieth century, there was an expansion of the criteria for nonresponsibility for crime. It sprang from the powerful currents of the movement toward liberalism and humanism and produced a vigorous debate, reflected in the articles in Part 1.

In 1954, Dession, a lawyer, Lasswell, a political scientist, and Freedman, a psychiatrist, participated in a symposium[10] that Robitscher has referred to as a precursor to the modern development of the interface of psychiatry and law.[11] Grappling with the dynamic flux of social demands for conformity and individually expressive nonconformity from the perspectives of law, policy science, and psychiatry, they agreed that the cognitions and perceptions of their fields shared common problems that could be appropriately responded to by the interaction of their respective disciplines.

Dession discussed the impact of deviation on those within the community who were empowered to make decisions concerning appropriate sanctions, whether positive or negative. He emphasized the influence of their own experience of events on their judgment concerning the outcome of their sanctions or probable effect on future events and speculated on the roles of psychiatry and law in the infliction of negative sanctions in the name of the community. Dession postulated four preferred values of public order, stated as principles: equality, which places primary value on the individual and holds that no prescription or negative sanction should be favored for the establishing or reinforcing of institutional patterns unless it facilitates full self-realization of all individuals; economy, which holds that punishment is never a good in itself; democracy, which requires that the power of decision in sanctioning should be as widely shared as possible; and the humanitarian principle, which claims that those who benefit by the sanction should be the largest possible identification unit or group consistent with freedom. The psychiatrist's concern for his patient's welfare may clash with the community's concern with danger to its security. The pursuit of just goals is endangered when preventive sanctions are based on predictions of future socially harmful behavior. Practices that may be helpful in therapy may be harmful as socially imposed negative sanctioning.

Lasswell suggested that psychiatrists contribute to the classification of

————

[10]George H. Dession, Harold D. Lasswell, and Lawrence Z. Freedman, "Law, Conformity, and Psychiatry: A Symposium" (New Haven: Yale Study Unit in Psychiatry and Law, Yale University, 1955); also published as separate essays in *Psychiatry and the Law*, Paul H. Hoch and Joseph Zubin, eds. (New York: Grune & Stratton, 1955), pp. 1–53. Reprinted in Part I of this volume.

[11]Jonas Robitscher, *The Powers of Psychiatry* (Boston: Houghton Mifflin, 1980), pp. 100–02.

goal values and institutional objectives in legislation by possibly anticipating the psychological impact of suggested changes in social policy. Their empirical ·data could provide a corrective to idealized versions of social behavior. Psychiatric pragmatism might differentiate between community-imposed stresses that promote either psychopathology or psychological health. Popular outbursts of hostility may create an environment in which the legislators introduce the most absolute bills with drastic negative sanctioning.[12] The psychiatrist could explore the motives for such extreme legislation. Clinical and behavioral science findings might assess psychological predispositions as well as help to estimate, anticipate, and appraise enforcement policy. Case studies by psychiatrists also could provide both substantive data and paradigms to aid legislators in the self-surveying and social-prediction process.

Freedman discussed the underlying phenomenon of the difference between the nonconforming, or deviant, individual and his society. He suggested possible psychiatric contributions to administrative and legislative aspects of government but also emphasized the limitations of clinical contributions to understanding social process. Psychiatrists must be cautious in projecting into the social environment insights gained in the course of treating individuals. They must be conservative in their assessment of the clinician's ability to predict future behavior, even of individuals. In his zeal to be scientific in theory and method, the psychiatrist must subject himself to relentless self-scrutiny lest he unwittingly substitute his own personal and social values for the scientific objectives to which he aspires.

In 1954 the Committee on Psychiatry and the Law of the Group for the Advancement of Psychiatry issued a report urging that criteria for criminal responsibility and psychiatric testimony be changed.[13] It described the limitations that psychiatrists and several of their legal consultants believed were implicit in the McNaughtan formulation, whose criteria were cognitive. However, as Maudsley pointed out in the mid-nineteenth century, powerful conscious and unconscious feelings were barred by such criteria.[14] Even if he is aware of the wrongfulness of the act and wishes to avoid it, a person might nevertheless be unable to restrain himself. He acts harmfully, irresistibly impelled by forces within him that he cannot control. In several states an exculpatory role was given to the so-called "irresistible impulse." However, this defense rarely has been successfully invoked.

The report on the Committee on Psychiatry and the Law also evaluated the competence and the limitations of the psychiatrist as an expert witness:

---

[12]A striking example is the torrent of proposed legislation to restrict or eliminate the insanity defense following Hinckley's acquittal.

[13]Committee on Psychiatry and the Law of the Group for the Advancement of Psychiatry, "Criminal Responsibility and Psychiatric Expert Testimony," GAP Report #26 (Topeka, KS, 1954). Reprinted in Part I of this volume.

[14]Sir Henry Maudsley, *Responsibility in Mental Disease* (1874; reprint ed., New York: D. Appleton & Co., 1897).

1) The psychiatrist can predict behavior statistically and determine, with fair accuracy, the classes of undeterrable persons. He can predict the tendency of behavior in the individual and, with fair accuracy, determine his deterrability. 2) He can, with fair accuracy, determine the degree of disorder of the accused relating to the mental state of the accused as it is relevant to his capacity to appreciate the significance of the charge and to cooperate in the preparation of his defense, and the causal connection of the mental state and the act charged. 3) He can make advisory recommendations for suitable disposition of the convicted. The committee pointed out that it was unable to fit any "scientifically validated entity of psychopathology into present legal formulae of insanity" and that the psychiatrist was unable to "determine degrees of legal responsibility calibrated to mental degrees of psychopathology." The report recommended that the psychiatric expert be freed from the necessity of testifying in terms of moral judgment.

Beginning in the mid-1950s, a series of legal developments altered slightly the rules by which responsibility was determined. In 1954 the appellate court in Washington, DC, held in the case of *Monte Durham*, that a man should not be made responsible for an otherwise criminal act when his behavior was the "product of mental disease or deficiency." The *Durham* decision was a judicial reaction to the limitations of the previous legal tests for criminal responsibility.[15] In 1962 the American Law Institute included a formula for legal responsibility in its Model Penal Code, which was prepared by leading American scholars and legal authorities. This would free from responsibility anyone who, because of mental defect or deficiency, had been incapable of appreciating the criminality of his act, or, if he had appreciated its criminality, nevertheless had been unable to control his behavior.[16] However, repetition of harmful antisocial behavior would not by itself free a defendant from responsibility for his crime. The repetitive criminal was then called the psychopathic personality, now known as the antisocial personality. The *Currens* decision[17] freed from responsibility those who were unable to control their behavior, and made that inability the crucial distinguishing factor rather than perceptual, intellectual, or emotional traits.

The decision in *Gorshen* v. *California*[18] resembled the centuries-old partial responsibility clause of the Scots. Mental disability might serve as a mitigating circumstance, affecting the nature and duration of disposition, whether penal incarceration or therapeutic treatment as an outpatient or inpatient. California had two separate trials in criminal cases where the question of mental illness was raised. The first trial sought to ascertain whether the accused person carried out the illegal act. If so, the second trial sought

---

[15]Durham v. United States, 214 F.2d 862 (D.C. Cir. 1954).

[16]*Model Penal Code*, American Law Institute (Philadelphia, 1962), p. 401.

[17]United States v. Currens, 290 F.2d 751, 775 (3d Cir. 1961).

[18]People v. Gorshen, 51 Cal. 2d 716, 336 P.2d 492 (1959).

to determine how his state of mind at the time related to the legal criteria for responsibility. This has since been repealed.

These variations in legal procedures affect, however, only a small fraction of the criminally accused. Federal jurisdictions and most states have followed the legislative example of the Model Penal Code. The impact of the *Durham* and *Gorshen* decisions had been mainly confined to the jurisdictions of the courts that pronounced them. By and large, until 1962 the question of criminal responsibility remained approximately where it was when promulgated by the law lords in the wake of McNaughtan. But coming as they did within a single decade, these defections from the McNaughtan formula reflected widespread dissatisfaction and seemed to presage a legal consensus certain to be more harmoniously adapted to contemporary social values and social sciences than the answer given by the English lords.

This period was a hopeful one, perhaps naive. It widened the range of testimony concerning mental disability allowed in the courtroom so as to be more responsive to the new knowledge of mental health professionals. It also provoked a strong reaction. In 1963, Szasz maintained that there is no such thing as mental illness, and he argued that everyone should be held responsible, that is, punishable for their illegal behavior.[19] In the same year, Wooten urged that criminal law discard the notion of *mens rea*,[20] and Goldstein and Katz proposed the abolition of the insanity defense.[21] And in 1966, Roche made a plea for the abandonment of the insanity defense.[22] Although their rationales varied widely, their recommendations foreshadowed contemporary changes in popular and professional views.[23]

The essays published in Part II of this volume were presented at a symposium held on 12–13 October 1979 entitled "Psychiatry and the Law: Reaching for a Consensus," sponsored by the Institute of Social and Behavioral Pathology at the University of Chicago. As anticipated, our reach exceeded our grasp. No consensus was achieved, nor should any have been anticipated. However, these essays are thoughtful, sometimes provocative, analyses of a contemporary dilemma. In the western democracies there exists no consensus establishing the legal threshold of toleration for harmful behavior inflicted by

---

[19]Thomas S. Szasz, *Law, Liberty and Psychiatry: An Inquiry into the Social Uses of Mental Health Practices* (New York: Macmillan, 1963).

[20]Barbara S. Wooten, *Crime and Criminal Law* (London: Stevens & Sons, 1963).

[21]Joseph Goldstein and Jay Katz, "Abolish the 'Insanity Defense?' Why Not?" *Yale Law Journal* 72 (1963): 852–72.

[22]Philip Q. Roche, "A Plea for the Abandonment of the Insanity Defense," in *Crime, Law and Corrections,* ed. Ralph Slovenko (Springfield, IL: Charles C. Thomas, 1966), pp. 146–64.

[23]In 1967, however, Abraham S. Goldstein published a powerful defense of the McNaughtan formula in *The Insanity Defense* (New Haven: Yale University Press, 1967).

persons with impaired intellectual and emotional states. These papers reflect the public policy debate, ranging from classical concern for the welfare of the polis to contemporary preoccupation with the vulnerability of the community. Within this spectrum fall essays that modulate the delicate balance between the need to defend the structure of society and the moral imperative to protect the psychiatrically disabled.

Quen treats the question of responsibility historically, and while doing so, has illuminated the contextual problems of law and medicine as well as the political, social, and economic value systems in which evolution has occurred. He reviews the history of the insanity defense in Anglo-American law. Insanity was originally a medical and not a legal term and describes several modern diagnostic categories. During the nineteenth century the word insanity was applied to "idiocy, senility, mania, melancholy, alcoholism, compulsive theft, and compulsive firesetting." Perhaps, considering its origins, a contemporary definition is unattainable. More importantly, considering its purported legal role, a legal definition is impossible. The McNaughtan jurists had used the precedents and knowledge of law. Hale and Blackstone discussed legal concepts of the psychological capabilities and thus competencies of minors at different ages for legal purposes.[24] Medicine had no direct part in this development until 1843, when physicians played a key function in the McNaughtan trial. That medical intervention initiated the debate concerning the appropriate role of the medical and mental health expert in determining responsibility for an alleged criminal act.

Anastaplo bases his reaction to psychiatric intervention in criminal trials on the Aristotelian argument that both the polis—the community—and man are by nature a unity: "the polis is among those things that are by nature and . . . man is by nature a political animal." Aristotle emphasized the centrality of man's relationship to his community. "A man who is no part of a polis," he wrote, "is either a beast or a god." Anastaplo believes that psychiatry favors those who endanger the decent opinions about good and bad within the community. Psychiatry, unlike medicine, developed at a time when "Nature was under a cloud." Politics is the master art and psychiatry must be subordinate to a decent political order. He decries the modern intellectuals, including psychiatrists, who depreciate nature and misconstrue natural right, and urges a return to the rationality of pre-Enlightenment and classical philosophy. To Anastaplo, Ibsen is the paradigmatic example of modern denigration of the community in favor of personal license.

Morris argues for the abolition of the insanity defense. He distinguishes four areas of concern: triability, responsibility, punishability, and treatability. The consideration of blameworthiness complicates and confuses these issues

---

[24]Matthew Hale, *The History of the Pleas of the Crown* (London: E. R. Nutt and R. Gosling, 1736), pp. 40–46; William Blackstone, *Commentaries on the Laws of England* (Oxford: Clarendon Press, 1765–69), 4: 20–26.

when the moral power of the state acts to punish a person who is, in "common" justice, not to blame because of psychological incapacity or pathology.

Carroll examines the range of proposals from those that would eliminate mental disease or defect as relevant to the determination of guilt to those that suggest that the law might rather define more closely the scope of knowledge or intent necessary to sustain a plea of insanity, restricting it to a specific conscious state in a severely delusional person. Another approach would be to limit the criteria to a defendant's lack of knowledge or intent required for the statutorily defined offense. Finally, *mens rea* may be interpreted as a moral category. In other words, was the defendant capable of such evil disposition that he may be held justly responsible and blameworthy for harmful behavior? In emphasizing the importance of moral blameworthiness, Carroll differs from Morris concerning the legal significance of the state of mind as an element in the crime.

The Supreme Court of the United States has held that the prosecution must prove beyond reasonable doubt every element necessary to constitute the crime charged. In the case of murder, this includes "adequate mental capacity as an implied element of the *mens rea* required to constitute the offense of murder."[25] However, Carroll distinguishes sharply between the questions of abolishing the insanity defense as a separate defense and the exclusion of evidence concerning the mental element of the offense charged. He concludes by stating that to abolish the insanity defense or prohibit evidence of mental disability raises the specter of the elimination of a mental element of true crimes and of offending a fundamental principle of justice "rooted in the traditions and conscience of our people."

Studies by Lifton and others have developed the concept of "coercive persuasion," which holds that the prolonged exposure to captors who control and manipulate the environment including food, ideas, and all sensory input may alter the will, belief, and behavior of captives.[26] Arens discusses the defense of coercive persuasion in civilian criminal trials. After the kidnapping of Patricia Hearst by the Symbionese Liberation Army, she announced that she had joined them; she later was tried for the alleged crimes in which she participated with them. Her trial reflected contemporary social and political values. Coercive persuasion may exculpate because the degree of psychopathological incapacitation may inculcate its victims with a perception

---

[25]In re Winship, 397 U.S. 358, 361 (1970); Davis v. United States, 160 U.S., 469, 491 (1895).

[26]Robert Lifton, *Thought Reform and the Psychology of Totalism* (New York: Norton, 1961); "'Thought Reform' of Western Civilians in Chinese Communist Prisons," *Psychiatry* 19 (1956): 173–95. See also Edgar Schein, I. Schneier, and C. H. Barker, *Coercive Persuasion* (New York: Norton, 1961). For a recent case see Vanessa Merton and Robert Kinscherff, "Coercive Persuasion and the 'Culpable Mind': The Court-Martial of Bobby Garwood," *The Hastings Center Report* 11, no. 3 (June 1981): 5–8.

of reality or propensity to behave consistent with the psychological conditioning to which they unwillingly had been subjected. Arens argues that the "pathological disorientation" found by the psychiatrists who examined Hearst was consistent with an insanity defense, but "its acceptance hinged exclusively upon judicial recognition of coercive persuasion as a full-fledged defense." In this, the defense was unsuccessful, and Hearst was convicted.

Henning resolves the apparent contradiction between a legal positivist or utilitarian approach, which would abolish the insanity defense, and the moral concern with blameworthiness, which requires that it be maintained. He advocates that different standards of sanity be applied to crimes of different degrees of severity and suggests that only in the more serious crimes should the question of criminal responsibility be invoked. Henning offers a rational set of alternative standards that would be graded according to the seriousness or severity of the alleged offense. The defense of mental incapacity or defect already is invoked most frequently in major crimes.

Stone deals with the legal response to the mentally ill person. Foucault, Szasz, and Laing view the patient as the victim of social and professional values. Lawyers have seen some patients as victims of diagnostic commitment and treatment procedures that violate their civil rights and deprive them of their civil liberties. Civil commitment has been justified by two overlapping principles: the government's role as the protecting parent to the afflicted individual, and its traditional role as the protector of society. Treatment facilities must be vastly improved before abuses of involuntary commitment can be remedied. Stone applauds efforts to limit the powers of the law but cautions against premature attempts at final answers. Psychiatrists must recognize the need for due process restraints, and lawyers reciprocally must recognize the need for appropriate care of the mentally ill. When therapeutic and punitive social actions are not distinguished, the moral concept of blameworthiness is eliminated as an element in criminality.

The rise in the crime rate in the United States, the apparent failure of our jails, and the inadequate reform and inept rehabilitation efforts have been accompanied by the suspicions and resentments of governmental initiatives that became especially intense from the mid-1960s to the mid-1970s. Ironically, this dynamic synergy of political reaction and radical politics resulted in a harsh reversion to simplistic dichotomies and Draconian punishments. Dinitz provides a perspective in developments in penology and criminology from the last quarter of the nineteenth century to the final decades of the twentieth century. His study required that he analyze the changing social environment in which the prisons exist. He demonstrates that the changing patterns of imprisonment reflect, and are illuminated by, the more general alterations in legal and the far wider social, political, and economic pressures and values.

Dinitz reflects on the remarkable fidelity with which the social and cultural attitudes toward trial and sentencing procedures have been paralleled by variations in our penological approaches. The progressive periods in American history have been associated with increased concern for the mentally ill offender in the courts as well as for the treatment and rehabilitation of all prison inmates. Conversely, periods of conservatism have been reflected in the courts by withholding the protection of responsibility criteria and by denial that rehabilitation is a rationale for imprisonment.

In 1982 the American Bar Association Task Force on Responsibility reassessed the responsibility formula. The task force recommended that the psychiatrist or mental health expert have a contributory, not decisive, role. The American Law Institute's responsibility formula would have been retained. The judge would have instructed the jury that the expert witness should describe his clinical evaluation of the mental health of the prisoner at the bar. He would have no other role in determining guilt or innocence. The ultimate legal question is based on assessment of the facts in the case, and the jury is the trier of facts.

As Quen states, although the term insanity came from medicine, the insanity defense originated in the law. Within the past century, mental health experts have become part of the judicial process; the consequent misunderstandings have led to mutual suspicion and disillusionment. Differences of opinion are likely to emerge when the issues require an understanding of human motive and action. They become inevitable when mental health experts are expected to respond in terms of legal, semantic formulas rather than in terms of their area of clinical and scientific competence.

———

The relationship between law and psychiatry often produces conflict. In trial, psychiatrists are asked to assess the defendant's state of mind at the time of the examination and also to assess retrospectively the state of mind of the defendant at the time of the alleged commission of the act. With these levels of complexity, there is rarely a case without ambiguities. Conflict on procedural matters reflects conflicts of sociolegal values. When values are in conflict, the inherent difficulties can never be resolved when they are debated in terms of process and procedure. Are the values those of the amelioration of social problems, the alleviation of social anxiety, professional projections of the expert, or are they the values of law confronted by those of medicine? The conflict in values may be inherent in the evolution of common law, which expresses the "common" sense of justice. Justice does not demand that every socially harmful individual be punished, even when that person does not fit the twentieth-century version of the "wild-beast" test.

The phrase "forensic psychiatry" is an old one. It connotes the rhetorical tactics of the courtroom. But the concern of psychiatry with the law is far wider, for whether he realizes it or not, every physician repeatedly deals with patients whose feelings of guilt, shame, dependence, or unresolved conflict are significantly affected by the legal environment in which they live and grow. The law's concern with the state of mind of those accused of offenses against society has preoccupied its practitioners for centuries, and there is still no final solution. It seems unlikely that there can be an ultimate resolution. Forms of human social organization are the products of cultural evolution, just as the form of human anatomy has emerged from biological evolution. Cultural evolution, of which legal codes are a part, is a never-ending process. Therefore, the role of the psychiatrist during a criminal trial may become less significant than his function in helping to prevent harmful social maladjustments.

There is no forensic psychiatry, no psychiatry of rhetoric, of law, or of debate in the courtroom. There is only the psychiatry of psychically sick or unhealthy people, a few of whom have aroused the anxiety, anger, and desire for revenge of aggregate man, who has reacted through rituals of law. There is a need for this sort of psychiatric concern. The sense of urgency does not arise from an increase in man's destructive, greedy, and polymorphous-promiscuous tendencies. This generation of human beings is not more brutal, erotic, or thieving than its predecessors. Rather, the capacity and range of the disturbed person to act beyond the boundaries of his family and community has extended to wider spheres of human impact. His biosphere is enlarged. Meanwhile, the technology of our sociosphere has increased its ability to permeate our environment and our inner selves.

There is a social contagion of delinquency as well as an epidemiology of mental illness with which physicians, psychiatrists, and social and behavioral scientists are, or ought to be, concerned. Disorganized communities and fragmented families predispose individuals to emotional distress, hatred, and violence. An environment in turmoil will reflect chaos in the inner conflicts and delinquent acts of its inhabitants. More hopeful than the psychiatrist's role in ascertaining the mental state of offenders is his potential contribution toward preventing those outward manifestations of personal conflict that may damage the life of the delinquent as well as the community in which he lives.

Words, whether wrought with marvelous elegance or crudely and awkwardly phrased, are not the final or even necessarily the prepotent determinants of how the law of responsibility operates. Empirically, the language of legal formulas for determining legal responsibility is probably less important in determining guilty responsibility than is commonly believed. The nature of the offense, the defendant's personality, the competence of the attorneys, and the emotional reaction of the jury seem to affect the outcome of criminal trials more effectively than the particular words of the responsibility formula.

For some, there has been an excessive emphasis on the topic of responsibility and criminal behavior as the point of interaction between law and psychiatry. For many, it has become an emotion-charged *idée fixe*, and for others a preoccupying moral question. For most, it leaves too little time or energy for other equally significant and quantitatively more extensive joint problems of law and psychiatry. But we cannot escape this redundant dialogue until it is resolved. When there is individualization in imprisonment, probation, and parole; when the psychiatrist becomes the diagnostician before and the therapist after the trial rather than the instrument of social arbitration during it; when deterrability by punishment and amenability to treatment are sensibly assessed in human individuals and not in hypothetical statistical entities, the problem still will not be resolved. However, we will be facing this essentially insoluble but inevitable human dilemma with our best available resources of mind, values, and methods.

Lawrence Zelic Freedman

ACKNOWLEDGMENTS

The editor wishes to acknowledge the helpful guidance of Philip G. Johnson, managing editor, and Carolyn McVeigh, project editor, of Scholarly Resources Inc., and of Sandra E. Schmidt, research associate at the Institute of Social and Behavioral Pathology. The editor also would like to express his gratitude to Mary Ann Dillon, Dr. John W. Crayton, and Sandra Schmidt for their invaluable assistance in the planning and facilitation of the conference on "Psychiatry and the Law: Reaching for a Censensus" held at the University of Chicago in 1979, from which most of the papers included in this anthology were prepared.

PART I

CRIMINAL RESPONSIBILITY AND PSYCHIATRY

[Part I in this series of essays consists of historical papers covering the period from 1950 to the publication of this book. Many of these essays were written by the editor and his colleagues, first on the Committee on Psychiatry and the Law for the Group for the Advancement of Psychiatry, then at the Yale Study Unit on Psychiatry and the Law, and finally at the Institute of Social and Behavioral Pathology.

The affiliations which were basic to the development of these ideas, essays, and public presentations were the American Law Institute, the American Psychiatric Association, the Center for the Advanced Studies of the Behavioral Sciences, and the Social Defense Sector of the Organization of the United Nations.

The essays also originated from work done in association with the American Law Institute in its preparation of the Model Penal Code, and with the American Bar Association in the Restatement of the Responsibility Formula following the attempted assassination of President Ronald Reagan.]

Criminal Responsibility and Psychiatric Expert Testimony

COMMITTEE ON PSYCHIATRY AND THE LAW*
GROUP FOR THE ADVANCEMENT OF PSYCHIATRY
(MAY 1954)

Although the McNaughtan rules have a history of over one hundred years in the American judicial system, psychiatric expert testimony in capital cases has brought little satisfaction to either the lawyer or the psychiatrist. These two professional groups, moreover, have not arrived at a common basis for criticism so the resulting discussions have been nebulous with little interchange in communication. As might be expected, the voluminous record of the contentions between them usually fails to disclose a realistic examination into the nature of the problem. However, a recent and rapidly developing knowledge of mental life now challenges traditional concepts and brings the central issue of responsibility and mental illness into sharper relief.[1]

Any attempt at a fresh approach would be hopeless except for the fact, insufficiently stressed in the tedious arguments over doctrine, that there has been a basic agreement that there are areas wherein the individual is not legally accountable for his conduct. Moreover, there is agreement that some part of the determination of responsibility should be subjected to the expert opinion of the psychiatrist as witness. In modern practice, expert psychiatric testimony is employed in every trial in which mental illness is raised as a defense. It is abundantly clear that not all individuals are accountable—even the McNaughtan rules accept this—and that the problem involves more than common sense. The psychiatrist can contribute much on the subject of behavior as it affects the legal issue of responsibility. It remains for the path to be

---

*Committee included Lawrence Zelic Freedman (chairman), Frank J. Curran, Manfred S. Guttmacher, and Philip A. Roche. Reprinted by permission of the Group for the Advancement of Psychiatry.

[1]"It is only within the last few years that psychiatry has been formally invited by legal, administrative and executive authorities to intervene in the problems of crime. It worked its way into penal and legal procedures from the outside, by modifying public opinion and by throwing light on the problems of delinquency in the course of purely medical studies, and the formal invitation comes when a generation of lawyers, prison commissioners and legislators has grown up in the intellectual tradition which social studies have created. Psychiatry, therefore, brings into its contacts with law a tradition of its own, cutting across the preconceptions of law and government which come from the pre-scientific tradition of society." Alex Comfort, *Authority and Delinquency in the Modern State* (London: Routledge and Kegan Paul, 1950), p. ix.

cleared for him to fully communicate to the court his knowledge in meaningful terms.

Attacks upon the law by psychiatrists and the defense of the legal position by lawyers have engaged a disproportionate share of our attention and exertions at the expense of significant psychological insights that can no longer be ignored. A reexamination not only of the basic premises of the criminal law but also of its actual operation is needed if lawyers and psychiatrists are to attain a better intercommunication and understanding. In assessing certain legal practices, it is proper to point out that on paper rules are one thing, but in action they are frequently something else. Thus, the manner of their employment has significant implications in the partisan group tensions of the trial.[2] In the adversary process, neither the limitations nor the actual contributions of psychiatry have been reckoned with realistically. A formidable difficulty that confronts both psychiatrist and lawyer is the simple fact that the investigator is inside instead of outside his material. One cannot investigate the inner nature of man by the same methods employed in the investigation of external nature. The study of human motivations is inextricably tied to those of the investigator, since he is himself a part of the social structure within and through which all motivations take form.

The unlawful act may be a surface manifestation of a more profound psychic disturbance, an indicator of breakdown in a system of psychic adaptive defenses erected to balance inner conflicts. In such cases, the act is not the conflict itself but a token, overdetermined compromise lived out in an attempt to attain relief from tension. This is the pattern of pathological behavior with which the psychiatrist is particularly concerned. If the psychiatrist is to discover the basis of such unlawful behavior, to understand the offender, and serve a purpose in the trial, he must go beyond the act itself and evaluate the total personality, both in its conscious and unconscious aspects. With such orientation and in such context, he should be prepared as a witness to convey his insight to the court and jury. The law, however, does not allow the psychiatrist to communicate his unique understanding of psychic realities in the trial situation. Often the mutual quest for the "whole truth" cannot get past a barrier of communication that leaves the psychiatrist talking about "mental illness" and the lawyer talking about "right and wrong."[3]

---

[2]"Of the great gap between the law in books and the law in action not even a first year law school student needs to be told; it is but an aspect of the wide gulf between precept and practice in every activity in which human beings with all their frailties have a part." Arthur T. Vanderbilt, *Men and Measures in the Law* (New York: Knopf, 1949), p. 37.

[3]The social attitude toward the psychotic stems from a source in common with the punitive attitude characterizing the community reaction to the criminal. Present-day legal procedures dealing with the psychotic represent a variant rather than a separation from the criminal process. The established commitment procedure for mentally ill persons rests upon the principle of welfare and has a therapeutic aim. The criminal procedure remains an accusatorial device. Whether the individual finds himself involved in either process, the essential effect upon his person is a disablement through legal sanction. F. N. Flaschner, "Analysis of Legal and Medical Consider-

A further extension of our knowledge of the forces of unconscious life invites a corresponding extension of its application in legal welfare to a number of persons whose antisocial behavior does not fit into the current medical description of the psychotic and who are likewise beyond the legal definition of insanity. With the increasing acceptance of psychological knowledge, a larger part of society should be exempt from mere imprisonment and at the same time removed by commitment from the opportunity for destructive behavior.[4]

As expressed in contemporary law, responsibility is regarded as a function of the intellect, of conscious volition with definable boundaries and degree. Modern psychiatry recognizes the role of the intellect but would give to the emotions and the unconscious a greater weight in the balance of forces in mental life and would assert that their boundaries and degree are not readily ascertainable. Turning again to the legal view, it seems to be premised upon the impossible notion that responsibility is something possessed by and possessing the individual. In this sense, responsibility is a materialization of guilt as determined in earlier days when a defendant was examined for the stigmata of demonism. If such were demonstrated, the defendant was guilty. Even today, as Mercier correctly observes, responsibility is "not the quality of the person who has inflicted pain, but a demand on the part of others that he shall suffer."[5] Such a frame of reference compels psychiatrists to take the social group emotional response into account. We have here the spectacle of the group versus the individual, not simply in terms of moral values but in terms of often irrational personal interactions.

In Anglo-American jurisprudence, the McNaughtan rules occupy a terminal position in a series of legal tests of responsibility first dimly developed in fourteenth-century England when insanity first became a defense to a crime.[6]

---

ations in Commitment of the Mentally Ill," *Yale Law Journal* 56 (1947): 1178–1209. In twenty-one states a trial by jury is a permissive feature of the commitment law for mentally ill persons. In Texas a jury trial is mandatory. Few commitment procedures spare the mentally ill person some stigmatization and in some six states voluntary commitment is yet to be provided.

[4]In the Middle Ages responsibility, identified with individual salvation, was attributable to everyone, animals, corpses, and to inanimate objects. Today individual behavior is no longer judged in terms of accountability to a divinity but rather in the light of biological and cultural forces. Today responsibility is generally disavowed in the small child and in certain psychotics and should be diminished in a larger intermediate group (mental defectives and neurotics) who cannot be fitted into conventional legal categories of either the sane or the insane.

[5]Charles Mercier, *Criminal Responsibility* (New York: Physicians and Surgeons Book Company, 1926), p. 41.

[6]In the early seventeenth century, Sir Edward Coke formalized the absence of felonious intent or purpose to the madman, and from such assumption that the "will is taken for the deed," enunciated that no felony or murder could be committed by a madman. It remained for Lord Hale to introduce the concept of "partial insanity" as distinguished from "total insanity," only the latter of which would negate intent. A person with mental disorder otherwise with the understanding of a fourteen-year-old child was nevertheless responsible, that is, punishable. The predecessor of the McNaughtan right-and-wrong rule was contained in Judge Tracey's so-called "wild beast" jury instructions in the Arnold case (Rex v. Arnold, 16 How. St. Tr. 695) in 1724,

The rules were formulated with reference to a specific case to define a change in the relationship between society (the crown or state) and the criminal. This change refers to the fate or disposition of a defendant, owing to something that existed within him. The rules departed from the inflexible position that for doing X the punishment was Y and ventured to examine certain aspects of the defendant's behavior to conclude that for doing X the judgment of society would not be Y but something different. For the moment, the essential point is not how this was rationalized but the fact that official attention was focused on the defendant's actions and his thoughts about them, thus extending far beyond a mere surface description of the forbidden act.

The crystallization of the right and wrong test was achieved in the reaction to the sensational Daniel McNaughtan case tried in England in 1843. His acquittal on the grounds of insanity invoked a debate in the House of Lords, which at length proposed five questions to the fifteen judges of England regarding the law of insanity. The answers of the judges can be reduced to two rules to determine the responsibility of a person who pleads insanity as a defense to a crime:

1) "To establish a defense on the ground of insanity it must be clearly proved that, at the time of committing the act, the party accused was laboring under such a defect of reason, from disease of the mind, as not to know the nature and quality of the act he was doing, or if he did know it, that he did not know he was doing what was wrong."[7] This rule was amplified with the comment that the knowledge of right and wrong refers to "the very act charged" rather than to "knowledge" in the abstract.

2) "Where a person labors under partial delusions only and is not in other respects insane," and commits an offense in consequence thereof, "he must be considered in the same situation as to responsibility, as if the facts with respect to which the delusion exists were real."[8]

The McNaughtan rules framed in 1843 did not constitute a decision upon an actual case but were given *extra curiam* and adopted in due course

---

and later reiterated by the eighteenth-century legal writer, Hawkins, as "those who are under a natural disability of distinguishing between good and evil, as infants under the age of discretion, idiots and lunatics, are not punishable by any criminal prosecution whatever." The trial of Lord Ferrer (19 How. St. Tr. 886) in 1760 brought execution to the accused, since in accordance with Hale's dictum no total want of reason was shown, and it was held that a partial degree of reason remained sufficient to restrain the "passions." In 1800, Lord Erskine obtained an acquittal of Hadfield (27 How. St. Tr. 1282) on the jury's acceptance of the argument that the existence of a circumscribed delusion negated responsibility, and on its disregard of its right-and-wrong formula. Two other cases before the McNaughtan case attracted notice, those of Bellingham in 1812, and Oxford (Rex v. Oxford C.P. 528) in 1840. In both, the defendant appeared to have identical types of delusional mental disorder, but Bellingham was convicted and Oxford acquitted on the defense of insanity. Such results throw little light on the problem.

[7]Henry Weihofen, *Insanity as a Defense in Criminal Law* (New York: Commonwealth Fund, 1933), p. 28.

[8]Ibid., pp. 28–29.

by the American courts, with the exception of New Hampshire and possibly Montana. In twenty-nine states the McNaughtan formula is the solitary test, and in seventeen others and in American military law it is still the main test supplemented by the "irresistible impulse test."[9]

Two applications of the test questions are employed in the state courts. In one, the defendant to be excused must be incapable of knowing the nature and quality of the act; in the other, he must be incapable of knowing right from wrong as to the act charged, and some courts have held that there is no distinction in meaning between these two phrases.[10] Keedy points out that the responses of the lords were specifically limited to a case "afflicted with an insane delusion," as was McNaughtan, and also that the test announced by the judges was the same as given to the jury by the presiding judge in the

---

[9]The federal courts early adopted the McNaughtan rules and referred to them repeatedly in their opinions. For example, in 1951 the circuit court for the District of Massachusetts in the case of United States v. McGlue, 26 Fed. Cas. No. 15,679, charged the jury that the defendant was entitled to the defense of insanity only if ". . . he [was] under such delusion as not to understand the nature of his act, or . . . to know that he [was] doing wrong, or . . . to discern that his act [was] criminal and deserving punishment. . . ." See also United States v. Holmes, a decision by the circuit court for the District of Maine, 26, Fed. Cas. No. 15,383 (1858).

The earliest decision of the Supreme Court of the United States on the subject of criminal responsibility of persons, allegedly insane, is United States v. Davis, 160 U.S. 469 (1895). The Supreme Court in this case, speaking by Justice Harlan, referred to the "discussion" in the House of Lords respecting McNaughtan's case and the opinions of the judges of England. The Supreme Court nonetheless departed substantially from the McNaughtan rules, holding that if all the evidence does not exclude beyond a reasonable doubt the hypothesis of insanity, the accused was entitled to acquittal. See also Hotema v. United States, 186 U.S. 413 (1902); and Matheson v. United States, 227 U.S. 540 (1913), the most recent utterance of the Supreme Court on this subject, in which it was held that there was no error in charging the jury in the language approved by the Davis decision.

As to the capacity of a defendant to stand trial in U.S. courts, a germane subject, the matter is covered in Sec. 4244, Title 18, U.S. Code, adopted 7 September 1949, *Statutes at Large*, vol. 63, p. 686. The statute provides in substance that if the defendant is so mentally incompetent "as to be unable to understand the proceedings against him or properly assist in his own defense," he may not be tried. Although the statute is plain, the principle enunciated has been misconstrued in the case of United States v. Gundelfinger, 98 F. Supp. 630 (W.D. Pa. 1951), where the existing dichotomy between the views of the psychiatrist and the bar as to mental illness is all too clearly outlined. For a judicial rationalization of the difference between these views, see Holloway v. United States, 148 F. 2d 665, 666-7 (D.C. Cir. 1945). The court seemed to believe that it was bound to apply the principle of the McNaughtan rules though it did not mention it.

Ohio 1834, Massachusetts 1844, Delaware 1851, District of Columbia 1853, Kentucky 1863, Indiana 1869, Connecticut 1873, Michigan 1878, Virginia 1881, Alabama 1866, U.S. Supreme Court 1895, Arkansas 1895, Vermont 1901, Colorado 1915, Illinois 1920, Utah 1931. *Pennsylvania* 1846, *Iowa* 1868, *Maine* 1870, *Tennessee* 1871, *Texas* 1880, *Wisconsin* 1883, *Louisiana* 1904, *New Mexico* 1910, and *Washington* 1930 all have the rule that is not clear. (States marked by italics are those in which the rule adopted has been changed in subsequent cases.) Weihofen, *Insanity as a Defense,* p. 66.

[10]Weihofen, ibid., pp. 43, 44.

McNaughtan trial.[11] In effect what was at first limited to a specific system of paranoid delusions was extended as a declaration of comprehensive law on insanity, applicable to any case presenting the defense of mental illness. This generalization has been of no less discomfort to legal scholars than to medical men who must grapple with it in open court. Many have joined in condemnation of the action of the judges upon "specific pathological notions" that only remotely conform to present-day psychiatric conceptions.[12]

It would be well, however, to remind psychiatrists of the words of Glover:

> The law is not primarily interested in psychopathology; it rarely goes further than to characterize certain end products of psychic tension (behavior) as socially undesirable and reprehensible, and to charge and sentence the offender accordingly. Even when, as in the case of the M'Naghten Rules, the law established a relative immunity from punishment for offenders suffering from some form of mental disorder, its concern is less with the *actual* state of mind of the individual than with the lack of social responsibility ensuing therefrom.[13]

Nevertheless, outside of the courtroom the law is very much concerned with psychopathology, either before or after the trial. Before trial it may be necessary to have a psychiatric judgment of the offender's mental capacity to stand trial, but the law does not require the psychiatrist to pass medical judgment within the narrow dimensions of the McNaughtan formula. Nor is he so restricted when he passes upon the mental condition of the convicted

---

[11]E. R. Keedy, "Irresistible Impulse as a Defense in the Criminal Law," *University of Pennsylvania Law Review* 100 (May 1952): 956–93.

[12]Weihofen, *Insanity as a Defense,* p. 31. Justice Frankfurter gave the following statement to the Royal Commission: "The M'Naghten Rules were rules which the Judges, in response to questions by the House of Lords, formulated in the light of the then existing psychological knowledge. . . . I do not see why the rules of law should be arrested at the state of psychological knowledge of the time when they were formulated. . . . If you find rules that are, broadly speaking, discredited by those who have to administer them, which is, I think, the real situation, certainly with us—they are honoured in the breach and not in the observance—then I think the law serves its best interests by trying to be more honest about it. . . . I think that to have rules which cannot rationally be justified except by a process of interpretation which distorts and often practically nullifies them, and to say the corrective process comes by having the Governor of a State charged with the responsibility of deciding when the consequences of the rule should not be enforced, is not a desirable system. . . . I am a great believer in being as candid as possible about my institutions. They are in large measure abandoned in practice, and therefore I think the M'Naghten Rules are in large measure shams. That is a strong word, but I think the M'Naghten Rules are very difficult for conscientious people and not difficult enough for people who say, 'we'll just juggle them. . . .' I dare to believe that we ought not to rest content with the difficulty of finding an improvement in the M'Naghten Rules. . . ." *Royal Commission on Capital Punishment* (London: H. M. Stationery Office, 1953), p. 102.

[13]Edward Glover "Isolating a Group of Delinquent Disorders," *The British Journal of Delinquency* (October 1950): 109.

offender for the purpose of sentencing, or after sentence upon the imprisoned offender.[14] Thus, pretrial and posttrial the McNaughtan rules are ignored. In dealing with any psychotic person, except one on trial for a criminal offense, the law does not separate the sane from the insane on the basis of knowledge of right and wrong. If such were the case, few if any commitments for mental illness could be secured. Before and after trial, the psychiatrist is called upon to give his professional judgment in a manner consistent with his competence. In the trial, his contribution is inadmissible.

Yet precisely here its function is most essential. Many dangerous persons are essentially undeterrable, and it is the business of psychiatry to supply the law with such knowledge as is necessary to detect such persons among whom may be counted several classes of mentally disordered offenders. In the trial the McNaughtan formula does not determine realistically who such persons are. Many undeterrable offenders are treated as if they are sane and sent to prison to be released at the termination of sentence, free to repeat the cycle. As matters stand, as a device of criminal-law administration, the rules touch only a fraction of undeterrable mentally ill. In this there is no security for the law-abiding community.

The rules place a premium on intellectual capacity and presuppose that behavior is actuated exclusively by reason and untrammeled choice. On the one hand, this overemphasizes the importance of the intellect, reason, and common sense; on the other hand, it underemphasizes the emotional pressures that energize behavior. Actually, in the psychic effort to rationalize forbidden behavior with reality, reason and choice are more often observed in bold relief after the act.

The rules are applied to the case in which knowledge that the act is wrong may be the very inducement to its commitment. This is a frequent

---

[14]From 1931 to 1941, one out of every forty-two felons sentenced to the Eastern State Penitentiary in Philadelphia was mentally disordered to a committable degree or developed such a condition. Many such individuals were probably psychotic on admission to the penitentiary and likely so at the time of their trial and sentence, but none presented a defense of insanity. This group represented a limited order of psychiatric screening and segregation from the general prison population that otherwise abounded in unexplored mental disorder. The record of 287 such mentally disordered prisoners indicates that only in exceptional instances did the trial court take cognizance that the accused was a mental suspect, when in fact one out of four of the group had an available documented history of mental illness prior to last arrest. This group accounted for 199 crimes against the person, of which 47 were homicide and 42 sex offenses. The group had engaged law enforcement agencies and the resources of the taxpayer to the extent of 1,503 arrests, 964 convictions, and 20 parole violations. The offender's average age upon last conviction was thirty, indicating the potentiality for future social danger. These cases had an average record of five arrests and three convictions. Summary reflections of this sampling lead to the disquieting realization that in each case the court overlooked at least five chances to find out the kind of person with whom it was dealing; that by omission, each offender was given other opportunities for crime, including murder; and that not until the mental disturbance had attained such flagrant appearance and threat did the court finally meet the problem realistically.

observation in children's behavior and common enough in many neurotic adults. And, ". . . except for totally deteriorated, drooling, hopeless psychotics of long standing, and congenital idiots—who seldom commit or have the opportunity to commit murder—the great majority and perhaps all murderers know what they are doing, the nature and quality of their act, and all the consequences thereof, and they are therefore 'legally sane' regardless of the opinion of any psychiatrist."[15] This consideration poses a difficult problem for the psychiatrist as witness under the present system wherein he must answer questions according to a tacitly understood convention. When the knowledge-of-right-and-wrong or of-the-nature-and-quality-of-the-act question is put, the psychiatrist as witness knows that if he answers "yes" he is saying that the defendant is legally sane whereas, for example, he may know from his technical insight and careful examination that the defendant is mentally ill and committed his offense out of unconscious need of punishment. This leaves the witness with his intellectual honesty at stake and with no escape, for suppose he answers "no"—the defendant did not know the difference between right and wrong. Now he has given the legal answer that conveys the psychiatric truth: the defendant is mentally ill. Next comes the cross-examination and the psychiatrist finds that he cannot relate any vital information about the defendant without contradicting himself. Such an imposition is not expressly intended by the law in words; it is nevertheless inherent in the law in action.

Often the psychiatrist learns too late that the existence of psychosis as such at the time of the offense does not automatically exempt the offender from punishment. He knows that the psychosis about which he is testifying involves a very distinct appreciation of society's judgments of right and wrong but finds too late that in affirming this he has answered so as to convict the defendant. Only in cases of disturbed consciousness or of idiocy can the psychiatrist make honest replies to the McNaughtan test questions.[16]

No entities of mental disorder can be abstracted out of matters solely confined to the faculty of knowledge as explicit in the rules. The test questions are not consistent with the experience of the psychiatrist as a scientist though they do have a meaning to him as a member of the community. Thus, the psychiatrist witness finds himself in a dual role, one as a scientist who brings technical information to the trial, in the outcome of which he must be disinterested; the other, as member of a social order who shares with his fellows its value judgments in answers to any questions of right and wrong.

---

[15]Gregory Zilboorg, *Mind, Medicine and Man* (New York: Harcourt Brace, 1943), p. 273.

[16]The test questions may be given responsive answers in cases involving actual disturbances of consciousness as in epilepsy, intoxications, deleria, fugue states, true amnesias, and in organic encephalopathies. The grossly feeble-minded person is presumed not to have acquired the knowledge of a responsible person.

Neither the bench nor the bar nor the public seems aware that the test questions do not test mental disorder but are a test of legal responsibility, that is, a device intended to facilitate the determination of guilt. In capital cases with the issue of mental disorder as a defense, this determination is pivoted on the answers of the psychiatrist on either side, and may have the effect of placing the experts themselves on trial. To the jury, the replies of the psychiatrist cannot be free of the implication that the test questions are medical criteria; in fact, the psychiatrist cannot be free either, since the test questions are addressed to him as a medical expert. As matters stand, the test questions have the effect of vesting the psychiatrist with the juryman's function. It may be contended that the test questions exact only medical opinion as to the right and wrong, or knowledge, from the psychiatrist and that from his answers the jury formulates the verdict. This is indeed the intention, but there is no escaping the fact that the moment the psychiatrist answers the issue of knowledge he has simultaneously answered to the jury on a nonmedical issue of legal responsibility.

Courts do not now permit the attorney to ask the medical witness whether in his opinion the defendant is responsible or irresponsible, holding this would be usurping the court's function. But the judge does permit, in fact he often insists, that the attorney read the legal formula of responsibility as laid down by statute or decision and then ask the expert whether the defendant does or does not fit this narrow legal concept. This permits the expert to answer a question that had previously been held objectionable, by the simple device of translating it into other terms. But it is after all the same question. Such obliquity is further compounded by the requirement of the McNaughtan formula that the medical expert translate his psychiatric findings into ethical terms of knowledge of right and wrong before the lawyer translates them into responsibility and irresponsibility.

The problem of the psychiatrist not only engages him as a participant in the trial but also imposes upon him a private ethical reckoning. The pivotal assumption of the rules is that a disorder of the cognitive faculty (knowledge) is the only basis for the determination of responsibility. This confines the psychiatrist to an exceedingly short tether, and it is usually his undoing. He is put to the exercise of relating his medical data to an unrelatable requirement. The ethical issue is clear here. It is the "using" of the psychiatrist. In Zilboorg's words, "the problem would suggest that there is something immoral in this forcible conversion of the psychiatrist to formalistic concepts of legal insanity—concepts which certainly have no clinical existence in psychiatry or in life itself, and which exist on paper only in our penal code...."[17]

---

[17]Gregory Zilboorg, "The Reciprocal Responsibilities of Law and Psychiatry," *The Shingle* 12 (April 1949): 79–96. In a dissenting opinion handed down in U.S. Court of Appeals for the Third Circuit, U.S. ex, rel. Smith v. Baldi, 192 F. 2d 540, 549, 26 October 1951, the dissenting judges saw fit to make note of the method employed by the lone psychiatric examiner: "prior to

A second assumption of the rules is that the existence or absence of such knowledge is readily determinable by the methods of psychiatry. This assumption is unwarranted. There is no developed scientific method of determining the existence of such knowledge of the nature and quality or the right and wrong as related to an act, or the lack of it. Nevertheless, the law in effect compels answers to invalid questions of knowledge, which cannot be met. As a rule, the defendant knows the facts of his crime and knows its unlawfulness and consequences, but he does not know the unconscious basis for it. The task of the psychiatrist is to perceive the unconscious basis of the unlawful act and the nature of the inner conflict, but in action the law would confine his exploration to the familiar territory of the conscious.

From the foregoing, the committee recognizes that in the interest of a comprehensive criminal justice, psychiatric expert testimony is indispensable and that its employment will likely increase; that the psychiatrist has an obligation and a competence to take part in its rational administration. But widespread dissatisfaction with this process as it exists calls for a renewed mutual collaboration of lawyers and psychiatrists in the reexamination and reappraisal of basic legal concepts, of the procedures governing expert testimony, and of the present state of our knowledge of psychic life.[18]

The committee submits that present-day knowledge of mental life limits the psychiatrist in the following respects:

1) He cannot fit any scientifically validated entity of psychopathology into present legal formulae of insanity. He cannot determine by scientific method the existence of knowledge as implied in the legal texts, excepting in cases of disturbed consciousness or profound mental deficit.

2) He cannot testify in any manner in terms of moral judgment. Any testimony

---

giving his testimony he had examined Smith on two occasions for about 'an hour' in the prison—about eight and a half months *after* the commission of the crime. The examination consisted largely of *talking with Smith, observing his demeanor and reading his confession to him to discover whether or not he could distinguish between right and wrong.*" The dissenting judges further observed that "the law, when it required the psychiatrist to state whether in his opinion the accused is capable of knowing right from wrong, compels the psychiatrist to test guilt or innocence by a concept which has almost no recognizable reality" (Emphasis added).

[18]Circular Letter No. 225 of the Group for the Advancement of Psychiatry reports the tabulation and preliminary impressions gained from a questionnaire on capital punishment, distributed to the membership of GAP, comprising of 150 members of whom 86 made returns. From this sampling of North American psychiatry the Committee on Psychiatry and Law was able to develop general conclusions of which several follow:

1) Only a few psychiatrists have an established competence in dealing with criminal matters.
2) American courts assume that any psychiatrist is qualified to testify affecting the disposition of an offender. A clearly defined and accepted standard of expertness is wanting.
3) Psychiatrists avoid giving testimony in criminal cases.
4) The psychiatric profession is in need of better definition of the actual role of the psychiatrist in the trial.

beyond professionally recognized medical data descriptive of the defendant's mental status, and informative to the court and jury, is beyond the province of the psychiatric expert testimony. Any expert testimony containing value judgments, namely, statements imputing the rightness or wrongness of behavior, of dislike, disapproval, disgust, or of defense, approval, or acceptance, has authoritative impact upon those charged with the making of verdicts. To be of social utility, and to be scientifically valid, all expert testimony should be free of moral and value statements.

3) He cannot, within the framework of present requirements, determine degrees of legal responsibility calibrated to medical degrees of psychopathology.[19] The severity of ego impairment manifest in symptoms or in acts appears to be a measure of lessened responsibility, but psychopathological features do not lend themselves to the making of a reliable and teachable guiding scale. The majority of offenders do not exhibit frank symptoms and are more often counted among borderline problems of diagnosis and analysis. Any attempt to scale responsibility in terms of symptoms will inevitably lead to endless forensic contentions over degree, fractions, and percentages of responsibility.

The committee submits that the psychiatrist as expert is competent to do the following:

1) He can predict behavior of the mass statistically and determine with fair accuracy the classes of undeterrable persons. He can predict the tendency of behavior in the individual and with fair accuracy determine his deterrability.

2) He can with fair accuracy determine the degree of disorder of the accused relating to: a) the present mental state of the accused as it is relevant to

[19]Mental illness is a behavioral expression of ego impairment. With this in mind, the psychiatrist attempts to take a measure of the ego, translated into some kind of intuitive scale and curve, which enable him to refer to the severity of the illness and to anticipate the effect of treatment. By corollary, the ego impairment would appear to be a direct measure of responsibility. Ego impairment implies lessened control in maintaining behavioral norms of social interaction. In law, such would be the basis of exculpation. The offender with impaired ego is said to have diminished responsibility. On this level of abstraction, the lawyer and psychiatrist can agree. The psychiatrist can determine that ego impairment exists and the lawyer can transpose the fact into his terms of intent and responsibility. Beyond this neither can move since in this area of observation no meaningful dimensions and scale have been worked out; thus, the question of how much is left unanswered. The matter is less troublesome by common-sense criteria in the case of the manifestly normal or of the manifestly psychotic, but such are exceptional; the routine case is that of the intermediate borderline which cannot be fitted into either normal or psychotic categories.

Certainly in keeping with our concepts of mental life and behavior there can be little question of differences of responsibility for given acts, but we have not as yet devised a formula for measuring them. Consequently, in workaday practice we perforce cling to the expedient of common sense in estimating diminished responsibility in all cases. Here the psychiatrist may do somewhat better than the man on the street, but not much.

his capacity to appreciate the significance of the charge and to cooperate
in the preparation of his defense; b) the causal connection of the mental
state and the act charged.
3) He can make advisory recommendations for suitable disposition of the
convicted.

It is not beyond the resources of the law to remove barriers to realistic
psychiatric testimony. The law can do much by:

1) Elevating standards of expertness of witnesses. There is little to bar
American courts from accepting any licensed practitioner as an expert in
matters of psychopathology. Despite the advances made in specialization,
and the establishment of boards of certification, the appearance in court
of unqualified experts is more the rule than the exception. The matter of
standards is chiefly the responsibility of the court which has the power to
insist on higher qualifications of witnesses.
2) Providing procedures to eliminate the withholding of essential data from
either side, when such data is not constitutionally protected. Partisan
experts seldom if ever jointly examine the accused and share the same
collateral sources upon which, in part, their opinions are established. Since
they do not possess the same data, it is almost certain that they cannot
meet in agreement—they cannot be judging the same material and observation. Adoption of procedures requiring the disclosure of the same data
to both sides would protect the accused and elevate expert testimony. This
has a beginning in the practice of the public defender who, with public
funds, seeks out essential evidence and could be extended whereby all
essential medical evidence is made equally available to both sides.[20]
3) Insulating the expert witness from issues of moral judgment.
4) Providing facilities equipped for exhaustive study of the accused when
there is presented the issue of mental condition. Forensic clinical psychiatry
has had scant recognition by the criminal courts in the United States. A
few court clinics are in operation as agencies for diagnostic screening and

---

[20]M. S. Guttmacher and H. Weihofen, *Psychiatry and the Law* (New York: W. W. Norton
Co., 1952), pp. 248–49, set forth remedies for the more glaring abuses and shortcomings of the
partisan method of presenting expert testimony. They are: "1) Requiring notice of the name and
address of any expert to be called and thus eliminating 'surprise' witnesses; 2) Requiring the
person to be examined to submit his person for examination by the experts; 3) Permitting the
filing of written reports, the conferring together of the experts and the filing of joint reports; and
4) Allowing expert witnesses to speak in terms of inferences or conclusions without the use of
the hypothetical question and so allowing them to testify in ordinary language which the judge
and the jury can understand. These recommendations are included in the Uniform Expert
Testimony Act, the adoption of which is urged. The authors further solicit the legal profession
to adopt the Model Code of Evidence, which would give the trial judge more discretion and
control over the conduct of the case, liberalize the rules of hearsay, and allow hospital and other
records and learned books to be admitted in evidence."

for nominal advisory assistance to the courts in matters of disposition. In the overall scope of administration, the courts employ psychiatrists only on occasion. Court psychiatry has yet to be recognized and developed as a clinical specialty and as a social-research discipline. With few exceptions, court psychiatry is mediocre, largely because the courts have done little to provide inducements. Hurried examinations and observation of offenders in prison cells, commonly without privacy, in some instances in the presence of an attorney, are conducive neither to good psychiatry nor as a career incentive to the well-trained psychiatrist.

The committee submits that good court psychiatry requires no less than the minimum standards of civil practice. Minimum standards are as follows: a) observation of the offender in a facility under psychiatric administration; b) a minimum-maximum term of observation to be determined by mutual agreement between the courts and the psychiatric facility; c) provision of facilities for psychologic testing; d) provision for social case work; e) provision for laboratory adjuncts including electroencephalography; f) provision for consulting services of medical specialists; g) organization of such services to operate in accordance with established standards of practice, diagnosis, supervision, and reporting and to provide for interval evaluations and to promote teaching and social science research.

5) Adopting the principle of deferring sentence in every case in which a question of mental disorder is raised.

The committee recommends that in institutions of learning there be established joint curricula for the instruction of law and medical students in the fields of common interest touched upon in this report, and that there be established facilities for multidisciplinary research in law and psychiatry. Such collaborative programs would bridge the long-standing insular separation of law and psychiatry.

The committee recommends the abolition of the McNaughtan rules and the substitution of a procedure based on the following principles:[21]

---

[21]Conclusions of the Royal Commission's report:

"(i) (Mr. Fox-Andrews dissenting) That the test of responsibility laid down by the M'Naghten Rules is so defective that the law on the subject ought to be changed.

(ii) That an addition to the Rules on the lines suggested in paragraph 317 is the best that can be devised, consistently with their primary object, for improving them; and (Mr. Fox-Andrews dissenting) that it would be better to amend them in that way than to leave them as they are.

(iii) (Dame Florence Hancock, Mr. Macdonald and Mr. Radzinowicz dissenting) That a preferable amendment of the law would be to abrogate the Rules and to leave the jury to determine whether at the time of the act the accused was suffering from disease of the mind (or mental deficiency) to such a degree that he ought not to be held responsible.

(We shall also recommend [paragraph 356] that, whether the M'Naghten Rules are retained, or amended or abrogated, it should be made clear that mental deficiency no less than disease of the mind is a possible cause of irresponsibility.)" *Royal Commission on Capital Punishment* (London: H. M. Stationery Office, 1953), p. 116.

1) That the substitute provide that the psychiatrist be permitted to explain fully the basis of his medical opinion.
2) That mental disorder not be regarded as a constant quantity.
3) That there be embodied in the substitute no medical or psychological theories.
4) That the substitute should not limit the defense to any mere categorizing of mental disorder by form or by symptom.
5) That the substitute clearly separate the legal and medical functions of the trial.

———

The committee is indebted to the following consultants who contributed to its exploratory studies: Hon. John Biggs, Jr., chief judge, U.S. Court of Appeals, Third Circuit, Wilmington, DE; Dr. Robert Waelder, psychoanalyst, Philadelphia; David M. Burrell, Esquire, Freeport, IL; Thomas M. McBride, Esquire, Philadelphia; Michael von Moschizker, Esquire, first assistant district attorney, Philadelphia; Professor Herbert Wechsler, Columbia University, New York City; Professor Louis B. Schwartz, University of Pennsylvania Law School, Philadelphia; Professor Arthur R. Pearce, University of Pennsylvania Law School, Philadelphia; George H. Dession, Lines Professor of Law, Yale University, New Haven, CT.

The committee acknowledges that in this inquiry there remain unresolved areas of disagreement. Three consultants do not concur with the committee's views and recommendations as set forth in the report for which the committee takes sole responsibility.

A Psychosocial Analysis of the Making of the Model Penal Code*

LAWRENCE ZELIC FREEDMAN

The writing of a model penal code is a rare and significant event in the history of a nation. Noncodified criminal law in the Anglo-Saxon tradition is an amalgam of common law buttressed by tradition and precedents plus all the various bills that have been passed by legislatures and parliaments and councils and edicts uttered by kings and governors over the centuries. Laws creating crimes are passed when community tension exceeds a threshold of tolerance for a category of acts. The severity of punishment reflects the anxiety, loathing, or envy that each transgression arouses at a specific point in time, space, and cultural evolution. All together these become a pastiche, uncoordinated, sometimes mutually contradictory or excessively harsh, sometimes obsolescent and unused.

A model penal code is an effort to integrate the best of the criminal law into a coherent, contemporary, rational pattern of legal response to crime. During the decade between 1952 and 1962 the American Law Institute, supported by a generous grant from the Rockefeller Foundation, wrote such a penal code for the twentieth century to serve as a model for the states and governing bodies. The author of this paper was invited to serve as a psychiatric advisor and as a member of the Criminal Law Advisory Committee.[1] The ten-year-long task was completed in 1962, and I have now attempted to reanalyze my observations, not only from the perspective of a participant psychiatrist but also, objectified by time, through the eyes of a behavioral science investigator. With this perspective I have attempted to elucidate systematically those factors—crucial, peripheral, and contributory—within the deliberating group that affected the consensus leading to the final version of the Model Penal Code.

---

*The preparation of this paper was aided by the Otho S. A. Sprague Memorial Institute and the Foundations' Fund for Research in Psychiatry. It was presented at the Institute of Psychiatry and Judicial Law, San Diego, CA, 9 May 1965. This edition is a slightly revised version of the original article reprinted from Ralph Slovenko, ed., *Crime, Law and Corrections* (Springfield, IL: Charles C. Thomas, 1966), pp. 213–31. By permission of the publisher.

[1]At this time the author was chairman of the Yale Study Unit in Psychiatry and Law and a faculty member of the Yale Law School and the Yale Medical School. His psychiatric colleagues

FRAGMENTARY LEGISLATION

It now seems likely that very soon I will be liable to arrest for carrying an illegal weapon should I break a milk bottle on my way home from a grocery store and do not make it to a trash can before a patrolling police car nabs me. In Illinois recently a legislative body unanimously passed a bill declaring that henceforth a broken bottle is an illegal weapon. The other legislative body will probably follow this lead. The governor may well sign the bill. He seems a sensible man but nonetheless dependent on and responsive to the will of the people as expressed through the urban leaders of the Democratic party. When these three events have occurred, I will have to add to the already long list of sins, which I warn my children against—lying, stealing, and hurting others—picking up and holding broken pop or beer bottles.

What set in motion such a unanimous aversion to broken bottles? Some weeks previously a Chicago judge had freed two men after one of them had cut an off-duty officer in the face with a broken bottle while he (the officer accompanied by a companion policeman) was attempting to arrest them for the crime of carrying a broken bottle. There are many associated factors affecting the judge's decision, but the most obvious legal points were that (a) it was not against the law to carry a broken bottle in Illinois, and (b) the officer who had drawn his gun had, therefore, no right either to make an arrest or to use such a degree of force against the men. The local newspapers, led by the *Chicago Tribune,* reacted with great publicity and continuous barrage of attacks against the judge, saying, *inter alia,* that he had stimulated contempt for the law and the authority of the police. It should be noted that the two men indicted for felonious assault, although only one of whom was accused of carrying the broken bottle, were members of a minority group and, being poor, had been unable to raise bail. At the time of their release they had been in jail for many months awaiting trial.

The judge, who only recently had assumed office, was and is a man of great distinction in Chicago. A brilliant graduate of one of our greatest law schools, he had, by the force of his character, integrity, and ability risen rapidly to a position of eminence within the city. Among the accomplishments for which he was widely admired was his success in obtaining reversal of a death penalty in an outrageous miscarriage of justice against one of the relatively few white men in Illinois's death row. The judge also happens to be black, one of the first of his ethnic group to achieve so powerful a position in the Illinois judiciary.

---

in the Model Penal Code project were the late Winfred Overholser, wise and kindly, and Manfred Guttmacher, then dean of forensic psychiatry in the United States.

In this case both the judge and the defendants belong to a minority group, albeit not the same ones. The ethnic origins of the accused criminals are commonly referred to in newspaper accounts often accompanied by the apparently significant information that the assaulted officer was white. The judge's ethnic identity has not been alluded to in any journalistic account that I have read. Instead, his "irresponsibility" is related to the recency of his assuming his role. The county sheriff was quoted as calling him that "rookie judge." Admired though he is and has been, virtually no one among the power-elite of the Chicago community has come to the judge's defense. The newspapers have kept the issue alive with news reports of the event itself. When that was thoroughly played out, descriptions of defiant behavior by delinquents against officers were prominently and frequently reported, making it appear that the judge's decision had triggered an epidemic of lawlessness and threatened chaos. Under these pressures and circumstances not a single legislator dared or cared to vote against a bill that made a broken bottle an illegal weapon.

On 1 January 1962 Illinois had adopted a coherent criminal code, based in large part on the Model Penal Code of the American Law Institute, whose emergence is the subject of this paper. The Illinois code had been drafted by a committee whose first chairman as well as drafting chairman were also members of the Committee of the American Law Institute. In addition, one of the Illinois committee's most effective members was the judge. He was simply following the provisions of that code.

This incident dramatizes because it juxtaposes so clearly the social mechanisms by which an outraged and frightened community, aroused by its newspapers, may enact through its legislature fragmentary bits of criminal law. A century from now, when all liquid containers are plastic and that law is still on the books, judges and legal scholars, not knowing how it came to be enacted, will puzzle over how this particular shard of criminal sanction happened to be passed only months after the state had adopted a model comprehensive code—the work of ten years of its best legal brains, built in turn upon the ten years' labor of the country's most respected jurisprudential experts.

THE MODEL PENAL CODE

This report is about the making of the Model Penal Code, but it is well to keep in mind the above-described vignette of emergent law; that particular incident arose out of the reactive turbulence of minority groups emerging into full citizenship, with journalistic enterprise reflecting and enhancing the prejudicial anxieties of the troubled populace. The quiet chambers in which model codes are written are, or at least seem to be, far indeed from this hit-and-run marketplace.[2]

The legal response to social offenders in the Anglo-Saxon tradition has found its expression in common law and miscellaneous legislation. Common law is under the misapprehension, like Topsy, that it just grew. It is only vaguely aware of its heritage, of its genetic endowment, and of the nutritive and conditioning factors that determined its present tradition. What moves legislators to enact criminal sanctions has never to my knowledge been studied systematically in the United States. Nonetheless, it is from this potpourri of the precedents of common law and the usually spasmodically and incoherently enacted laws at the municipal and state level that determines how most ordinary criminals will be treated most of the time in most of the American states in the mid-twentieth century. Only rarely in Anglo-Saxon cultures have there been attempts to create a coherent, integrated, internally consistent body of penal law.[3] It never had been done before on a national scale in this country during this century. Probably another century will elapse before a similar attempt is made.

These observations describe a special event and experiment in nature which is unlikely to be replicated during our lifetimes and which will have enormous and increasing influence on our lives in the coming decades. Already, Wisconsin and Illinois have adopted penal codes essentially based on the Model Penal Code of the American Law Institute. The proposed penal code of Puerto Rico derives from it. Several other states have adopted parts of the Code, and many more are in the process of adopting it substantially, either its entire corpus or significant elements such as the responsibility provision.

If, therefore, we can ascertain how this document came into being we will know a great deal about how an important legal, social, and psychological event in our lives and that of our children, and theirs, came into existence. More than that, however, we will have some evidence in this nexus of the impact of science and law, of what science does have to offer law, and what the law now is willing or capable of accepting from science. We may be able to make some informed hypotheses concerning the role that *pure legal precedents* and logic, as compared to social and private values, play in decisions concerning penal practices in our culture.

This paper is the product of careful restudying of the variations in the tentative codes over the years as well as the rather complete notes which I

---

[2]See Slovenko, ed., SYMPOSIUM ON THE LABOR-MANAGEMENT REPORTING AND DIS-CLOSURE ACT (1961).

[3]The Louisiana Criminal Code of 1942 is a notable exception. Louisiana's private law is rooted in the French Civil Code, but its criminal law is based on the common law. However, employing civilian technique, Louisiana formulated and in 1942 enacted a coherent and integrated criminal code.

made during the committee meetings which preceded each of the interim alterations in the code.

The Participants

The participants were from four vocations, each with its own values, perspectives, and methods: judges, professors, behavioral scientists,[4] and professionals. From the laity there was also a foundation representative and a chairman of a parole board. For a couple of years a distinguished critic and professor of English struggled to act as a moralist, reflecting the ethical sense of the community at large. He finally gave up and resigned, possibly because the rest of the committee, unlike the chief reporter, somehow never got the message that he was there as a moralist and persisted in turning toward him for assistance in grammatical construction. This confusion was further compounded by his tendency to make not moral evaluations but psychological observations. Strikingly absent from the list of participants were such vitally interested people as legislators (who must enact or reject all proposed criminal laws), victims, and criminals.

The judges were men whose main task was to oversee legal procedure, determine guilt, and decide on, but not to carry out, punishment. The professors had no community-wide service function but were entrusted with the task of studying, comparing, and teaching the factors presumably or putatively relevant to achieving a model penal code that approximates excellence. The behavioral scientists' main function was to investigate with the best available clinical, inductive, and deductive methods the psychological, physiological, and social questions relevant to the individual's adjustments to his community. They were expected to know what legal controls might be workable in the light of human psychological predispositions. The professionals were men directly involved in the custody and management of the defendant before and during trial and of the prisoner after the trial.

The professors had had the longest academic education. The judges were, for the most part, very intelligent college and law school graduates.

---

[4]I have grouped the three psychiatrists, who were in essential agreement with each other on all basic issues, with the behavioral scientists because it was mainly as students of human behavior that their role was perceived by themselves and their colleagues in the committee. The three psychiatrists were hardest to classify in this four-part system since they were professors teaching in universities, behavioral scientists studying human behavior, and professionals. One administered the largest federal mental hospital in the country, in which were kept large numbers of mentally ill offenders; another directed the oldest medical court clinic in the country; and the third directed a prison psychiatric clinic. All were, moreover, in direct contact with offenders as their therapists or diagnosticians. None of the psychiatrists were judges, although there are those, as you know, who believe that they have usurped that role as well.

They had had no formal training to prepare them for a career of judging since no such preparation existed at that time, nor does it today. The professionals, particularly the penologists, had the least academic experience or institutional training for their roles. They were men who had come up from the ranks and had had to educate themselves. They were the self-made men of the Criminal Law Advisory Committee. But so, perforce, were the judges, as judges.

In hierarchal status the most prestigious judges ranked first and the professors of law next. They were followed by the behavioral scientists and the professionals. Status was judged by the various tokens of superordination or subordination that marked group deliberation. However, the final decisions of the group, which culminated in the Model Penal Code, by no means reflected this status hierarchy that I have constructed.

There were changes within the committee over the ten-year period, both as to the professional roles of its members and to its personnel. What was impressive was not this change but the extraordinary consistency of the core members of the reportorial staff as well as the committee. These were occupationally stable people with an unshakable middle-class foundation.

Invoking Operations

The intellectual, social, and forensic operations that the participants used to decide and to persuade themselves and each other I have classified as "invoking operations."[5] The most commonly invoked operations, in the order of their frequency and apparent importance, were: 1) statutory law, 2) common law, 3) social values, 4) sciences, 5) logic, 6) tactical considerations, 7) group dynamics, 8) metaphysics, and 9) common sense.

1) *Statutory law* and 2) *common law*. These require no discussion. 3) *Social values*. These social values might be based on the religious, professional ethics, and class standards or personal, idiosyncratic preferences of the speaker. More commonly the speaker justified his stand on the basis of the social values of the entire community as he understood or inferred them. Since next to legal precedents itself the mores of contemporary society were the most powerful invocation, considerable ingenuity was displayed in justifying this wide ethical or empirical generalization especially when, as frequently happened, two or more discussants disagreed as to the nature of these shared cultural values. Most commonly cited were personal observations, a private

---

[5]The word "invoking" seems especially appropriate since it not only accurately refers to citation of cases in evidence and to rational appeals for support but also because it carries, as I intend it to, overtones of invocation, of calling for aid and protection by dimly limned incantations.

sense or intuition or the data, actual or alleged, of the fourth most important referent, science. 4) *Sciences*. These included the physical, biological, psychological, and sociological sciences. 5) *Logic*. This referred to rational, coherent discussions rather than to the science of normative formal principles of reasoning. 6) *Tactical considerations*. These concerned the likelihood that the parent-sponsoring group or the government or legislators or the public would agree to accept the proposed program. 7) *Group dynamics*. Deliberately or unwittingly considerations of professional loyalty, position of respect, and factors more directly arising from the formal roles as well as personal relationships within the committee itself could be, and were, at least inferentially, invoked. 8) *Metaphysics*. Under this heading I included any philosophical discussion that was abstruse, not limiting it to the ontological science of cause or to the cosmological science of fundamental causes and the processes in things. 9) *Common sense*. Everyone, of course, knew what common sense was. It is how he himself thought about things.

Attitudes

By and large the members of the committee were progressive men. Their very presence on a committee to create a model penal code was evidence of their dissatisfaction with the status quo and of concern with making progress in this field. However, the notion about how best to accomplish this and how much should be accomplished was not uniform. The range of legally liberal to conservative attitudes was relatively wide within the judges and professors and behavioral science groups. It was somewhat narrower in the professional category. The committment to legal conservatism proceeded from the professionals who were most reluctant to abandon traditional method, to judges, and from law professors to behavioral scientists, who were least bound by such precedents. There were also differences within each category according to subcategory; for example, trial judges more conservative than appellate level judges and psychiatrists less conservative than sociologists.

I do not know the political complexion of the group in the organizational sense of their Republican or Democratic party membership. On the basis of the numerous discussions in which I participated over the ten-year period, both within and without the committee rooms, I would guess that there was about an equal distribution between the parties, with perhaps a slight predominance in the Democratic party. However, both Republicans and Democrats would have been classed among the moderates of their party. Within this restricted range, it is probably fair to assume that there was some positive parallelism between the degree of general political conservatism and legal conservatism or, reciprocally, of political liberalism, and legal liberalism as expressed in the committee deliberations.[6]

It was my impression that any one of the invoking operations might be alluded to in order to justify one or another point of view. There was a predictably greater predisposition among the professors to use legal precedents, particularly statutory. The judges as well appealed to legal precedents, but they gave somewhat greater emphasis to adjudicated cases and common law. The professionals, penologists, and district attorneys cited the hard facts of personal experience with criminals. The behavioral scientists used as their authority clinical observations, field surveys, and some experimental data. These disciplinary differences were in turn associated with the greater likelihood that the data of the behavioral scientists would be cited by them to justify less controlling sanctions than would the empirical data of the professionals. The comparative law and historical legal perspectives of the law professors provided them, as a group, with data with which they urged slightly less stringent control provisions than did the decision-making experience of the judges at the trial level.

Influences deriving from the discipline of origin—the occupational referent group—distinguished the committee members, and influences associated with the subgroup within each occupational group affected attitudes toward issues. Status relationships between these occupational groups and within each occupational group influenced discussion and made possible reasonably accurate predictions concerning how participants might be listened to. However, the discussants who were listened to with the greatest obvious tokens of respect were not necessarily the most influential framers of the code itself. Indeed, overall, the tone of the Model Penal Code was more reflective, for example, of the conservative stand of the professionals than of the liberal role of the leading judge. The leading drafters frequently invoked tactical suggestions, insisting that the code had to reflect the art of the possible.

All these valences and countervalences culminated in countless scored points. If this pointillism was not as inspired as the art of Seurat, the final result did blend into a coherent and reasonably harmonious pattern.

Judge Learned Hand and the Impact of a Great Personality

No single participant, of course, fits any generalization entirely. A few glimpses at one of the code makers, as he reacted to the issues and was responded to by his colleagues, may sharpen the focus somewhat of our image

---

[6]These views on the correlation of the political and legal attitudes of the committee participants are, of course, impressionistic and not based on consistent objective evidence as to their political affiliations.

of the committee at work. I have selected an extraordinary man, Judge Learned Hand. Judge Hand was the only man whom I thus far had met in my professional life whom I continued to think of as a great man even after I came to know him well. Most others on the committee shared my attitude to some degree. In the sense that his presence dominated our assembly, he was not typical. But it cannot be accurately stated that his respected position resulted in a penal code reflecting his views, as a mirror reflects by refraction the image of the person who stands before it, deflecting all the rays of light impinging on him and blotting out all others.

Learned Hand, when he joined the group drafting the code, already had entered his seventh decade and had behind him a half century of legal celebrity. One was immediately struck with his vigor, his wit, and his leonine, yet benign, appearance. Of height medium, his physique stocky and rugged, his face his most magnificently impressive feature, its contours and bony structure were block-like, his skin a healthy brown and pink complexion, its deeply etched lines conveying at once virile strength and sensitivity, his hair by now gray with streaks of black, his startlingly great, black, bushy eyebrows framed, dominated, and reinforced the overall impressiveness of his physical presence. Over the almost ten years that followed there was little to alter in this description of him as he lived into his eighth and final decade. Even when he conferred with us for the last time from a wheelchair, vigor was a characteristic that dominated his intellect and permeated his physical set.

Judge Hand showed, during those first sessions, legal erudition combined with personal warmth that included all. His questions and his responses were unfailingly constructive and reflected interest in and respect for the person with whom he was carrying on the dialogue, whether or not he agreed with him.

Obvious as my admiration for Judge Hand is, I trust that the reader will not lose sight of the fact that this discussion of his participation in the decision-making process may serve as a paradigm, not in spite of but precisely because of his special endowment. Psychiatrists have discovered that observing the distortions of human personality in the mentally ill led them to a theory and a method of observing normal personality. The reciprocal of this is that a particularly gifted personality may reflect with greater intensity principles essentially applicable to all who fall into the same general class. Furthermore, Judge Hand's frank sense that he and we were men, fallible, each with a childhood that not only trailed behind but also sat right there beside, behind, and within us at the august tables of deliberation, made him the most rewarding person to record for our purposes, for he ranged from the highest levels of abstruse legal, logical, and philosophical abstraction to the concrete images of his own childhood. He was able to talk spontaneously not only within the narrow constricts of the assigned role of model penal code maker but also as the man he was—as a friend, citizen, and convivial male amongst males.

In committee, Judge Hand was a seeker rather than a seer. He more frequently asked than told. He saw the need for decisions and he made them, but he saw more clearly than most judges how inadequate was the information upon which these decisions had to be made. In discussions he paid everyone that high and rare compliment of listening to what was said. What he heard could, and sometimes did, cause him to shift his own view if he felt he had learned something new or had been presented with a more ethically, logically, or legally powerful alternative to his own previously held opinion. Above all, he was aware, to a startling degree, of the potent personal forces within himself and within lawmakers, police, and penologists (no less than victims and criminals) that affected his decisions and their legislative and administrative acts.

When one of our colleagues apologized in embarrassment for having let "holy hell" slip out in the heat of an exchange, Judge Hand grandiloquently asked the chairman to permit him to go on record, submitting his belief that "holy hell is a helluva good phrase." By this he not only dissolved the embarrassment of our colleague, in the ensuing good-natured laughter, but he also invited us, as he so often did, to remember that we were somewhat ridiculous. It jolted us to the recognition that the same man used far saltier language during recesses without self-consciousness, as we all did, and to the more important awareness that this fiction of our ascetic sanctity imperiled our very effort, for it removed us to a degree from earthy, searing realities that we were attempting to respond to effectively.

It was suggested that no one be held criminally responsible regardless of his mental state before the age of eighteen instead of sixteen as is now generally the case. Judge Hand argued vigorously but ineffectively to raise the age of jurisdiction of the juvenile or family court to twenty-one. A trial court judge objected that "young mobsters should be held responsible for their crimes." To this a legal aid attorney observed that the criminal law in its conventional courts had not stopped these young offenders. Perhaps, therefore, it was time to try a new attack. A state supreme court judge also opposed the trial court judge's point, saying that it reflected the traditional attitude that the more serious the crime (that is, the more shockingly inconsistent with our community-shared morality and background) the more severe the penalty. He felt that this was inconsistent with our increasing emphasis on the modifiability as well as the motives of the individual offender.

A professor soothingly and academically interjected at this point that we needed to be concerned about what he called the "mores of the community." "How far," thereupon demanded Judge Hand, "how far will we defer to atavistic feelings of revenge and how far will we concern ourselves with the effects of punishment." He continued, "if I thought that it might prove effective, I might be able to override my own feelings of shock at the possibility of trying a child even under sixteen." "But," he concluded, "I must suppose that a child under sixteen cannot be so influenced" (in the way we wish and with this public trial method). An erudite law professor here interjected his opinion that we do not know the effect of the various forms of punishment and asked: "Is shock level the determinant" (of the severity of punishment)? Judge Hand then referred to some evidence in the Report of the Royal Commission on Capital Punishment that the sense of "shock" was indeed a real determinant of decision in capital offenses.

Now, another trial court judge emphasized that even the present age establishing a person as responsible to the full force of criminal law when he had passed his sixteenth birthday had itself been arbitrarily selected. "Chronological age," he said, "is not important. Emotional age is." He pointed out the recidivistic rates which proved, he felt, that conventional prisons were inefficient and ineffective as well as inhumane. Deterrence of repetitious criminal activity depended, in his view, on adequate therapy supplied when most appropriate—during younger years. Determination of a man's rehabilitability seemed more important to him that the determination of his alleged responsibility. A penologist averred that even under the present system of freeing from criminal responsibility those under sixteen, younger boys repeated their offense. They were saying, in effect, "there is nothing you can do to me. I'm not responsible." He implied that if the upper-age level of juvenile court jurisdiction were raised from sixteen to eighteen, as had been suggested, the same irresponsible attitude and repetitious delinquency would extend as well to seventeen and eighteen year olds.

Judge Hand, however, with relentless logic and consistency, took precisely the opposite tack. "Since," he said, "the age limits are arbitrary, why choose eighteen?" He suggested again that twenty-one would be the most reasonable age, since it would then include all persons who were legally minors. The customs of civic and fiscal responsibility would be consistent with those of criminal responsibility. The criminologist who had been mainly responsible for the draft of the issue under discussion—raising the age limit of juvenile court authority from sixteen to eighteen—said that offenders between the age of eighteen and twenty-three are more recidivistic and need to be "handled" more. This young adult group, as he saw it, was better handled as a distinct group, criminally and punitively, than with children. A law professor offered the suggestion that whatever the upper-age limit, a juvenile court could waive its jurisdiction in special cases. However, a trial court judge complained that the juvenile courts in his area never waived their jurisdictions, and, in fact, there was a tendency for these courts, even now, to aggrandize their positions.

All of this was followed by another round of dialogue in which each of the previous debaters reiterated his original point, with heightened emphasis and greater intransigency. A law professor then suggested that we "tidy up this question of the law involved." He distinguished between cases in which the issue of responsibility might be important and the far more frequent instances in which it was simply irrelevant, as, for example, in the question of waiving traffic violations. A state supreme court justice ended this phase of the discussion by warning that we "shouldn't throw this too much in the hands of the experts."

Having thus heard myself warned against, I joined the rest of my colleagues in a break for a delightful lunch.

The problem of responsibility took what was, for a layman psychiatrist, an unexpected twist. What was the responsibility and liability of a man who violated a law as a result of his own lawyer's advice? The arguments went back and forth until Judge Hand told a story. He often told stories as sort of parables to make his point. He recalled that "when that man whose name . . . begins with 'S' . . . was being tried for contempt of the Senate. . . ." The name Sinclair (an oil man who, on the advice of his attorney, had refused to answer certain questions before a Senate investigating committee) was supplied, and he continued. "Federal Judge Bitts, a tiny man who perched high on the great bench with his head cocked on one side. . . ." Hand then imitated Judge Bitts's characteristic gesture and recalled to others in the room who had known Bitts how they had loved him. He resumed his narration, enacting with considerable skill how Sinclair's attorney, with excessive deference, declared that "Your Honor, if anyone should be punished for Mr. Sinclair's refusal to answer the Senate's questions, it should be me, because Mr. Sinclair was following my advice." Judge Hand dramatized also the attorney's even more urgent plea that nobody, including the attorney, be in fact punished. "But," he continued, "Judge Bitts answered out from tilted perch: 'Well, some sick people are unlucky enough to have poor doctors and . . . they die. And some law-breakers are unfortunate enough to have poor lawyers and . . . they're sent to jail.'" Judge Bitts then sentenced Mr. Sinclair to sixty days in jail for contempt of Congress. Rather wryly, Judge Hand concluded: "I thought that was a little unfair . . . but . . ."

Judge Hand, like E. M. Forster, recognized that what was important was personal. Even though the legal issue of responsibility refers to culpability and hence punishability, he always viewed the problem as refracted simultaneously from the perspective of legal society on the person, and the perspective of that person at bay. Whatever the issue, he used himself as his laboratory of humanity to test the elements of the issue, to see whether they tested true. The committee was discussing a new proposal that not only physical but also excessive mental distress caused to minors by their parents be brought into the sanctioning range of the code. There was uncertainty as to the significance of excessive force resulting in such mental distress. Judge Hand, who happened then to be sitting by my side, was moved to recall his childhood. He described the severe restrictions of his Calvinist upbringing with its austerity, its Yankee harshness. The punishments were quick to come and relentlessly imposed for infractions.

Mainly, however, Hand's severe mental distress had not been occasioned by corporal punishments. His was caused by the extraordinarily powerful and persistent presumption of guilt and sinning that permeated his household. He told how, as a child, he used to have to recount all his sins of the day, begging for forgiveness for them with the shaky presumption that Jesus Christ, The Saviour, in His Mercy, might do so, but with absolutely no assurance that He would. I think that this great judge, with his vast legal authority, erudition, and responsibility never for an instant forgot what it was to be like a little boy who had sinned and repented, but who could never, ever gain assurance that he would be freed from personal responsibility, culpability, and the imminent threat of punishment for his crime.

Judge Hand's specific contribution to the particular provisions of the final draft was surprisingly limited when compared to his position in the discussions. There were many possible explanations for this seeming paradox. Hand himself was a complex man. Passionately committed to the democratic ethos, he could not be easily politically typed as a liberal in the contemporary political sense. Indeed, as judges know well, his ruling in the first Smith Act case and other decisions reflected his deeply held view that the limits of judicial review ought to be more tightly drawn than is presently the case. Social welfare alone, in his view, was not sufficient to justify the extension of the precedent of judicial review to judicial legislation. Holding it essential that there be a supremacy of judicial review, he nonetheless derived this principle, not from the Constitution but as an imperative necessity for effective government. On the other hand, he deplored the role of courts as governing agencies. Typically, he has said: "For myself, it would be most irksome to be ruled by a bevy of Platonic Guardians, even if I knew how to choose them which I assuredly do not."

So seriously engaged in this enterprise that he attended his last session in a wheelchair, he nonetheless saw the ultimate absurdity in our efforts to divide humanity into neat geometric cubicles, to establish sharp lines between the bad and the mad. With sometimes ribald wit, he epitomized the humor of the effort by men who themselves were barely mastering the tempestuous and unpredictable thrust of sex mainly through the enervating passage of years, solemnly declaring when and how and under what conditions others still carried along by these imperative sexual currents might be deemed criminally innocent.[7] He recognized judging no less than code making, as examples of the great, necessary, inevitable, but in a sense impossible, tasks that mankind set for itself because it had to. Like Judge Jerome Frank, for many years his dear friend and brilliant colleague on the bench, he saw the pompous vulnerability of the rituals by which the judges themselves and the

---

[7]Perhaps the most clear-cut example of his role in liberating the penal code was his cogent and insightful defense of tentative drafts covering sexual offenses that omitted adultery and homosexual relations between consenting adults from the penal code. In this instance, his effectiveness, particularly in the parent body, the American Law Institute, sprang as much from the respectability that his support lent to the proposition as to his legal persuasiveness.

public hid the all too vulnerable, tentative man behind the black robes and surrounded him with respect-evoking formulae so that both could be reassured concerning the majesty and inevitability of justice.

SUMMARY

This resumé of a retrospective analysis of the making of the Model Penal Code has presented some vignettes from observations extending over a ten-year period. It allows these conclusions: 1) Very little empirical data was available from any of the sciences—physical, behavioral, or social—upon which to base decisions. 2) Even when some such data was available it served mainly as a vehicle for the promotion of a priori values rather than as an antecedent conditioning for arriving at socially relevant decisions. 3) Nonetheless, even this partial role of the clinical skills and social sciences affected, however subtly, the tenor of the code. No major policies can be credited to them but certain attenuations may be. 4) All of the listed invoking referents were at one time or another introduced to justify choosing one or another decision. There were discernible and roughly classifiable occupational and personal determinants that made one group or person tend toward one set of invoked operations predictably more than another. These referents and operations seemed to be chosen to fit the argument as a rhetorical, persuasive or forensic device rather than as an inherently consistent method of analyzing the problem in question. 5) There were clear status differences between and within the vocational groups that affected how their comments were received in committee discussions. 6) This hierarchy of prestige was, however, only indifferently and in some cases even inversely related to the final provisions of the drafted code. 7) The vocations of the participants provided the best predictive base as to how they would respond to particular issues. 8) The participation and contributions of one especially influential member of the Advisory Committee, a distinguished judge, are described in some detail to illustrate how complex and diverse may be the range of individual determinants for decision making; it extends from childhood experience to legal principle. 9) This analysis also shows how change can be affected when there is a coalescence of values between different disciplines, even though the final agreement springs from quite disparate backgrounds, attitudes, and motives. 10) In the formation of criminal law, in the marketplace, immediate social stresses (economic and ethnic) and their exploitation by mass media out of journalistic motives remains prepotent over the most rational and authoritative model code.

Mental Disease or Defect Excluding Responsibility: A Psychiatric View of the American Law Institute's Model Penal Code Proposal*

LAWRENCE ZELIC FREEDMAN
MANFRED GUTTMACHER
WINFRED OVERHOLSER

It is a truism that in any decision-making process the freer the flow of relevant information the greater the chances that the decision will be rational and just. Any impediment to pertinent communication increases the probability that irrational or, in the court of law, unjust decisions will be made. The clinical insights of psychiatry can accurately reflect the state of its knowledge and be efficiently utilized by courts only when the procedures for testifying do not suppress or distort the information. The fewer the restrictions imposed on the psychiatrist testifying in court, the greater the resources upon which the courts can draw.

Decisions concerning the legal criteria for excluding responsibility obviously belong to other members of this committee. The considerations that we are presenting arise from and are restricted to our area of training, competency, and primary interest—mental disease and mental defect. Only so far as the proposal attempts to incorporate psychiatric disease need the committee grant our advice any more weight than that of other interested laymen. However, so far as it does we think it reasonable to hold that the unanimous opinion of the three psychiatric members of the Advisory Committee ought to be weighed as representative of the thinking of many of our colleagues in psychiatry upon whom the success of any formula depends.

There is now a body of experience based on the history of the McNaughtan formula, which may guide us to avoid a repetition of difficulties

*This is the minority report of the psychiatric members of the Advisory Committee to the American Law Institute preparing a model penal code. The preparation of this paper was supported by the Foundations' Fund for Research in Psychiatry. This edition is a slightly revised version of the original article reprinted from *The American Journal of Psychiatry* 118, no. 1 (July 1961): 32–34. Copyright 1961 American Psychiatric Association.

arising from earlier efforts. For example, a serious impediment to meaningful communication between psychiatrists and lawyers in the McNaughtan formula is the psychiatrists' mistaken assumption that McNaughtan makes an attempt to define insanity, which they consider in error. Lawyers see it as a statement of the conditions under which an accused person might be exculpated from guilt and from being stigmatized as a criminal.

The traditional reluctance of psychiatrists to testify in courts under the McNaughtan formula arises in large part from the frustration of language that the law requires of them. Many lawyers have failed to realize that freedom of psychiatric testifying is not identical with extension of psychiatric concepts in the procedures and decisions of the courts. Courts can only benefit from having the greatest possible clarity of exposition of psychiatric testimony, no matter what standards it sets for responsibility.

Section Four of the Model Penal Code of the American Law Institute, devoted to Responsibility, has a dual function.[1] It sets up the criteria by which, according to law, mental disease or defect may exclude responsibility. Responsibility is not a qualitative or quantitative intrinsic attribute of a person; it is, in this context, a legal judgment. Since, however, "the deed does not make the criminal unless the mind is criminal," the state of mind must be ascertained and a pathological state of mind is a psychiatric problem. However, the gauge for determining legal exculpation is not suitable for the differential diagnosis of psychiatric disability.

So, Section Four also sets up standards, it guides, and it limits the communications of the psychiatrists concerning mental disease and defect to the judge and the jury who are to make the legal decision. It is this second, and to some extent competing, function that concerns us. Confusion arises from this paradoxical effort to combine in one formula: 1) the criteria by which the courts will hold a man not legally responsible (i.e., punishable), and 2) the conditions for the exposition of the psychiatrist's knowledge.

The question clearly should be: How may the courts optimally elicit testimony from the psychiatrist concerning psychopathology so that its own legal question concerning responsibility may be answered with maximum information at its disposal?

The two major formulae, competing to supplant McNaughtan, are the

---

[1]The proposed American Law Institute formula: Section 4.

1. A person is not responsible for criminal conduct if at the time of such conduct as a result of mental disease or defect he lacks substantial capacity either to appreciate the criminality of his conduct or to conform his conduct to the requirements of law.

2. The terms "mental disease" or "defect" do not include an abnormality manifested only by repeated criminal or otherwise antisocial conduct.

proposed American Law Institute prescription and the Durham decision.[2] In our view both are refreshing and encouraging advances over McNaughtan and reveal significant agreement. The similarities between them might be summarized as follows: 1) each is intended to free from responsibility a man who has committed an illegal act that is the result of, or the product of, mental disease or defect; 2) each includes mental pathology—illness, disease, or defect; 3) each rejects exclusively cognitive or intellective approach; 4) neither formula, presumably, is primarily concerned to define mental illness but rather to indicate what degree of severity of mental illness protects an individual against the punitive and stigmatizing impact of criminal law; and 5) each incorporates the concept of causality, with the words "product of" and "as the result of." Both "product" and "result" refer to the cause. Cause is the circumstance, condition, event, which necessarily brings about or contributes to a result.

Within this framework we state our reservations concerning the American Law Institute formula. We hold that the subtlety, complexity, and obscurity of its psychological entities and its actual intrusion into the field of psychiatric diagnosis unnecessarily limit the contributions of psychiatry, present and potential, and needlessly restrict the medical and psychological resources upon which the court may draw. The legal requirements concerning appreciation of criminality and conformance of conduct and the negative definition that repeated criminal or otherwise antisocial conduct is not mental disease effect a gratuitous entrance into medical and scientific arenas that is unnecessary and may be harmful to the law's purposes.

Specifically, "substantial" and "capacity" are psychologically vague, ambiguous, unclear, and complex quantitative concepts. More importantly, "to appreciate the criminality" is an involved cognitive phrase at least as likely to lead to confusion as "knowledge of right and wrong." Further, since criminality is an illegal act with an accompanying mental state, is there not a logical inconsistency or tautology here? For if the offender cannot "appreciate the criminality," then his act is not criminal, and if it is criminal then he must have "appreciated" it.

"To conform his conduct to the requirements of law" is an inverse restatement of irresistible impulse that has proven to be an almost unusable defense. To lack "substantial capacity to conform his conduct to the requirements of law" is to have an irresistible impulse.

The terms "mental disease" or "defect" specifically exclude "an abnormality manifested only by repeated criminal or other antisocial conduct." To refer to mental disease and then to limit its meaning is to rob the court of the worth of the psychiatrist's expertness precisely to the degree that it limits his

---

[2]The Durham decision states that an accused is not criminally responsible if his unlawful act was the product of mental disease or mental defect. 94 U.S. 228, 214 F.2d 862 (App. D.C. 1954).

ability to transmit clinical information. It predisposes to failure in communication. The phrase "mental disease or defect" should serve as a focus for the communication and description of the combined behavior, feeling, ideas of a person so as to inform judge or jury.

If the courts wish to determine whether mental disease or defect exists, then the law must use not only the semantics but also the substance of psychiatry. It cannot, for example, meaningfully adopt psychiatric words and then appropriate to itself the right to establish psychiatric diagnosis criteria even by exclusion. It legally excludes forms of behavior which may themselves be symptomatic of pathology, for antisocial behavior may be the manifestation of illness. Repeated illegal or antisocial conduct is a manifestation of a personality, and this personality may be a sick one. There is a quality of behavior referred to as alloplastic, most commonly found in the psychopathic personality in which the symptom of psychopathology consists in the acting out. The manifestation of a man's abnormality may consist precisely in his repeated or otherwise antisocial conduct. To exclude such conduct from "mental illness" is to make a psychiatric judgment eliminating behavioral or conduct disorders.

Apparently there is no insistence on legal formulae in diagnosing physical diseases, so why in this case? If the physician were similarly forbidden to use one outstanding symptom as criterion for physical illness, the absurdity of such an approach would become apparent, or if he were limited to two tests it would be considered unscientific.

If the intent is to exclude the so-called psychopathic personality from irresponsibility, it is hard to see how it can succeed in this way. If the committee does not want to excuse as psychiatrically ill individuals the so-called psychopathic or sociopathic personality, this formula will not serve that purpose, for its use depends upon the testimony of psychiatrists; those who consider psychopathic or sociopathic personality a mental disease or defect will so testify and those who do not will not.

In summary, essentially the Model Penal Code formula has added to the cognitive criteria volitional criteria. It has eliminated behavioral criteria except when they are combined with other phenomena.

The Durham decision permits free communication of psychiatric information and the American Law Institute creates road blocks to such transmission. The Durham formula puts no limitations on psychiatric testimony except those which are implicit in the present state of the discipline. The American Law Institute formula requires psychiatric judgments as to substantial capacity, demands essentially cognitive criteria concerning capacity to control, and insists upon including legal criteria in the old tradition by attempting to eliminate the psychopathic personality.

Neither the Model Penal Code nor the Durham formula resolves the problems of psychiatry; no legal formula can. Psychiatry is an incomplete scientific and medical specialty. Indeed all medicine and science are developing and hence are incomplete. This is reason to encourage its contribution rather than to emphasize its limitations in the courts.

For these reasons we recommend the adoption of the historic practice of the New Hampshire Court, as recently reformulated in the case of Monte Durham.

Deviation and Community Sanctions*

GEORGE H. DESSION

The general topic of this symposium—psychiatry and the law—specifies two areas of social process in which individuals seem to experience exceptional difficulties in the pursuit of their objectives. Possibly that is what brings us together. My prime concern is with that joint part of the two areas that seems to present the greatest difficulty, namely, the infliction, under our joint auspices, or at least with our joint participation, of negative sanctions (e.g., criminal or otherwise severe penalties or measures) on individuals in the name of the community. These difficulties suggest the significance of a symposium effort such as this to compose the differences of perspective and of focus that have distinguished our respective disciplines in facing problems of negative sanctioning in the past.

The significance may indeed be critical, considering that the composing of such interdisciplinary differences appears to present problems of the same nature, if not of the same generally obvious magnitude, as those presented in any effort toward composition of differences between nations or cultures that do not share the same goals, identifications, and predispositions. In the contemporary world (and here I have a friendly dispute with our symposium title), we find not the law but rather a diversity of systems of law and public order, just as we find differing conceptions of the well-ordered or "healthy" personality and of the institutional patterns most likely to produce such personalities and facilitate their best functioning. Under these circumstances the composing of interdisciplinary differences between persons who share the same general culture and hence enjoy exceptional opportunities and facilities for communication may constitute one of the most strategic approaches to implementation of the total policy of any given community. I hope that this may first be achieved in our own.

DEVIATION

The sanctioning processes that now concern us take the form of community responses to individuals who do not (or are thought not to) conform to

---

*This edition is a slightly revised version of the original article that appeared in *Psychiatry and the Law*, ed. Paul H. Hoch and Joseph Zubin (New York: Grune & Stratton, 1955), pp. 1–12. Reprinted by permission of the publisher.

community norms. But "nonconformity" in our language is a loaded word, variously applied to past martyrs who were subsequently esteemed to have rendered their communities exceptional service as well as to persons whose contemporary designation as degenerates or criminals failed to improve through time. For that reason I shall adopt the more neutral term "deviation." I do not use it synonymously with "crime," for reasons that will be more fully developed in my discussion of sanctioning processes. I would broaden it to include all deviation which, if not responded to by recourse to a sanction-equivalent such as a welfare program to prevent it, or a positive sanction such as the offer of a reward or incentive to do otherwise, touches off severe negative sanctioning of the deviate. By the same token I would exclude deviation that the given community experiences with tolerance or relative indifference.

Definition aside, it may now be useful to consider this phenomenon of deviation a little further. We will always be speaking of events—and usually of past events—but in the light of their impact on the expectations of sanctioning decision makers with respect to probable future events. ("Events" include both acts and nonacts such as intrapsychic changes.) By deviation we sometimes refer to a large continuing complex of past events, e.g., a public nuisance condition such as a metropolitan slum subject to a sudden influx of rural or small-town immigrants, a home in which children are reared without parental affection or parental example conforming to the mores of the community, or a market structure characterized by a scarcity of wanted consumer goods coupled with a surplus of consumer dollars. We sometimes refer to a smaller complex of past events, e.g., a deviant personality. And we sometimes refer to a single deviant overt act. This three-way classification of deviation reflects three very different focuses of attention and implies quite different types of response. Given the first, one is likely to ask: What condition should be abated? Given the second: What individual should be isolated or reconstructed? Given the third: What act should be prohibited and what deprivation prescribed for the transgressor? The difference between these questions sharpens when one considers that a deviational act may not be symptomatic of a deviational personality (for example, in the case of an accidental, situational, or transitional offender), and that a dangerously deviant personality may exhibit no tendency toward overt aggression prior to his ultimate explosion into violence (for example, the overly passively conforming "good child" who years later goes berserk and commits a few seemingly senseless murders).

Deviation, of course, implies a norm, and perhaps something should be said at this point concerning values. I think that a workable conception of "community norms" or "law" must include an "ought" as well as an "is" component. I say this because a statement that such and such is "law" involves both a summary of the past behavior of people and a forecast as to their future behavior, and behavior is presumably not unmotivated. Then, too, one needs a frame of reference for the most rigidly empirical kind of evaluation of the consequences of any given past or prospective sanctioning decision. Having said that, however, like Dr. Lasswell I am content, for purposes of this discussion, to postulate values, and in this case the values that I take to be most widely shared in our national community. It includes, of course, a strong preference for wide, rather than narrow, distribution of the power to make decisions of importance to the community and a wide, rather than narrow, distribution of other human values such as respect.

SANCTIONING PROCESSES

There is probably no area of social process more in need of continuing empirical study and comparative evaluation than that comprising community responses to individuals who do not conform. Historically, in this area much always has been at stake for the community and for the individual, and there usually have been significant differences of opinion concerning the appropriateness of any given response. This latter is understandable enough, especially where the nonconformity is so disturbing to such a large number that the response takes the form of an invoking of severe legal, or at least social, negative sanctions. The response is then that of a group in which real anxiety has been aroused concerning a person whose suspect behavior engenders widespread fear or hostility. But if the disagreement is symptomatic of the emotional tension that must inhere in such responses, it also reflects the lack of an empirically based and generally accepted body of knowledge concerning the productive use of such sanctions. I have already referred to the diversity of forms of public order that obtain in the contemporary world, and I suppose it is obvious that these stem not merely from diverse value preferences but also from diverse conditioning, diverse expectations, and diverse identifications.

The critical role of these community responses becomes apparent when one considers their strategic impact on the forces constantly at work shaping the pace and direction of social change. If sanctions are wielded on behalf of a minority, sources of tension in the community are intensified. If they are intended to promote the best interests of the community as a whole but are ill devised in respect to know-how and technique, the community is unlikely to achieve its purpose and may even suffer an unwanted change in structure. If sanctions otherwise unobjectionable are invoked in an arbitrary manner, the liberties of individuals are, to that extent at least, curtailed without compensating benefit to anyone.

These considerations become more pressing in periods of heightened tension, ideologic conflict, and accelerated social change, just as they recede in periods when a community is enjoying a large measure of external security and internal stability. Our discussion here is necessarily pitched in the contemporary context of continuing world crisis. The stakes involved in the achievement of a widely preferred, rather than an imposed, form of public order have become sufficiently obvious to focus attention on the thrust and the consequences of sanctioning responses, be they responses in the name of a community with which one identifies or in the name of a hostile or competing community.

Our sanctioning responses are, of course, oriented in terms of our preferences in the matter of public order, so far as we know how, but they are also conditioned by our experience as we have interpreted it. Does not much of this latter stem from periods in which a relatively high measure of security and stability were enjoyed? Propositions valid in the one context may or may not hold in the other. In this spirit it may be useful to attempt to restate our public order preferences and to reexamine some of our predispositions, both the adaptive and the unadaptive, in this branch of the art and practice of government. Such effort may help to clarify our own thinking, and it may assist in communication with a wider audience. Even in our half of this bipolarizing world there are many who do not necessarily assume that the goal values of any given one of the component communities are what the community in question thinks they are and who do not share all of the predispositions of that given community.

To persons outside the culture of a community, the actions of the community are likely to speak louder than its words. To borrow a concept from the Anglo-American law of "evidence," there is such a thing as "speaking conduct." For the free community, e.g., one where many, rather than few, participate in important decisions, and in that sense checks and balances obtain, this poses special problems. Such a community necessarily speaks with many voices. For those conversant with the local culture, the harmony may not be too dissonant, the design not too unintegrated. For a larger audience or community in the making, this may not be the case. If the community that is to embrace our preferences in the matter of public order is to expand, it may well be that the dissonances must be rendered more harmonious, the overall design be tightened up. For us that cannot be achieved through the suppression of dissonant components. That could lead only to a more primitive pattern, expressing a more primitive concept of public order. Our problem is to achieve a higher synthesis, to find a rearrangement of the components and of the tensions between them, which will result in a more clear and significant statement, a more dynamic and satisfying design.

Who, in the sense of this inquiry, are the deviates and how, consistently with our values, should we treat them? Against what hazards should they be protected? The focus is on persons charged with crime, but just as the criminologists are finding it useful to work toward functional-developmental categories rather than to content themselves with the purely legal symptomatic classification of offenses and offenders, so here I suspect that functional

This proposition needs no belaboring. What may be worth exploring are a few of the differences in respect to goals and perspectives that psychiatrists seem to experience in the course of such contribution.

Differing value orientations between psychiatrists and community decision makers sometimes do seem to be involved. The psychiatrist is ordinarily therapy-oriented and professionally conditioned to think of his prime obligation as that to his patient. There can certainly be no quarrel with this, and no difficulties arise so long as the patient is not also a defendant in a sanctioning proceeding or otherwise in serious conflict with others. Where he is, however, the situation becomes more complicated. The community, too, is interested in the patient and in health and therapy generally, but its resources for the purpose are limited and hence must be used selectively, and on top of that the community has a great range of other interests. If total community policy is to be served, a rather complex arbitration may be involved. To take a very simple illustration, I imagine that a psychiatrist in military service may often have to weigh the probable impact on a combat unit's morale of an otherwise indicated release of one of its members from active duty. In this situation I imagine that the psychiatrist might feel pulled in conflicting directions.

Now let us imagine a situation in which there is no patient-physician relationship, but in which the psychiatrist is called upon to examine and report on a person he has never previously seen, as, for example, where the issue is court commitment. And let us further assume that after an examination typical under the circumstances, the psychiatrist is satisfied that this person qualifies as a potentially dangerous and aggressive psychopathic sex offender—though, to be sure, the person has thus far committed no overt offenses beyond indecent exposure. Here again we have problems of conflicting values. The community, if it has enacted one of the recent types of sex offender laws, has manifested some interest in the prevention of seriously aggressive sexual offenses and some willingness to rely on expert prophecy, but it may be assumed that the same community would be, generally speaking, very loath to authorize the infliction of severe negative sanctions on suspicion, however well founded the suspicion might appear to be. The common law requirements for conviction of an attempt, e.g., not merely proof of intent to commit the crime but also of overt action reasonably adapted to that end and carried to a point where there is a dangerous probability of success, manifest this second interest in civil liberty. In such a situation (assuming that commitment, even though coercive and indeterminate, is to be to a "hospital" for "treatment"), I can imagine that many medically oriented might be less troubled than many litigation-oriented.

I may be wrong in my supposition in this last instance, and in any event I have no impression that these allegedly preventive laws were primarily sponsored by psychiatrists. They do, however, suggest another interesting question: Should laws that undertake to define classes of persons who shall be subject to preventive sanctions (or, for that matter, correctional sanctions) speak in psychiatric or nonpsychiatric terms? And in what terms should the psychiatric witness who is heard on such issues be questioned and speak? Let me try to put it more concretely. Should we ask whether a person is a defective delinquent, psychopath, or character neurotic, or should we ask such questions as the following: What is the probability that this person will behave in such and such a fashion in the future, specifying the sorts of situations in which the answer assumes that he will find himself? What is the probability that such situations will occur? On what past events do you base these estimates? What have been your opportunities to validate estimates of this sort?

I raise this question because I am wondering whether the verbal categories that psychiatrists use in describing patients and in talking to one another in the physician-patient and therapeutic context may not involve value judgments which, however consistent with total community policy in that context, may be less so in the different context of social negative sanctioning. The difference I have in mind, of course, stems from the absence of coercion in the private medical practice situation and its omnipresence in the second. Here, however, my role in this discussion shifts. I would welcome discussion of this question.

Legislative Policy, Conformity, and Psychiatry*

HAROLD D. LASSWELL

There would be no occasion for this discussion if public officials always laid down standards that people would live up to, or, putting it the other way around, if people would live up to whatever is prescribed by the duly constituted authority of a democratic body politic. The relation between legislative policy and conformity is an ever present problem, whether the issue is posed by new legislation or the revision of old statutes. We are especially concerned in the present symposium with the actual and potential role played by the psychiatrist in relation to the compliance problems of legislative policy.

When new legislative proposals are under consideration the following questions are pertinent:

1) What degree of compliance will probably occur immediately on the announcement of a prescribed norm with its accompanying sanctions?

2) What degree of compliance will be reached as a result of a given level of enforcement activity?

When it is a matter of revising statutes, the following additional questions arise:

1) What trends have there been in the degree of compliance (and noncompliance)?

2) How has compliance been affected by the activities of enforcement authorities?

3) What factors other than enforcement have influenced the degree of compliance to date?

Since psychiatrists have special knowledge of human conduct, and particularly of motivations relating to authority, it is rational to involve them in legislative deliberations. This is constantly happening, often at the initiative

---

*This edition is a slightly revised version of the original article that appeared in *Psychiatry and the Law*, ed. Paul H. Hoch and Joseph Zubin (New York: Grune & Stratton, 1955), pp. 13–40. Reprinted by permission of the publisher.The viewpoint developed in this paper and in the one by Professor George H. Dession has been worked out in a joint seminar at the Yale Law School, conducted over a period of years. Separate authorship does not therefore imply independent responsibility for the results.

of the legislature, often at the initiative of private persons and associations, including psychiatrists themselves. Legislative committees invite physicians or medical associations to appear before them to submit material or even to aid in drafting. Participation in lawmaking may come about at the initiative of officials in the executive branch of government (at the local, state, federal, or international level). Some of these officials are qualified psychiatrists employed in civilian or military agencies who, in the ordinary course of business, propose or comment upon proposals on the way to the legislature. Psychiatrists having no official employment may be invited by their colleagues or other public servants in the executive branch to give advice and suggestions. Since members of the profession are in frequent contact with courts and the courts are involved in reports and recommendations, psychiatrists often affect legislation by way of the judicial branch. Advisory committees of psychiatrists may be set up by judicial, executive, or legislative organs to provide continuing consultation. Special commissions may be the channel of communication between government and psychiatrists.

A comprehensive inventory of the impact of the profession on legislation would take into account the many unofficial activities undertaken by private persons and associations, including psychiatrists.[1] At the instigation of private parties, or at one's own initiative, there may be appearances before legislative committees and other bodies with some role to play, in fact if not in name, in legislative policy. Besides addressing officials directly, there may be lectures given to civic and other associations, appearances on radio and television, films for classroom or more general use, pamphlets, articles in magazines of general or special circulation, and books.

In the cases referred to here, the psychiatrist is called upon as a qualified expert on certain phases of human conduct. This is the area with which we are presently concerned, with special reference to the whole network of activities coming within the purview of legislative policy. By concentrating upon these participations of the psychiatrist, we are leaving to one side the many additional roles that may be taken by the psychiatrist who is also an active Republican or Democrat; Protestant, Catholic, or Jew (and so on through the group identifications outside the profession). If we were considering the whole range of activities engaged in by members of the profession, it would doubtless appear that training and experience in the profession would influence at least some of the psychiatrists' beliefs, faiths, loyalties, and operations.

---

[1]There is no comprehensive examination of the impact of psychiatry on legislative policy, although important clues are found in standard histories of the profession, in legislation in various fields, and in the political process. See, for example, *One Hundred Years of American Psychiatry*, published for the American Psychiatric Association, New York, 1944; David B. Truman, *The Governmental Process: Political Interests and Public Opinion* (New York: Knopf, 1951); and Oliver Garceau, *The Political Life of the American Medical Association* (Cambridge, MA: Harvard University, 1941).

Insofar as these eventually impinge on legislative policy, they have a place in any study of the historic impact of psychiatry on legislation. Our scope is much more restricted, since the principal purpose is to raise some questions about the content of the legislative problems to which it is rational to expect that members of the psychiatric profession can make explicit contributions. It is a matter of clarifying the relevance of psychiatric knowledge to one of the main recurring problems of legislation, which is what to do in reference to existing or anticipated noncompliance with the prescriptions officially laid down by legislative bodies. Shall the prescriptions themselves be modified in the direction of greater, or less, comprehensiveness and severity? Shall efforts at enforcement be increased or decreased?

POLITICAL EQUILIBRIUM

It is helpful to think of the political process of the community as a dynamic equilibrium with many component factors. An examination of any community (town, city, region, nation) indicates that a "steady state" is maintained which, if interfered with by outside factors, tends to be reinstated. Cyclical fluctuations may be part of the steady state itself, since the magnitude of change in any direction determines the strength of the self-correcting drives that are mobilized in the opposite direction. A rough equilibrium relationship appears to obtain between statutory prescriptions, enforcement activities, and compliance. A flurry of legislation (perhaps precipitated by reports of what other communities are doing) may result over short periods in increased enforcement activity, though with high levels of noncompliance. It is not difficult to understand why noncompliance is likely to be high when new statutes go into effect. People often find that they are faced by new learning problems: to stop at a red light; to fill out a long tax form; to reorganize their bookkeeping methods. Besides learning problems, there may be motivational problems. The new arrangements may be bitterly resented in many quarters, and rumor may support the expectation that administrative snafu will lead to early repeal. Official agencies of enforcement perhaps failed to receive new appropriations sufficient to permit the enlargement of staffs.

The "built-in" tendencies that sustain the community equilibrium typically go into action, with the result that discrepancies are reduced between legislation, enforcement, and compliance. Learning errors may be overcome, and resentments may die down. Enforcement agents may be increased, or the technique of administration may be improved. The most offensive and difficult requirements may be cut out of the revised statutes.

It is not to be understood that the steady state means that the tendency is to eliminate all discrepancies among prescriptions, enforcement, and compliance. In reference to every comparable set of policies, research may show that the community equilibrium position is characterized by comparatively high levels of noncompliance and nonenforcement. This is particularly well known in municipalities where high levels of compliance may be maintained in the middle- and high-rent residential wards so far as ordinances against gambling and prostitution are concerned. At the same time the downtown high mobility wards may show high levels of noncompliance, coupled with slack enforcement. In the residential areas the limited amount of active enforcement, on the other hand, may be prompt and potent. Hence, we infer that the steady state of the municipality in question is characterized by territorial specialization in efforts at enforcement and in the facts of compliance.

We note that the equilibrium of a community may be upset at the enforcement or compliance level, rather than by a flurry of legislation. A strong "syndicate" may move in from another city and may upset the balance by attempting to spread organized prostitution and gambling to the residential areas, thus arousing intense civic activity designed to "abolish crime" with a law enforcement mayor and council (culminating as a rule in restoring the previous "territorial" adaptation). The equilibrium may be disrupted by a vigorous "law enforcement drive," originating with an ambitious prosecutor, for instance, or a reform association stimulated by some dramatic exposés. After some initial changes, the older influences may succeed in reasserting themselves, restoring the previous equilibrium.[2]

In describing governmental activities we have employed the three categories traditional in the United States: legislative, executive, judicial. Valuable as this breakdown is for many purposes, it is convenient to employ a more differentiating classification. The first functional component already has been referred to, namely, the making of *prescriptions*. The prescribing function is typically performed by constitutional conventions and legislative bodies. They lay down formal requirements of a general character for the guidance of decisions. Another function is *recommendation*. Among us it is carried on by political parties, pressure groups, and private persons. There is the function of *intelligence*, or the supplying of knowledge of the past and estimates of the future. (In modern communities the media for the gathering and dissemination of news are the principal structures specialized to the job.) We speak also of an *invoking* function. This is the making of a provisional characterization of an act as constituting a violation of, or a conformance to, community prescription. The official who issues a warrant of arrest is performing an act of invocation. The *applying* function is the final assessment of an act according to conformity or nonconformity and is typically performed by courts. The *appraisal* function is closely connected with intelligence, though

---

[2]Cyclical fluctuations in offenses are often described in more or less explicit relation to the larger equilibrium of the community. An example is "The Correctional Cycle" in Lowell J. Carr, *Delinquency Control* (rev. ed., New York: Harpers, 1950), pp. 223ff.

specialized to assessing the effect of past policy. The *terminating* function is the ending of official prescriptions such as treaties or compacts.[3] It is obvious that the psychiatrist is involved in varying degree with all functions and hence with all structures (and substructures) engaged therein. So far as legislative prescription is concerned, the chief participation by members of the profession is in recommendation, intelligence, and appraisal. In connection with his therapeutic and administrative activities the psychiatrist is also involved in concrete cases in which the other functions are predominant, such as invocation (asking for commitment), application (litigation), and termination (of court orders). (It is within the scope of Professor Dession's paper to deal with these postlegislative functions.)

We obtain another perspective on the role of psychiatry when we consider the legislative process as a whole. The prescriptions of a body politic fall into two broad categories: *constitutive* and *legislative*. The two differ in generality, the former referring to the most important arrangements by which community decisions are authorized to be made, and the second to the most inclusive prescriptions within this framework. The constitutive prescriptions deal with the overriding goal values of the body politic, the peaceful procedures by which basic patterns of public order can be modified, the organs by which decisions pursuant to fundamental goals are to be made, and the procedures by which the organs of decision are chosen. In the United States the formal prescriptions at the constitutive level are found in a written charter—the original instrument as amended. In some nation-states no one document has the status of a charter, although several may be accepted as fundamental authority, e.g., the Magna Charta and the Petition of Rights in Great Britain. When we study preliterate societies, it is necessary to rely upon oral tradition to identify the basic provisions.

For many purposes it is convenient to classify legislative prescriptions into codes according to the degree and kind of community intervention entailed.[4] The following classification results: supervisory, regulative, enterprisory, corrective, and executory.

The *supervisory* code lays down the rules governing private agreement and private wrongs. Our civilization has a strong bias in favor of respecting the initiative of individuals in the making of arrangements with one another. We like to think of the officials of government as umpires who are resorted to only under special circumstances, as when the parties disagree about the

---

[3]On functional analysis see Lasswell and Abraham Kaplan, *Power and Society: A Framework for Political Inquiry* (New Haven: Yale University Press, 1950); Myres S. McDougal, "The Comparative Study of Law for Policy Purposes," *Yale Law Journal* 61 (1952): 915–46. See also *American Journal of Comparative Law* 1, no. 1.

[4]The classification is for use in comparative legal study and does not necessarily correspond to the labels attached to "codes" or to the topical subdivisions of the "collected statutes" of any one body politic.

meaning of an obligation or one of the parties is accused of evading performance. The community code lays down the requirements to be met by the private agreements that government officials accept as enforceable. However, the initiative for alleged violations of an understanding come not from the government but from private parties. Once the machinery of the community is invoked, the matter may be withdrawn if at any point the parties are able to compose their differences. The coercion of the body politic is, however, available to enforce the judgment made by public officials when the parties at interest are unable to settle their disagreement. When we examine the supervisory codes of a modern industrial society like the United States we find that the "law of contract" and of "tort" falls in this broad category. Tort is part of the supervisory code because, like contracts, it has to do with relationships among private parties.[5] Even when agreements have not been made among individuals in the community, disputes may arise in which it is alleged that a standard of conduct has been violated, and that deprivation has resulted that ought to be cured by a compensating deprivation. The community prescribes a code of conduct in which is stated "who is to compensate whom for what and how." Here again the officials of the community do not act until a private party takes the initiative, alleging a deprivation, and pointing to a target from whom compensation is sought. At every step of the ensuing proceedings, the community is ready to withdraw if the parties are able to settle their differences.

It often happens that private arrangements, which are permissible when considered separately or that occur with a certain frequency in the community, add up to an aggregate whose effects violate basic community policies. In the United States a fundamental policy is to preserve an economic system of competitive private enterprise. The implementation of such a policy calls for rules by which private monopoly can be identified and either prevented or abolished. In order to protect the structure of competitive private economy the government may intervene to compel the dissolution of corporations, according to the rules of a *regulative* code. The regulative codes of a free society are designed to defend or foster the attainment of institutional structures that foster the general sharing of all values.[6]

The third legislative code is *enterprisory*, which refers to the activities to be performed directly by the community acting through governmental

---

[5]Although the recognized categories of "tort" and "contract" in the Anglo-American legal system fall readily into the supervisory code as here defined, the fit is not perfect since the line between individual and governmental initiative is not always clear-cut in the judicial process. Examples readily suggest themselves in the law of workman's compensation, domestic relations, and in the commitment of the mentally ill.

[6]In general, then, we define the regulative code as implementing the constitutive code by adding further specification of the standards to be applied in evaluating the aggregate pattern of activities left to private arrangement.

institutions. In modern nation-states it is taken for granted that the raising and equipping of armies and the conduct of relations with other countries come within the province of government. There, of course, may be many variations from one nation to another. It is the task of the operational code to authorize direct activities and to lay down the basic outlines of their execution.

The fourth code is *corrective*. It is founded upon the expectation that the prescriptions laid down in all community codes are likely to be breached. The corrective code classifies such situations as "destructive" in varying degree, and the participants as "precipitators" or "recipients" of damage. Situations are destructive according to the degree of damage that has been or is expected to be done to community values. The most important distinction to be made among the precipitators is between those with "destructive intent" and those with "no destructive intent." If the act with damaging results was unintended, there is no basis for charging it to the individual who precipitated it. Rather the damage is a common risk of living in a given society. Hence, it is appropriate for the community as a whole to shoulder the burden of reparation and relief. Intended damage is a different matter. One aim of the community is to do away with "externalized destructive intent," with failure to control destructive drives. The existence of a deliberate offender means that the community has failed to achieve a social process in which people have the will and the skill to refrain from dangerous acts. When the community is confronted by such a failure, the problem is not only how to repair whatever damage has been done, if possible, but also how to act toward the precipitating person. The corrective code deals with the categories to be employed by the community in reference to these individuals. When no destructive intent is present, the situation comes within the purview of the other legislative codes.[7]

---

[7] We are reaffirming the ancient maxim: "No crime without criminal intent." This removes from the purview of the corrective code some of the material found in our ordinary penal code when the consideration of intent is excluded. Typically, these exclusions are what we classify as "regulative," since they impose deprivations as a convenient device for protecting the political and social structure irrespective of the intentions of the targets of community coercion. The category of "absolute liability," for example, may ignore either the fact or the degree of damage done as well as the intent. Unlicensed possession of firearms may carry "automatic" penalties. In this connection what is called "negligence" is especially interesting. A duty may be imposed upon some individuals to maintain greater vigilance than persons engaged in ordinary pursuits. Thus the courts have held that junk dealers have a duty of alertness in regard to stolen property. The policy objectives of the community are quite clear in this connection, since one of the ways to reduce offenses against property is to impose barriers upon the disposition of stolen goods. If the damage from lack of alertness is great, or is viewed as potentially significant, the offense may be called "culpable negligence" even though no intent enters. Since we are including "unconscious" as well as "conscious" intent in our definition, some of the cases now commonly viewed as involving no destructive intent come within the purview of the corrective code. If it can be shown, for instance, that X is "accident prone," he is a correctional problem, and community values are not properly served by leaving him to be dealt with by private initiative

The *executory* code prescribes "who acts how" in putting prescriptions into effect, and gives particular attention to the use of positive or negative sanctions for the purpose of improving the probability of conformity to community norms.

Although the findings of psychiatry have an important bearing on legislative questions arising in connection with every code, it is not difficult to identify the areas in which the specialized competence of the psychiatrist has immediate and obvious usefulness. We speak especially of the corrective and the executory codes. Since the corrective code deals with questions of destructive intent, the psychiatric viewpoint is of major relevance. The executory code deals directly with persons in the hope of changing their future conduct; and this enterprise must draw heavily on current knowledge of human behavior.

Whatever the code concerned, the weighing of facts and estimates of conformity are invariably involved in legislative policy. Psychiatric knowledge has had, or can have, an important continuing impact on legislation by providing a basis of inference about all pertinent human activities. The chief relations to be discussed are:

1) clarifying goals and values and institutional objectives;
2) disclosing the causes and consequences of conformity and nonconformity; and
3) estimating and appraising enforcement policy.

Clarifying Goal Values and Institutional Objectives

The overriding goals sought by legislation in a democratic body politic are to be discovered in written constitutional charters and in unwritten practice. In what sense is "conformity" a goal of democracy? Not conformity in the sense of discouraging initiative or outspokenness but conformity to the prescriptions laid down by duly constituted authority. The public order of a democratic body politic aims at protecting dissent without indulging rebellion, nullification, and other forms of overt lawlessness. It is a challenge to the public order of popular governments, either to disobey the clear requirements

---

through the invocation of tort liability. On the variety of community policies at stake in certain kinds of "crime" see the information and analysis of one category of offenses in Jerome Hall, *Law, Theft and Society*, 2d. ed. (Indianapolis: Bobbs-Merrill, 1952). A preliminary organization of the entire correctional field in terms of community values and institutions is George H. Dession, *Criminal Law, Administration and Public Order* (Charlottesville, VA: Mitchie Casebook Corporation, 1948).

of the statutes or to increase the use of private coercion in the relations among neighbors in the internal politics of private associations, pressure groups, or political parties. The institutions of the body politic are designed to exercise a formal and effective monopoly of coercion and to turn this coercion against any violator of this monopoly, or anyone who defies the lawful prescriptions of the community.

No one seriously disputes these principles. But the reaffirmation of the principle of obedience is not enough. The plain fact of experience is that many legislative norms are violated. Do the specialized investigators of human conduct have anything useful to say in addition to reaffirming the maxim that all laws are to be obeyed? If the specialists have nothing to contribute save a reiteration of the principle, they are not worth turning to since moralists and laymen are quite capable of reaffirming the same principle, either at the level of doctrinal sophistication or popular folk culture.

(a) *The request for specification.* We suspect that the potential contribution of the psychiatrist to legislative policy is sufficiently distinctive to distinguish psychiatrists from laymen, ethicists, or theologians. In common with all specialized students of human behavior, psychiatrists seek to discover the causes and consequences of man in culture. The principal task is to improve the methods and available findings about the factors that explain the occurrence and the results of the values and practices of specific societies and of society in general. Within this frame of reference the specialists on psychiatry supply the contributions that come from their professional concern with health and disease, and with particular kinds of disease. Like all behavioral scientists, they are explainers of values and practices; it is not incumbent upon them to advocate comprehensive systems of value, or to rival the theologians or the philosophers in arguing the transcendent truth of any given set of social values.

It is quite impossible for the distinctive skills of the psychiatrist to come into play until relatively unambiguous specifications are given to words. He cannot study the causes and consequences of "conformity," or of "democracy," or "human dignity," until these terms are given definitions that are sufficiently explicit to enable concrete cases to be identified for study. The working definitions do not need to be comprehensive; it is only necessary for them to be definite.

The need of specification affords a clue to the nature of the psychiatrist's contribution to legislative policy. He asks if the legislator intends to consider that conforming conduct in the community is an "absolute" value to be achieved at any price (in terms of other values). If compliance is absolute, in this sense, what are the subordinate values, together with their specifications, that the legislator is willing to sacrifice? Once these definitions are clear, the psychiatrist can aid the legislator by reporting on the past and estimating the future. On the basis of appropriate methods, it is possible to report on the cost of the degree of compliance obtained in the past and to anticipate the cost of obtaining total compliance in the years ahead.

In our society the reply of the legislator to the request for specification of conformity as an "absolute" typically produces a disclaimer.[8] With rare exceptions our legislators regard themselves as operating in a world of multiple values, and "the demand for compliance" may not even be accepted as a top value. Instead, it may be conceived as a specification of another value or values. It may simply be regarded as one of the many specific patterns of "right or wrong" (the rectitude value). The prevailing view is likely to be that in a "perfect" society there would be no discrepancy between prescriptions and compliance, and that enforcement efforts would be confined to information and education, with no need of utilizing negative sanctions. In the meanwhile, it is taken for granted that discrepancies will be found, even though a good deal of weight is attached to the desirability of sustaining as far as possible a nondiscrepant relationship. If pressed to state in general terms the degree of weight attached to obtaining compliance, the legislator will typically hedge and object that he cannot be guided by abstract principles in the complex situations that confront him and his colleagues.

The psychiatrist's demand for specification does not necessarily fall on barren soil, however. It is quite feasible for legislators to cite many of the values (with explicit practices) that they regard as pertinent to the making of legislative policy. By careful interviewing (and by the examination of legislative debates), it is possible to identify a number of value-institutional patterns that apply to the problems with which the legislators of a given time and place are grappling. If a concrete set of studies is under contemplation, it is useful to devise a set of categories for the purpose of classifying the statements relating to values and practices.[9] Some of the pertinent patterns are matters relating to the *power* value. That is to say, the specific patterns are related to the decision-making process at home and abroad. National security is a phase of power, and some conformity problems are interrelated with the security of the country. Disunity spells vulnerability, and if vigorous enforcement attempts on behalf of a proposed statute are likely to result in intensified opposition among minorities and to precipitate lawlessness, it may be doubted

---

[8]A sophisticated examination of the working politician in a democratic system is L. D. White and T. V. Smith, *Politics and Public Service* (Chicago: University of Chicago Press, 1939). Case studies in public administration provide ample indications of the role of legislators as viewed by administrators and political scientists. Consult Harold Stein, ed., *Public Administration and Policy Development, A Case Book* (New York: Harcourt Brace, 1952); Stephen K. Bailey, *Congress Makes a Law: The Story Behind the Employment Act of 1946* (New York: Columbia University Press, 1950); Stephen K. Bailey and Howard D. Samuel, *Congress at Work* (New York: Holt, 1952); Bertram G. Gross, *The Legislative Struggle: A Study in Social Combat* (New York: McGraw-Hill, 1953); and Dayton D. McKeon, *Pressure on the Legislature of New Jersey* (New York: Columbia University Press, 1938).

[9]An advantage of the value or policy orientation is that it accustoms the student of comparative law to operate with a comprehensive though provisional set of categories for the examination of the social process in any contemporary or historical setting.

whether the time is ripe for the new measure. Secession, rebellion, and desertion to the enemy are examples of the most extreme results that may be envisaged if conformity is insisted upon. Besides power, the *respect* value is at stake in situations involving conformity. Social class (and caste) relations come in the respect category, and legislation designed to block the rise of new social formations by strengthening the ancient disabilities that they have suffered is likely to provoke the sharpest protest and most vigorous efforts at nullification, despite the satisfaction with which the "policy of restoration" may be viewed by the older social classes. Some problems of conformity directly involve the value of *well-being* (safety, comfort, health), as in the case of failure to abide by sanitary and health regulations. Nonconformity to compulsory educational statutes poses many questions, such as community losses from lack of enlightenment and skill in the rising generation. Nonconformity in the market may undercut the structure of the competitive economy and put great monopolistic combines in command of the production and distribution of wealth. The cost of administrative and judicial measures of enforcement enter into the reckoning of economic factors. Some hotly controversial matters may alienate friends and divide families, in this way affecting the realization of congenial human relationships (affection) in the community or discrediting the church as a sponsor of standards of right and wrong in the eyes of the humbler classes in society (in this way undermining the rectitude consensus and creating a sense of injustice).

In the course of obtaining the clarification of policy goals, it is usual to find that values which were initially posed in "absolute" terms change their position in the context. "Retributive punishment" is a good example. The specific demand to "boil the kidnapper in oil" may presently be justified in terms of its alleged effect on other values. "We've been too soft with kidnappers; they should be tortured. That will cut down crime." Such an approach implies the goal of deterrence and opens the way to data about the past and probable future impact of "boiling" on kidnapping. It is also likely that the legislator will seek to justify his statement of preference for retributive action by reformulating it as a necessary deviation from some more comprehensive definition of morality, and to refer the definition of morality to a source transcending the social process and inaccessible to empirical study. Retributive justice is thus put forward as "moral" by definition, and derived from "God's will" or a "metaphysical norm" by definition. Since the psychiatrist is a specialist on empirical inquiry he does not, in his professional capacity, match nonempirical assertions with legislators.[10]

---

[10]In many discussions of retributive justice the shift to the consideration of side effects takes place so rapidly that the advocates of retribution as an end in itself do not specify criteria for the degree of suffering to be imposed upon the offender. The discussion often veers to the power value, as when severe penalties are justified as a means of avoiding riots and other evidences of public dissatisfaction with the treatment of offenders.

Can the specification of objectives lead to the ordering of values to serve as a guide to the work of investigation in contributing to the eventual judgment of the legislator? So far as concrete specifications go, the psychologists, and especially the students of opinion, have worked out procedures for exhibiting the rank order of preference involved. But it is rarely feasible at present in our culture to obtain the cooperation of legislative committees in taking opinion tests. If it is a matter of ranking highly abstract statements of preference, it is doubtful that any clarification can be obtained. Most of us would agree that both of the following propositions are acceptable: the conception of mutual respect implies that the majority has some regard for the opinions and sentiments of those who constitute the minority; the conception also implies an obligation on the part of minorities to have some regard for the opinions and sentiments of the majority. Does this help us grapple with concrete cases? This may well be doubted. The "middle range" between the statements affirming the overriding goals of the community and the specifics of concrete situations cannot be usefully filled in by the proliferation of principles. The process of eliciting specifications of meaning from the legislator prepares the way, not for the multiplying of "principle" but for observed data and future estimate. In this way the context in which the legislator must make up his mind gains in clarity and pertinence to the full-scale policy goals of the body politic. It is the act of specification and the act of receiving information and estimates of the future that improve the likelihood that the legislative process can result in the making of rational and valid prescriptions.

(b) *Confronting conflicting specifications with data.* We turn now to a brief consideration of the acts following upon specification that may be influenced by the psychiatrist. The data provided by the psychiatrist may show that the specifications of policy objective made by legislators conflict with one another. It is not a question of alleged inconsistencies in the wording of statutes, frequent as these may be. It is a matter of incompatible results as ascertained by inquiry or as indicated by an informed judgment as to the probable facts.

Legislators do not necessarily change their specifications because data show that one objective is achieved at the cost of other policy goals. Assume, for instance, that data concerning "punishments" inflicted as "retributions" fail to "deter" offenders; that on the contrary, offenses multiply owing in part to the sense of "righteous indignation" against "unendurable provocation" by legislative majorities. It is for the legislator to view the whole context and to make up his mind whether to relinquish retributive punishment as a value in itself, or simply as one working definition of rectitude or whether to continue his support of the policy.[11] We have noted that the psychiatrist is stepping

---

[11]The information supplied by Dr. Kinsey about the relationship between sexual activity and statutes pertaining to sex has not moved many legislators to change official norms.

outside his specialist role if he matches overall statements of preference with the legislator.

(c) *Confronting derivational claims with data.* The contribution of the psychiatrist to the clarification of public policy may be the result of using data to confront "derivations rather than specifications." We have called attention to the fact that the social values affirmed by a legislator may be justified by alleging that the value is derived from a source transcending the social process. In his distinctive role the psychiatrist does not have access to a natural order that issues a preference; he sees only sequences in which value preferences arise within the social process and not outside it.

There are, nevertheless, certain contributions that the psychiatrist can make in his scientific capacity when normative statements allegedly derived from a transcendent source are introduced into the discussion of legislative policy. He can sometimes raise a doubt by reporting observations about those who put forward and accept some of these statements. It is within his competence to report (if he does in fact make such observation) that persons who desire the suffering of others are likely to be recruited from among those who have experienced relatively unloving, contemptuous, or cruel family environments. This does not, of course, dispose of the preference problem; the argument can always be made that ethical truth is unaffected by the discovery of factors that explain why it is accepted and propagated.

In addition, the psychiatrist can sometimes cast doubt upon the usefulness of seeking to invoke transcendent factors in view of the availability of empirical explanations. Historically, the profession of psychiatry, or at least of some psychiatrists, played an important part in undermining the witchcraft "hypothesis." The phenomena seemed intelligible without introducing supra-empirical elements.[12]

(d) *Confronting legislators with conceptions of "health" and "disease."* Since psychiatrists are physicians, and to a certain extent physiologists and biologists, they are accustomed to operate with the conception of health and disease. It is not surprising to find that they often employ these fundamental terms in addressing themselves to legislators. Does this result in the clarification of basic community objectives?

In modern psychiatry many specialists are aware of the transformation that has occurred in the frame of reference of health or disease. The transformation has come about in the course of discovering the social—the "interindividual" or "interpersonal"—as distinct from the solitary (individual) as the distinctive context of psychiatry. A parallel reconstruction is occurring in all medical science, though for many reasons the pace is especially swift among psychiatrists. The transition from the "cell" or "tissue" or "organ" view of

---

[12]The standard reference is Gregory Zilboorg (with George W. Henry), *A History of Medical Psychology* (New York: Norton, 1941).

the individual organism has grown out of the problems implicit in the conception of "functional" disorder. When a disorder is categorized as functional, the frame of reference has moved to the social process. The processes within the organism are no longer decisive in supplying the criteria for an estimate of health or disease, or any synonymous term such as "integration" and "disintegration." In many cases the intensive examination of the individual shows that though organically intact conflicting systems of drive sustain the behavior disorientation. For present purposes the significant point is that in arriving at an assessment of the presence or absence of disease, joint consideration must be given to the entire context of person-to-person relationships and to the system of internal interaction. A judgment of behavior disorder is necessarily made from a point of view in which the social context is taken into account.

It is the introduction of meanings (of social values: of systems of expectation, demand, identification, and operation) that constitutes the revolutionary change in the physician's frame of reference. Not only are these features of the context pertinent for a tentative diagnosis of disorder, but they are also among the determining factors in the etiology of a disorder. Inner conflicts appear as outcomes of exposure to past situations in which value deprivations or indulgences were imposed upon the person. Thus, a search for the determining context includes both the social environment and the person. Particular practices of child rearing in the home—to choose the most obvious instance—become part of the disease process. Difficulties centering around the giving or withholding of affection, the encouraging or discouraging of infantile curiosity (enlightenment), and scores of other practices come into the picture. The symptoms that are localized within particular individuals, such as somatic disturbances, turn out in the modern perspective to represent localizations of damage in a total context of social interaction. The interactions are the locus of the disease process, not the symptoms.[13]

Given the new context that is emerging in modern medicine, only candor and calmness can obviate the appearance of head-on collisions between psychiatrists and legislators. In the name of well-being ("healthy" hence "well integrated" human beings), psychiatrists may challenge the value specifications of legislators. If the psychiatrist lays the cards on the table, he can clarify his own definitions in the same way that he challenges the legislator to specify goal values and institutional objectives. For instance, if the physician stigmatizes as destructive those social patterns that contribute in significant degree to the incidence of anxiety-driven personality systems, he will be able to provide guidance to legislative policymakers as knowledge expands. With this frame of reference, psychiatrists can estimate the probability that the

---

[13]Some reminders: Harry Stack Sullivan, "Conceptions of Modern Psychiatry," The First William Alanson White Memorial Lectures, *Psychiatry* 3 (1940): 1–117; Jurgen Ruesch and Gregory Bateson, *Communication: The Social Matrix of Psychiatry* (New York: Norton, 1951).

measures under contemplation by legislators are likely to contribute to, or reduce, the occurrence of anxiety-free persons.

To the extent that data warrant his recommendations, the psychiatrist, in common with other behavioral scientists, is reappraising the patterns of current culture and fostering redefinition. The legislator's conceptions of democratic character are open to question when confronted by the physician's conceptions of health and disease. If both can be brought to specify definitions, there need be no permanent misunderstanding.[14]

(e) *Disclosing the motives for extreme legislation.* It is unlikely that psychiatrists have had much effect on the self-awareness of modern legislators, although this may be one of the long-range results of an expanding science. Popular outbursts of hostility create an environment in which the legislator who obtains a tactical advantage is the one who is willing to introduce the most "absolute" bills with the most drastic sanctioning requirements. If popular sentiment quickly dissipates, we may hear no more of the proposal. But some persons are prone to impose their will on others, in the name of righteousness, and push through unenforceable statutes that give rise to chronic difficulties of enforcement and compliance. With the spread of psychiatric understanding such compulsive characters may not themselves be changed, but their influence may be diminished by inducing greater resistance to fanaticism that parades in the name of virtue.

During prosperous and secure periods, however, popular government is more amenable to extremism of a different kind: a movement in which standards and sanctions are disproportionately low, and there is easy acquiescence in slack administration and casual compliance. Many incentives are offered to the legislator to shirk his responsibility for severe discipline in the public interest. It would be too much to expect psychiatry to improve public morality by the spread of insight into frivolousness and irresponsibility. However, it is conceivable that during periods of comparative security a chief contribution of psychiatry will be in disclosing the motives to "buck passing" among the nominal leaders of a body politic.

Disclosing the Causes and Consequences of Conformity and Nonconformity

The psychiatrist usually feels on solid ground when he considers some of the factors involved in conforming or nonconforming conduct. Psychoanalytic psychiatry puts the stress on unconscious factors, making for the acceptance or rejection of authority in the home and in later contexts. It is evident

---

[14]The most striking position is taken by physicians who assert that medical inquiry has shown the dependence of the bodily and physical integrity of the person upon affection and

that some personality systems contain incompatible drives toward dependent conformity at one pole and extreme rebelliousness at the other. (That these matters are immediately pertinent to administrative and judicial agencies which are engaged in invoking and applying legislative standards is the point to which my colleague devotes extended consideration.) The present question is whether at the level of legislative policy the disclosures of psychiatry concerning unconscious and early conditioning of behavior are helpful.

It may appear at first glance that some recurring problems of legislative policy can be little benefited by the scientific knowledge and interpretations of the psychiatrist. There are many cases in which a policy that is strongly supported by local mores deviates from the mores of the nation as a whole. (Examples are the opposition of Tennessee and Kentucky mountain folk to federal taxation and the position of blacks in various localities.) These cases are to be distinguished from the situation in which there is a demand for legislative action on behalf of ideals of conduct, which though generally accepted, are expected to be widely violated. (Familiar instances are gambling, prostitution, and assault with intent to kill.) The "mores" are the accepted standards; the "countermores" are the deviations from the standards that are, in fact, expected to occur. (We do not include as part of the "culture" those infrequent acts that are regarded by the participants in a culture as shocking and inhuman, such as the sexual violation and torture of a small child. Ordinary rape is countermores since it is expected to occur with some frequency, despite the mores standard.)

Think for a moment of the problem presented when federal legislation is proposed to attack the various discriminations to which blacks are subject. If we accept the fundamental goal of human dignity, how can we tolerate the continued victimization of blacks? Shall we not invoke lawful coercion, if necessary, to fight local campaigns of resistance to legislative policies that are in clear implementation of basic constitutional and societal values?

Among the costs of coercion from the center is countercoercion (or nullification) at the local level. Where local sentiment is intense, it may appear that scientists have nothing to offer. But this is not necessarily so. There are moderating elements in the conflict, and the findings of psychiatric medicine can be counted among them. It has provided a supplementary factual basis for compassionate attitudes toward human error and prejudice. The stress that has been put upon the unconscious and the ego ideal, and especially upon the persisting effect of early experience, suggests that deep-lying attitudes are

---

respect. This approach has most in common with the problem of democratic leadership and eliteship, to say nothing of the reduction of human destructiveness. Scientists and physicians who adopt this view are therefore committed to explore the entire process for the purpose of discerning and abolishing whatever impairs the self-respect of human beings. This is a value-oriented medicine. Lasswell, *Power and Personality*, T. W. Salmon Memorial Lectures (New York: Norton, 1948), pp. 117–18.

transmitted by a social process that incapacitates many individuals from learning, save under exceptional circumstances. In good faith respect for human dignity can be interpreted to mean patience with those who have been systematically indoctrinated with error.

But what of the targets of human indignity? Can we quietly tolerate their continued victimization, with all the personality deformations that result? Does not psychiatry suggest the salutary role of assertiveness in putting a stop to environmental intrusions? On balance these countervailing considerations appear to support a policy of continuous moral pressure designed to divide the consciences of the local minority against itself. The result can be furthered by offering positive inducements in support of policies that hasten the social transformations that work against the older attitudes (increased industrialization, further opportunities for experience elsewhere, etc.).

Estimating and Appraising Enforcement Policy

The examination of enforcement policy presents many dimensions that come within the scope of the psychiatrist's conception of his special function. The legislator must choose more than the policy objectives to be sought by his prescriptions. He must select the sanctions (the deprivations and indulgences) to be authorized in dealing with those who deviate from the norms laid down in the statutes. In addition to the *sanctioning* problems are what may be called the *service* problems, the latter referring to the operations to be engaged in by administrative officials prior to the invoking or application of sanctions. The service activities include campaigns of enlightenment and the adjustment of government policy in order to diminish provocations to deviation.

"Sanctioning law" is a comparatively uncultivated field in the sense that it does not figure in the curriculum of the law schools. Nevertheless a great deal of research has a direct bearing upon it. In many ways the greatest success in the study and guidance of policy has been in the granting or withholding of parole. Legislative reference bureaus are constantly confronted by problems of sanction law, since the draftsmen of the bureaus are in practice given a great deal of scope in formulating the clauses in which "penalties" are prescribed. It is not inaccurate to say that at present the sanctions found in the statutes represent concessions to the whims of overburdened legislators (and draftsmen) rather than inferences supported by great bodies of analyzed experience. Devices like the suspended sentence are provisional solutions of the problems involved, provisional in the sense that they "pass the buck" to administrators, and in the further sense that they often provide no adequate criteria for the exercise and review of discretion in concrete cases. When the legislature fails to provide some standards of purpose, or some criteria for the implementation of purpose, the gate is left open for trouble. The difficulty takes the form of resentment against "administrative arbitrariness," whether in "unreasonably severe" or "soft" decisions. In any case the legislature has failed to provide a degree of clarification of community objectives that enables the courts to provide a stable frame of reference for the review of challenged administrative acts. To the extent that psychiatric knowledge enables the legislator to foresee the probable consequences of various sanctioning alternatives, psychiatrists can contribute to the growth of a stable body of doctrine and application in this area.

It is perhaps worth emphasizing the point that sanctions may be positive or negative, that they may invoke any or all categories of value (and practice), and that they may vary in severity and mildness. Positive sanctions are more often relied upon in the implementation of the regulative code than in other codes. Some nations support the existing structure of society by honoring distinguished service by improving the power position of the individual, perhaps making him an appointive member of the legislature. Economic inducements (tax exemptions, tariff protections) may be offered to new enterprises in order to preserve the competitive market by facilitating entry. Honors and titles (emblems of respect) are standard rewards. Medical attention, access to educational opportunities to acquire a skill, and access to secret information are among the indulgences given to those who measure up to various requirements. There also may be commendation for high standards of integrity (rectitude), and opportunity may be provided for enjoying affection at home among friends.

In the corrective field we are accustomed to rely upon negative sanctions and to impose deprivations in terms of any value. We disqualify the individual from voting or holding office, which is a deprivation in terms of participation in the community power process. We inflict an economic deprivation by levying fines. We deny enlightenment by cutting him off from sources of information. We interfere with his physical well-being by making him liable to hard and debilitating labor. We deny opportunities to acquire or exercise skill. We refuse the claim that a given act is a religious exercise and condemn it as immoral and unlawful. We cut him off from family and friends by solitary confinement. We attack his respect position by branding him as dishonorable.

Much of what we have called corrective and executory codes is traditionally discussed as "criminal law and legislation." The confusions involved in the traditional usage have been increasingly clear. One connotation was that in "criminal" matters the community takes the initiative. This does in fact contrast with the "supervisory" role of the community; however, the distinction is not applicable to the field of "regulation," where the community may take the initiative. Another traditional idea is that "criminal" law was concerned with imposing stigmas upon nonconformers. Under modern codes, however, penalties may be looked upon as business expenses carrying no actual disgrace. Another older connotation was that "criminal" law and procedure dealt only with severe deprivations, while civil procedure specialized in comparatively mild and unstigmatized deprivations. But this idea is also inapplicable, since many deprivations inflicted by civil process are severe and humiliating, as when firms are reorganized by consent decree.

By considering together all the sanction problems relating to any legislative objective, we open the way for a wider variety of positive and negative sanctions than when the issue is phrased in "civil" or "criminal" terminology, or when "tort" and "contractual" liabilities are isolated for special treatment. In general it is helpful to separate the norms of the corrective code from the connotations arising from long juxtaposition with "punishment."

In the examination of policy alternatives in the field of sanctions, a thorough knowledge of predispositions is essential. We know the predispositions of any individual or group if we can predict, with high probability, the response that is called forth by any category of environmental exposure. The prediction may be "retrospective" or "prospective." For instance, if we examine individual A by one or more procedures of data gathering and analysis, we may come to the conclusion that he has a potent drive to make authority ridiculous and that the cues by which he recognizes an "authority" are the ordinary emblems of a policeman, judge, or business owner-executive. The procedure used may be an interview, supplemented by a test (projective or nonprojective). The conduct observed in the interview and test situations, including the words produced in the interview and in response to the test, constitute the data available for interpretation. The interpretation is retrospective when it proposes the hypothesis that subject A, with probability above chance, has performed destructive acts against past authority objects. The prospective prediction may be that the subject will kill, mutilate, blackguard, or, in some other specified way, inflict damage upon authority objects in the future (with a specified probability).

Psychiatrists are accustomed to describe predispositions on the basis of interviews, tests, and other procedures of observation. From the standpoint of sanction policy the key questions may be simplified as follows:

1) What is the probability that persons with x traits (established by procedures y and z) will perform act k under conditions m?

2) What is the probability that conditions m will occur if persons x are left free to go about their usual activities?

3) If the probability of m is high, what is the likelihood that response k will be significantly reduced if persons x are exposed to environmental changes o, p, and so on?

Putting these general questions in more concrete terms, it will be seen that we are formulating rather precisely the question whether we are confronted by deterrence, reconstruction, or exclusion problems. By a deterrence problem we mean one in which the individuals or groups involved are capable of being educated. If so, they will modify responses (k) that bring socially imposed deprivations rather than indulgences. The performing of act k in the past may have been the result of poor educational opportunities or insufficient motivation. Given clear expectations of indulgence or deprivation, and an opportunity to acquire missing skills, act k will rarely occur in the normal course of living. That is to say: although situation m will recur, ordinary campaigns of education, coupled with positive and negative sanctions threatened and applied in a given number of cases, will be enough to prevent x meeting m with k.

The problem is one of reconstruction if group x cannot be influenced by ordinary informational and deterrence activities to meet situations m, if they are likely to appear very often, with some more acceptable response than k. On the other hand, if group x receives intensive opportunities to become modified, with an excellent prospect of being modified, x will then be regarded as able to meet m without response k. The reconstruction may be entirely "somatic," as by the removal of brain tumors that determine the appearance of k under the circumstances m. The reconstructive process may call for "social" rather than somatic therapy, as by the use of interviews with a physician, supervised living with other subjects, and the like.

If it is improbable that members of group x will be sufficiently changed by available methods of education or reconstruction, the problem is one of exclusion from ordinary participation in the social process. This may be necessary because the group in question is organically defective, and current therapy has no tool at its disposal capable of meeting the challenge. Or the problem may have no known organic basis (in defect, or disease); nevertheless, it may be beyond the scope of therapy to bring about the requisite change in conduct. Exclusion may imply death, banishment, or restriction upon full freedom of participation in the life of society.

The foregoing cases have been discussed as sanction policy questions as to the classification and disposition of groups of persons who have performed intended acts of a destructive character. The conception of intent is taken to include conscious and unconscious orientations—in a word, motivational factors. These are the categories referred to in the corrective code. It does not include all of the sanctioning problems that emerge in connection with all the codes of the body politic. For instance, retributive punishment may be prescribed, not for its effect on deterrence or reconstruction but as a postulated value in itself (with or without derivational elaboration in terms of a transempirical source). The deprivations are imposed as part of regulative policy, not as correctional measures, and have no place in a corrective code.

Another set of sanction problems is closely intertwined with deterrence, reconstruction, and exclusion. It will be noticed that when we considered the conduct of group x we considered the predispositions of the members of the group to perform act k in situation m. And we had in mind the "normal range" of environmental situations in which m would occur and operate as a provocation. Both the predispositions of group x to perform act k and of various members of the community to participate in situation m are part of the culture pattern. Legislative policy needs to consider not only the cluster of factors that predispose act k but also the cluster of factors that predispose the acts called situation m. If situation m is the leaving of money lying about in the open, with no established routine of making records of receipt, deposit, and expenditure, acts k may be frequent despite deterrence, reconstructive, or exclusionary measures aimed at convicted offenders. The problem of legislative policy is to consider the ways and means open to bring about a reduction in the occurrence of m, if it is taken to be a provocative and hence destructive situation in which the unauthorized taking of money occurs (acts k). In order to change the culture pattern m, which may be viewed as a regulative policy on behalf of rectitude ("not stealing") or wealth ("rewards for contributions to production"), the legislators may employ service or sanction measures. The service measures may be educational and may include free instruction in procedures for the handling of cash. The sanction measures may be positive or negative, including honorific citations for the introduction of efficient fiscal methods and the imposition of fines for failure in this area. The "psychopathic" appropriator of funds may recur with constant frequency unless the situations that help to produce him are changed. Since these are presumably in the recurring adjustments of family life, they are less amenable to legislative revision than situations of the type that we have been discussing.

Now the sanctions threatened or imposed on actual offenders are designed to influence the conduct of other groups besides the overt offenders. Hence, we speak of "deterrence" problems not only in reference to the offender but also the potential performer of act k who learns to control any impulses in that direction by hearing about the actual or threatened sanctions of x. Usually the only information available to the legislator about past deterrence is the analysis of the rates of past offenses. But other sources of knowledge can be tapped, such as interview information about acts contemplated but not completed, or acts begun and not carried through. In this area the information accessible to psychiatrists has high potential relevance.

In the same frame of reference we may consider the "reconstruction" problems that are potential among persons who have not performed act k. Nevertheless, they are among those who are strongly predisposed to perform k in situation m (whether "rendering aid or comfort to the enemy" or "sex deviation"). The tradition of Anglo-American law, at least, has been to wait until a destructive predisposition came together with a provocative situation before apprehending the individual, even when the predisposition to k was so strong that reconstruction rather than simple deterrence would be necessary to dispose of the predisposition. Under the impact of modern developments, we are witnessing a trend toward the apprehension of persons who have not performed k, but who are suspected of being highly disposed to perpetrate the act when situation *m* arises. The problem confronting legislators is whether to go along with this tendency and, if so, how to reduce the dangerous implications for the sacrifice of some of the cherished values of the common-wealth.

The most subtle form of the problem appears in connection with "preventive" surveys of the population. To an ever increasing extent we are becoming accustomed to medical examinations for the purpose of detecting the incipiency of cancer, tuberculosis, and other somatic disorders. It is but a step to add behavior disorders and to create situations in which the examination is fully compulsory (or all but compulsory) and that result in compulsory (or near compulsory) detention of the subject. In connection with educational institutions, job applications, and induction into the armed forces, the medical examination is already a well-rooted practice in our culture.

The legislator may well ask whether the available body of knowledge at the disposal of students of behavior is so reliable at present that the sanctions available to the community can be wisely applied to preventive custody as a result of examinations unconnected with the performance of specifically forbidden acts. When the psychiatrist advises the legislator, he may be equally well advised to adopt a strict and candid point of view in outlining the current map of knowledge. In a society with our traditions on behalf of the official invasion of privacy, there is a strong presumption—rebuttable in terms of all values at stake—against detention on "suspicion," not of overt deeds but of the potential intent to perform. In a sense the problem in this area is to protect against excessive zeal, to prevent an excess of prevention.[15]

The considerations that arise in connection with sanction law, as with the examination of goals and the factors that bear on conformity, point to the need of linking psychiatric knowledge, and estimates of the future, with other sources of information and prediction. The psychiatrist is accustomed to work with patients who seek him out, and for the most part he deals with patients one by one and in the hope of altering the structure of predisposition that led to behavior disorder. The legislator needs to have much of this knowledge expertly summarized for his benefit. But he needs to have it integrated with a much larger map of knowledge and of future potentialities. For instance, not only can he use information about the frequency of the occurrence of act *k* in situation *m* and the record of recidivism on the part of offenders treated by deterrence or reconstructive methods, but he must also know whether the occurrence of situation *m* can be reduced to a level that renders it insignificant as a provocation (and at what cost) and whether even without changing *m* it is possible by altering pre-*m* situations (at home, in the neighborhood, in the school) to cut down significantly upon the predispositions of those who move

---

[15]The sex offender statutes are arousing opposition in the name of the traditional safeguards of individual liberty.

from pre-*m* exposures into situation *m* (and at what cost in terms of wealth and other values a given level of change can be brought about).[16]

Since the frame of reference of psychiatric medicine has been the disordered individual (not the destructive social situation), and for the most part the psychiatrist's techniques of therapy have been addressed to the changing of predispositions by dealing with patients one by one in hospital environments relatively isolated from the rest of the community, it is not surprising that psychiatric findings require supplementation. It would be desirable to bring about this flow of supplementary and complementary information by integrating the observations made by psychiatrists with other specialists in the behavioral sciences. The aim would be to provide legislators with the results of a self-surveying process that would put the case studies of the psychiatrist in the perspective of the situational chain characteristic of the whole society (national or local) and to provide a provisional map of the future in which the policy alternatives confronting the legislators will outline and evaluate the costs and gains (in terms of all clarified values) of alternative policies for dealing with overt intentional offenders who are deterrable, reconstructable, or amenable only to exclusion; of policies for dealing with potential intentional offenders by deterrence, reconstruction, or exclusion; of policies for reshaping the provocative or developmentally warping situations of the society.

---

[16]We assume that information about past events and estimates of future probability do not provide an "automatic" guide to the legislator. The total context of rational and valid decision making comprehends the clarifying of goal values and the invention, evaluation, and selection of alternative policies. This is more than simple extrapolation of the past into the future. The decision maker must continually assess the degree of reliance to be put upon "fact-form" statements brought to his attention. What is involved in being candid about the present state of knowledge is indicated in E.R. Hilgard, L. S. Kubie, and E. Pumpian-Mindlin, *Psychoanalysis as Science* (Stanford: Stanford University Press, 1950).

Conformity and Nonconformity*

LAWRENCE ZELIC FREEDMAN

Psychiatry is a therapeutic discipline, law a sanctioning one, and policy science a decision-making one. The practitioner of each wants to influence the behavior of men. Each is concerned with those who conform and those who deviate. Each shares the challenge of effecting changes in individuals and in the community, of practicing techniques while he gropes for a valid theoretical basis for his action. Each shares the urgency of participation in a social process without the luxury of the resource of a solid body of scientific knowledge with which to implement it.

The most obvious characteristic of psychological illness is the difference that separates the sufferer from other men. The most obvious characteristic of social deviation is the difference that exists between society and the nonconforming individual. It is this phenomenon of difference that brings our specialties together today.

So comprehensive have been the challenges put by my colleagues and so searching and psychologically wise have been their responses to their own questions, that they have, between them, quite accurately outlined both the present contribution of psychiatry to community stability and its potential value. I shall, therefore, confine myself to a restatement of a few representative issues raised, as I see them, from a somewhat different perspective.

In recent years legislators, administrators, and decision makers have sought help from the methods and data of the social sciences. The social scientist has wished to learn the insights of the clinician. The clinician has completed the cycle by becoming concerned with the impact of social dynamics on his patients. So, concepts of social values, social structure, consensus, and conformity now seek validation through the investigation of such individual psychological phenomena as man's aggressive impulses, the role of frustrations and their genesis, sexual drives and their sublimation, instincts and their vicissitudes.

The psychiatrist, who was trained as a healer, struggles to gain perspective in order to respond to this burgeoning insistence that he participate in

*This edition is a slightly revised version of the original article that appeared in *Psychiatry and the Law*, ed. Paul Hoch and Joseph Zubin (New York: Grune & Stratton, 1955), pp. 41–52. Reprinted by permission of the publisher.

71

the sanctioning processes of the community. He is asked to diagnose nonconformist behavior that is an overt manifestation of a psychological illness. This
is a familiar task in an area in which he is an expert. Now he is requested to
diagnose social deviation, which is a form of personal license, or social revolt,
or social learning. These are subjects in which he is professionally a neophyte.

As a citizen, he makes judgments concerning the social implications of
his scientific observations. As a member of the community, he allies himself
with or against its value system. But as a psychiatrist, social deviation
perplexes him. Specialist in the field of psychopathology, he has very recently
become a scientist concerned with psychological dynamics of the hypothetically normal persons in our culture.

Law, policy science, and psychiatry have approached common problems
with different vocabulary and dissimilar techniques. We who are taking part
in this discussion must, therefore, try to clarify our areas of interest, agree
on our methods, and on the meaning of our verbal symbols. Can we agree
to postulate goal values and discuss their implementation without involving
ourselves in an investigation into their origins? Unfortunately not, for the
main contribution of the psychiatrist springs from his insights into the origin
and development of the values of the person in his family and community.
The only way we will ultimately be able to predict or bring about changes in
human behavior will be through understanding the sources of such behavior.

A prerequisite of such a goal is some understanding of our own vocational
values. Professional values determine what kind of data we get, where we
get it, how we treat it, what kinds of theories we evolve, and what we seek
to accomplish. We, in this symposium, are attempting to integrate our functions, our data, and our values. It would be unrealistic to ignore our irrational
links with our professional past. We want to share experiences, but, just as
the neurotic cannot function in a mature fashion until he has become aware
of what motivates him, we must share our insights before we can clearly
define areas of agreement or disagreement.

The codified law attempts great precision in its definition of criteria for
conformity. Policy science takes its norms for conformity from the knowledge
of the social and clinical sciences. Psychiatry is least clear in conceptualizing
conformity criteria, and, in fact, is not sure that it should be doing so. The
lawyers and policy scientists have had the advantage of a system of public
judgments. Historically, they have benefited from relatively crude but effective
empirical systems of trial and error, out of which some consensus of public
affirmation or rejection of a given form of behavior could be tested. Traditionally, psychiatrists have retired to the seclusion of the clinic with their patients,
and their judgments were necessarily private.

The function of law seems to have been the enforcement of community
values through governmental action. Group attitudes, crystallized in legislation
and judicial decision, were buttressed by tradition. Policy science is a bold
new program that attempts to implement the wisdom of philosophy, social

science, psychology and psychiatry, and to serve as adviser to the decision makers of our culture.

Psychiatry, a medical specialty, has been eclectic in its methods, drawing its data mainly from biology and natural science. It has reflected the values of the community as they related to personal physical integrity. American psychiatry now derives its data mainly from psychoanalysis, clinical sources, psychology, and the social sciences. Treatment of the sick individual has led to concern with social mental hygiene. This has raised troubling questions: What is social deviation and when is it psychopathological? What are the criteria for a psychologically healthy community? The psychiatrist talks the language of the scientific method and has the professional need to consider his social preference as having resulted from scientific observation. He is in danger of replacing the semantics of social morality with that of psychological morality without changing the substance. The same caution applies to law and policy science.

We have not as yet devised adequate criteria to differentiate nonconformity, deviation, and conformity. "Conformity" usually refers to overt activity that is consistent with the behavior patterns of the group. But conformist behavior may be accompanied by an inner psychological quality of harmony or by violent antisocial impulses and fantasies. Deviation is not necessarily a pathological or criminal variant. Criminal behavior is activity that is defined by society as intolerable and that is responded to with sanctions. Conformity and nonconformity to social norms are not opposite but are relative forms of behavior in a continuum. They have meaning in the sense of the dynamic interaction between the person and the members of his community who approve or disapprove.

When the clinician attempts to assess the social climate of his patient, he is impressed with the stresses and contradictions in the environment that are conducive to nonconformist behavior. He observes inequities of economic, social, and racial privilege, of prejudice, of changing patterns of family structure and child rearing. He considers the complexities of aggressive and sexual behavior in our culture. Infantile gratifications and frustrations, punishments and rewards awarded or withheld by father, mother, or siblings are the earliest pressures toward conformity. Yet, the practices of child rearing have fluctuated violently during the last decades. Within our memory, specialists have advised mothers to condition for conformity, later to promote spontaneity, and now back to a sort of conforming spontaneity.

Uncertainty exists in the community as to what constitutes juvenile delinquency and how it should be responded to. In a recent study, we found that the most important determinant in the disposition of certain kinds of childhood antisocial behavior was the social agency that happened to handle them. The police invariably sent the children to the juvenile court; the social agency with equal predictability sent such youngsters to the child guidance clinic. Those handled by the police and courts tended to understand that they were "naughty" ; those in the hands of the social agency that they were "sick." Often the behavior of these children violated the middle-class mores of the community agency rather than those of their own family or community.

In older teen-age groups all socioeconomic classes in our culture seem to be floundering for some standards of conformity. Psychiatric specialists in that age group are sometimes unable to decide if they are dealing with "adolescent turmoil," psychopathy, or even with schizophrenia. Much that was formerly defined as social deviation is now considered "normal turmoil," springing from the lag between biological and social maturation in the conventions of our culture. The greater part of adolescent behavior has been shifted from the deviate to the conformist category by the simple expedient of the parents' accepting it.

In the larger community there is comparable ambiguity in patterns of response to nonconformist behavior of children and adults. The approval or disapproval of the social group, expressed through its religious, political, and other institutional symbols, form powerful reinforcing agencies to ingrained social propensities. Even when effectively integrated, however, the rapid changes of our community mores and practices make the lessons of childhood frequently inapplicable in maturity. There are confusing and contradictory directives as to its criteria for conformity. Besides its changeability, our social organization promotes deviation by setting up contradictory and mutually exclusive, yet equally prized, goals.

In aggression, the problems of private anxiety and public order fuse. Every man chips away covertly or with courage at the edifice of social conformity. The laws of civilization, as Freud saw, are necessary to protect us from the "normal" individual. Here, too, the standards are obscure and shifting. The quanta of aggression that a given culture tolerates or stimulates present a problem of social titration, which the ordinary person must react to with exquisite precision. We hardly need point out the enormous anxiety that the need for its control arouses.

There seems to be no consistent pattern of aggressive expression that an individual can learn and adhere to in our culture with certainty that he will thus remain within the limits of conformist standards. Aggressive patterns of early infancy are transferred to the wider context of the play relationships and with growth and maturation to the larger political and other interpersonal activities. Faulty handling of aggression is a problem faced in the psychoanalysis of every neurotic. It takes no expert to know that a reservoir of homicidal aggression resides in the mass of men, which can be tapped whenever it is attached to a suitable public symbol. Whether aggression is provoked by frustration as Freud first thought, or is a part of man's inherited biological tendencies as he later observed, it is unquestionably universal. Of course, it is not necessarily destructive and unmodifiable; usually it is adaptive to frustrations and energizes forms of response that are accepted and rewarded in our western culture. Recent workers have postulated the existence of some form of "social instinct" and impulse to cooperate, yielding to aggression only after thwarting.

As in aggression, the sexual mores in our society are shifting, varying widely in time and in its covert and overt aspects. Deviation from the social ideal is the statistical norm. Faced with contradictory and conflicting codes, individuals have no way of knowing whether they are or are not conforming. Kinsey's discovery that genital heterosexual intercourse within a monogamous setting is only one of many patterns of sexual expression led him to the conclusion, expressed at an earlier meeting of this group, that "current concepts of normality and abnormality in human sexual behavior represent what are primarily moral evaluations. They have little if any biological justification." "The problem presented by the so-called perversion," he stated, "is a product of the disparity between the basic biological heritage of the human animal and the traditional, cultural codes."[1] Demonstration that what has been considered deviation was in fact a prevalent form of behavior led to the assertion that common practice demonstrated normality. By and large, this approach is rejected in contemporary psychiatric thinking. Kubie has pointed out that it is "incorrect and misleading to assume . . . that because something is widespread in human behavior it must therefore be regarded as normal."[2]

What is conformist sexual behavior and what is deviant? What is "normal" and what is pathological? Overt behavior may, at least hypothetically, be measured, but the accompanying psychological subjective experience is not identical with the act. Further, what is the relationship between sexual nonconformity, sexual crimes, and sexual psychopathology? An evolution in attitude seems to be now under way concerning certain forms of sexual perversion. The revelation of the wide practice of extramarital, extragenital, and homosexual erotic stimulation seems to be increasing publicly expressed tolerance for such behavior. The anxiety of the community now seems to be aroused more by the expression of aggressive rather than sexual drives. Judgment as to the degree of aggression involved rather than the form of sexual behavior now seems to determine whether it is stigmatized as criminal. In all these areas much more remains to be learned than we now know. We must develop the techniques for studying them. Any role we play in the management of the political affairs of men, whether they be judicial, legislative, or administrative, ought to maintain this perspective.

Thus far, the main involvement of the psychiatrist in the social process

---

[1]A. C. Kinsey, et al., "Concepts of Normality and Abnormality in Sexual Behavior," in P. H. Hoch and J. Zubin, eds., *Psychosexual Development in Health and Disease* (New York: Grune and Stratton, 1949), p.32; Kinsey, et al., *Sexual Behavior in the Human Male* (Philadelphia: W. B. Saunders, 1948).

[2]L. S. Kubie, "Psychiatric Implications of the Kinsey Report," *Psychosom. Med.* 10 (May 8, 1948): 97.

has been as an "expert" in judicial procedures. He has served a useful social function, but he has probably never been free from the suspicion of the judiciary and laity concerning his scientific legitimacy. The psychiatrist has always reacted with irritation at the insistence that he testify according to cognitive criteria set up over one hundred years ago. Since then, the importance of conative, unconscious, and early developmental factors has been recognized. Especially rankling has been the demand that he testify concerning "responsibility." He has felt that this term describes a metaphysical judgment, or a degree of social accountability, but not a medical or psychological diagnostic entity.

The issue is cogently discussed in the recent report of the Committee on Psychiatry and Law of the Group for the Advancement of Psychiatry.[3] The report evaluates the competence and the limitation of the psychiatrist as an expert witness. It describes his area of expertness as follows:

> 1) He can predict behavior of the mass statistically and can determine with fair accuracy the classes of undeterrable persons. He can predict the tendency of behavior in the individual and with fair accuracy determine his deterrability. 2) He can with fair accuracy determine the degree of disorder of the accused relating to (a) the present mental state of the accused as it is relevant to his capacity to appreciate the significance of the charge and to cooperate in the preparation of his defense, and (b) the causal connection of the mental state and the act charged. 3) He can make advisory recommendations for suitable disposition of the convicted.

These doctors point out that they are unable to fit any "scientifically validated entity of psychopathology into present legal formulae of insanity . . .," and that the psychiatrist is unable to "determine degrees of legal responsibility calibrated to medical degrees of psychopathology." The report recommended that the psychiatric expert be freed from the necessity of testifying in terms of moral judgment. This is a fair and honest statement. It demonstrates how the clinical skills of the expert can be utilized by the judiciary. But the repeated phrase "fair accuracy" clearly delineates the limits of our knowledge.

The involvement of the psychiatrist in the legislative and administrative functions are more recent and not nearly as extensive. The monumental decision of the Supreme Court, integrating the educational facilities of black children and white children, cited psychological justification for its thesis that segregation was harmful and violated the constitutional rights of the minority.[4] There are few comparable illustrations of the introduction of psychosocial ideas into administration or legislation.

---

[3]GAP Report #26, "Criminal Responsibility and Psychiatric Expert Testimony" (Topeka: GAP Publications Office, 1954), p. 6.

[4]Brown v. Board of Education of Topeka, official report of the Supreme Court, vol. 347, p. 483; Bowling v. Sharpe, ibid., p. 497.

Administratively, the psychiatrist commits the psychotic nonconformist to hospitals and runs the hospital. Legislatively, he makes recommendations concerning such things as the treatment of the psychiatrically deviating sex offenders, and frequently he is listened to. He makes observations on national and international relations, and is frequently not listened to. Psychiatrists can play an important preventive role in civil defense in helping maintain individual and group patterns of behavior under the stress of war.[5] In all such functions he has much to contribute, but he has far more to learn. For in his public, as well as private, functions, he is asked if he can predict. Can he foretell the behavior of potential deviates in his social environment? Can he anticipate the effect on the individual of this legislative act or that administrative edict? Can he prognosticate what will happen to the offender and to society if the courts treat a particular antisocial act with stringency or with leniency? If a man is sent to prison, can the doctor give a valid opinion as to how he will behave if he is paroled back to the community?

The psychiatrist responds in terms of probability of anticipated behavior of the person. But probabilities are statistical and not individual. Only when there is extreme psychological deviation may such predictions achieve a high order of probability. Even then it is necessary for him to be able to prophesy with equal certainty the future existence of the social context in which his patient or subject is to function. What hypotheses can be formulated, which will be empirically grounded, which can provide valid and reliable guides for predicting conformist behavior, or which can state the conditions that will minimize or control deviant behavior?

The two main techniques used in research of deviant behavior are the statistical and the individual. The statistical method consists of compiling large numbers of cases in time and subjecting them to manipulation, usually attempting to correlate sociological with psychological variables. The individual technique consists of investigation, usually by psychiatrists using the interview technique, of conscious and unconscious elements in the personality of the offender. For example, the development of sexual fantasies, of aggressive impulses, of antisocial tendencies is studied. But one cannot measure quanta of emotional stress or libidinal drive, nor can one extrapolate units of social dynamics. We have not yet devised means of studying definable, conceptually and behaviorally discrete "units" of social and personal interaction. Most of our knowledge has come from the empathic, intuitive "sharing" of experience between the therapist and the patient, the investigator and the

---

[5]GAP Report #4, "Commitment Procedures," April 1948; GAP Report #3, "Report on Medical Education," March 1948; GAP Report #6, "Research on Prefrontal Lobotomy," June 1948; GAP Report #11, "The Position of the Psychiatrist in the Field of International Relations," January 1950; GAP Report #13, "The Social Responsibility of Psychiatry: A Statement of Orientation," July 1950; GAP Report #19, "An Introduction to the Psychiatric Aspects of Civilian Defense," April 1951 (Topeka: GAP Publications Office).

subject. Such observations have to be communicated through shared intellectual concepts, and transmission has depended upon the shared experience of the observer and his fellow scientist. This has created the anomalous situation that the conclusions reached seem suspect to those whose research traditions demand methods readily duplicated by any interested scientist.

Psychoanalytic treatment has contributed significant findings concerning conformist and nonconformist behavior. In analysis, therapy and research are combined. The distressed human being, motivated to communicate with a therapist so as to gain relief from his symptoms, is probably the only subject who remains in intimate communication with a competent observer over a sufficiently long period of time to furnish primary data concerning unconscious genetic and dynamic factors. But we do not know yet how far we are justified in projecting onto the social environment insights gained as a result of therapeutic relationships with the individual. Psychiatric analyses should not be confused with their social analogies. Community dynamics that resemble those in the individual do not necessarily duplicate them.

The intensive life history derived from the clinical study of small numbers developed mainly by the analyst must be integrated into the extensive field study techniques that have reached such a high level of development by the sociologists and social psychologists. The development of techniques for weighing all variables in such a way as to make reliable predictive scales is the challenge.

Research thus far has usually been artificially isolated in technique and subject. Community studies have focused on delineating the relationship of culture to conformist and nonconformist behavior, and there has been investigation of individual traits, frequently quite sophisticated in design, method, and statistical approach. But too often validity and reliability have been achieved by a limitation of area of interest and a compartmentalization of factors so as to make much of the results pure, but sterile. Another example is the efforts that have been made to correlate physical habitus with deviant propensity. Few such studies have included ethnic and geographical differences, nutrition, genetic factors, physiological as well as anatomical measurements, within the context of social and psychological milieu.

The subjects of study also have been restricted. The psychopathic personality, the aggressive and sexual criminal, the "driven" or compulsive personalities, mainly those whose inner tensions find release through aggressive, antisocial activity, have aroused the interested concern of investigators. But probably the largest number—the least apprehended, the least comprehended—are the "white-collar" nonviolent offenders. Yet, scant research attention has been paid to them. Experimental subjects ought not to come predominantly from reformatories or prisons as they now do. Imprisonment is the result of a chain of social and legal selective factors. That a person was caught up in the system does not even absolutely establish that his behavior was significantly different from that of his fellows. We need more evidence that the qualities described as pathognomonic for delinquents are discrete. Since we do not have adequate controls, we do not know if they appear in individuals leading seemingly conformist lives.

My colleagues already have suggested a much larger number of questions as well as possible "causes" or "reasons" for nonconformist behavior that ought to be studied as part of the whole. What we require are interdisciplinary teams working in small areas over a long period of time and consisting of specialists collaborating as well as training each other. They would be capable of carrying out cultural, constitutional, psychological, genetic, and dynamic studies. Such an inquiry would make paired comparisons of deviant behavior with conformist social behavior. There would be adequate sampling from the whole population. The investigators would be competent to interpret the interaction of the single personality and the community forces, not in fragments but holistically and dynamically.

There already have been projects that can serve as working models for the development of such study units. Perhaps the best example of such an interdisciplinary integration is that of the Gluecks.[6] They examined matched groups of delinquent and nondelinquent boys and included biological, social, psychiatric, and psychological factors and developed predictive tables of a remarkably high level of reliability. The impressive analysis of *Authoritarian Personality* was also the work of a team of gifted researchers from related disciplines.[7] They devised questionnaire and interview techniques to study authoritarian personality types and their psychological, developmental correlates.

Such politically oriented studies make significant contributions to our knowledge of social pathology. They also serve to remind us of the responsibility that is ours as we attempt to apply scientific information to promoting conformity. The suggestion previously made that one day we may be asked to provide insights to be used in determining whether potential deviates should be taken into preventive custody is a troubling one to me. As long as the psychiatrist is fundamentally a therapist, as is now the case, the problem of such community functions as commitments is a medical one. As he becomes a political and social consultant, he should be certain that his essential curative role is not forgotten.

"Life, liberty, and the pursuit of happiness" expresses the humanistic orientation shared by the psychiatrist, lawyer, and policy scientist. Increasingly, but mistakenly, the pursuit of happiness is thought to be the particular province of the psychiatrist. It is beyond his power, even when he is therapeutically most successful, to produce happiness. The effect of therapy is in a sense more negative; it eliminates internal impediment toward self-realization.

---

[6]S. Glueck and E. Glueck, *Unraveling Juvenile Delinquency* (New York: Commonwealth Fund, 1950).

[7]T. W. Adorno, et al., *Authoritarian Personality* (New York: Harper & Brothers, 1950).

Whether self-realization will mean happiness for the individual and whether it will mean a degree of conformity consistent with social stability is, to a significant extent, a function of the kind of world the lawyers and policymakers have helped to design for him.

We, in this country, are entering an era in which the deviation of men, which troubles society, lies not alone in overt acts but also in their ideas, in the propensities of their personality that drive them to unconventional or heretical associations. Our society is rapidly developing a system of extralegal negative sanctions against those who, although they may conform completely behaviorally, deviate in their attitudes. Political and social crisis has opened up avenues of communication between groups that were formerly intellectually and ideologically isolated from each other. They now view each other with baffled dismay. Heightened social anxiety has obscured differences, which were formerly so clear, between nonconformist ideas that are the private right of man and disloyal activities that are harmful to the community.

Nonconformity seems to be a consistent characteristic of human society. The clinician dealing with his individual patient sees the inevitable matrix of this socially observed fact in the "biological and psychological uniqueness of the individual, in polarity of love and hate toward the same individual, in the conflict between strivings for independence and dependence, between the urge to creativity that sets one apart and acceptance with a sense of oceanic union with the group." As a doctor he accepts his social responsibility, but he solicits caution in using his still evolving investigation into the nature of man to implement conformity to goal values, however desirable they may be.

Psychoanalysis, Delinquency, and the Law*

LAWRENCE ZELIC FREEDMAN

Twentieth-century culture has fed avariciously on the constructs, models, language, and clinical observations of psychoanalysis. But the corpus, civilization, and its skeleton, the law, have not grown noticeably robust on it. This difference, though paradoxical, is inevitable. Culture is the sum, at any point in time, of the emergent creative values, the fluctuant aesthetic tone, the amorphous manner, the nuances of living style. One man may write a poem, a play, a book, compose music, paint a picture, survive a personal sequence of struggle, live a private life. Any man, through his work, whether physical, intellectual, political, or artistic, may seek solutions to his immediate, idiosyncratic dilemma. When he is creative, his solution is novel. Those who spontaneously associate themselves with him because his emergent solution seems to resolve their own predicaments may absorb a powerful cultural change relatively quickly.

Civilization is the totality of laws, rules, institutions, rituals, mores, and traditions that order the lives of the cives, city-state nations, of communities of organized conglomerates of persons. The formal structure of government, the controlling precedents of a society, maintain continuity and stability. Their primary function is to forestall the chaos of anarchy, whether by social control or by social example. Civilization, so defined, yields slowly to novelty.

One cannot argue seriously against those who hold that the official rituals of a society and the complex, variegated cultural values of its individual participants and aggregate groups are so interdependent as to make any effort to distinguish between them hopeless. Similar ambiguity afflicts the words delinquency, law, and psychoanalysis. We must depend, however, not on a specious and therefore dangerous illusion of semantic precision where none exists, but must acknowledge that we communicate through shared understanding, through apperceptive and empathic communality. However vague and inherently antithetic this may be, a clear awareness of the inherent ambience

*This is a slightly revised version of an article that first appeared in *Modern Psychoanalysis: New Directions and Perspectives,* ed. Judd Marmor. Copyrighted 1968 by Basic Books Inc., New York. Reprinted by permission of the publisher.

and limiting finiteness of verbal symbols, whether spoken or written, is preferable to the illusion of exactness where it does not exist. This degree of insightful lucidity is especially important when we attempt to collate the relationship between law, which is essentially a system of social prescriptions semantically defined, and psychoanalysis, which attempts to treat the ineffable, the verbally inexpressible.

In the mid-twentieth-century United States, civilization exists within a diversity and heterogeneity of cultures, of ethnic and national origins and recency of arrival, ranging from the indigenous Indians—really Mongolian immigrants from eons past—to Puerto Ricans still flowing into our urban centers. Both, like the blacks, are culturally depleted, economically deprived, and politically victimized. There are, in this country, a few men whose riches are unparalleled in world history, and there are whole communities that are chronically impoverished. Our citizens range from aggressive atheists to articulate agnostics, to those who noncommittally withdraw. There are also powerful organizations of ancient religions and a bewildering kaleidoscope of made-in-America variants of religious ritual and churches. A wide spectrum exists, as well, in education, skills, and aesthetic sensibility.

The American civilization whose principles are set out in the Declaration of Independence and the Constitution of the United States, and modified in our courts, legislature, and referenda during the two centuries since, encompasses all these cultures. It is identical with none. Within this civilization and under this Constitution, with its puissant thrust of states' autonomy and separation of powers, how do we educate those whose heritage is discrimination, whose ancestors have been enslaved, and whose skin is pigmented? How do we respond effectively and decently to lawbreakers who, as a consequence of their lifelong estrangement, have become identified with different cultural values than those who apply the sanctions? How do we achieve an equilibrium between equality before the law for the putative offender and protection for victims of harmful persons? What just balance can we achieve between freedom for impulsive expression and legally reinforced inhibitions?

A judge of the Federal Appellate Court asked the attorney general of the United States to help adapt procedures of arraignment for the poverty-enslaved black so he might achieve actual, substantive equality before the law. This request was rejected by the attorney general on the grounds that the law seeks not equality but justice. The procedural protections of the accused exist, said the attorney general, not for the defendants' sake but for ours, that is, for our civilization. The law-compliers and the law-enforcers are encased in a sense that justice will be done. The attorney general did not say so, but he was certainly aware that most men accused of crime who have suffered through their life from social injustice do not expect to get legal justice. The judge was sensitive to the significance of the operations of the law to the men from deprived subcultures. He had expressed a parallel awareness of the wide-ranging distortion of the perspective of the mentally ill toward lawful behavior when he and his judicial brothers had earlier freed, from century-old legal practice, the narrow cognitive criteria for the determination of responsibility (*Durham* v. *United States*, 1954). He had articulated, for the first time in American courts, considerations concerning the relationship between the unconscious motives, described by psychoanalysis, and the legal intent, inferred by prescription of legal codes (*Miller* v. *United States*, 1963). Thus, the same judge who had introduced concepts of the unconscious into courts also had widened the arena of relevant psychiatric testimony in criminal cases beyond the unrealistic constrictions of "knowledge of right and wrong." He had indicated as well his awareness that the social context of early development and adult role affects a man's sense of equality, of law, and of justice.

But the law has been concerned with the unconscious determinants of socially harmful behavior for centuries (Freedman, 1965). Acts contrary to the common welfare, to the rights of other individuals or to the prerogatives of the state, have not been judged criminal, however destructive they might have been, unless they reflected evil intent. The Law of Moses provided, as did criminal codes before and since, sanctuary for antisocial acts that were unlooked for, unintended, or adventitious, as it did for all acts of the unequivocally mad. As civilizations have developed, they have expanded the perimeters of this area of immunity from legal punishment.

The essential, hopeless, and honored task of the law has been to discover how to quantify accident, how to calibrate the degree of madness that exculpates. The limits of accident impinge on the borders of negligence. The frontiers of the democratic freedom to be different merge into the boundaries of psychotic syndromes. In recent decades the increasing diagnostic and therapeutic precision of psychoanalysis has helped to extend the legitimate area of concern of psychiatry from the institutionalized psychotic to the irrational personality, not readily recognized by lawyers as "insane" or by the laity as "mad." Personality deviance, whether subjectively felt or behaviorally expressed, has come within the widening ambit of psychoanalytic concern. In most jurisdictions, however, the law of responsibility remains fixed at a level of psychological understanding that reflects a period in history when the preoccupation of alienists was with the insane in institutions mislabeled asylums, as prisons were mislabeled penitentiaries.

One of the many ironies that makes life stingingly unbearable and wryly tolerable is that while impulsivity, like accident and madness, has become legally mitigating, the law's delays have themselves increased. Three centuries ago Hamlet's suicidal soliloquy keened over the law's delays. And his audience of bumpkins, bourgeois, and orange girls recognized this as a real, legitimate, if insufficient, vector toward self-immolation by suicide.

Perhaps the law's delays and the law's tolerance of impulsivity are reciprocally related. Lengthening time lags between the act, the accusation, and the legal judgment in twentieth-century America, while still perhaps inviting but rarely precipitating suicide, any more than it did in the ambivalent prince, is a basic feature of its process and function if not of its structure and intent. We might regard the common bind of compulsivity and impulsivity, inhibition and spontaneity as reaction formations to each other, reflections of the nexus of a human dilemma. This is the crossroad where the essential social stabilizing role of law through compulsion and inhibition meet, sort out, and in some yet unknown and still confused way discover a set of workable balances. If these speculations are justified, then this mix of private impulsivity and public inhibition reflects a sort of essential social symbiosis that is antipathetic but crudely workable. It is an amalgam of private wishes, initiative, and intents, and public precedent, restriction, and ideology.

Spontaneity, impulsivity, and creativity are always a potential source of danger to the state. But they are also necessary ingredients if the body politic is to escape stagnation and collapse. To legal organizations, the creative person is like the lover or spouse whose fickle partner bedevils and enrages but without whom life has no savor. Through its government, society enforces concordance and imposes order in the service of coherence and continued coexistence of its members. But some individuals require a sense of personal adventure, of emergent boldness, of private novelty if they are to wish for continued existence. Society needs them if it is to make cultural experiments and adaptations in the evolution of its civilizations. If either through its laws or tyranny it stifles them, it risks atrophy and fossilization. But uncontrolled spontaneity and the impulsive power of the mob also threaten orderly government with extinction. The delicate titration of impulsivity is, then, part of the shared chemistry of culture and civilization and law. Somewhere between the fossil and the dodo, viable laws must play their meaningful role.

This imperative need to achieve optimum balance between impulsivity and inhibition is shared as well by mid-twentieth-century psychoanalysis. Once, in a state of bemused if scientific inspiration, Clarence Day (1920) speculated that due to our evolutionary origins as the descendants of monkeys, impulsive, erratic, squealing, simian activity is labeled with some understanding and affection as "human." Even when such behavior is socially harmful, we may excuse it, we often envy it, and we might glorify it through our mass communications media. Spontaneity carries a positive valence for us in our culture. Similar acts carried out deliberately, with what the law calls "malice aforethought," provoke community anxiety and may elicit its vengeance. If, Day fantasied, we had been happily descended from elephants, thoughtful and planned behavior, even when socially harmful, would be considered elephantinely deliberate. It would, therefore, be humanly understandable, lovable, and forgivable. Simian impulsivity would evoke social fear and legal punishment. The thoughtful, deliberate, and reflective pachydermal criminal would be, at least, predictable, and hence held to be a better social risk than the unpredictable anthropoid delinquent.

Impulsive behavior is contrasted with thoughtful and rational conduct by the conventions of common sense as well as the precedents of the law. When spontaneity gets one into serious trouble with the criminal law, the differential ingredient deciding one's fate is often time. States' and defense attorneys, judges, and juries attempt to ascertain, with exquisite precision, the interlude of time that separated the onset of the conscious idea and intent of harmful behavior and the carrying out of the illegal act. If the interlude is very short, the behavior may be tagged impulsive. The punitive sanctions against such impulsive behavior are far milder than when intent and planning can be proven. Rarely, a legal defense of "irresistible impulse" provides complete protection from punishment. Delay leads to the presumption that conscious cognitive processes have intervened. Harmful acts after deliberation are prima facie evidence of evil intent, of a cold heart and an evil mind. If too long a time has elapsed between the thought and the act, severe punishment may be inflicted.

Impulsive behavior gratifies the immediate wish. It is characterized by minimal lapse of time between self-awareness of the action tendency and its realization. Frequently there appears to be a simultaneity of impulse and idea, kinesic tension and act. Psychoanalysis, like law, does not yet provide a better operational calibrating instrument to distinguish impulsive from other forms of behavior than this measurement of time. For the law, however, the duration of this crucial variable extends from the conscious recognition of the intent to the beginning of the act. Psychoanalysis has demonstrated that an unconsciously or preconsciously impelling motive may anticipate by days, months, or years any conscious self-awareness of its existence. The impulse is an inference retrospectively derived from the act.

A number of states, here and in Canada, have added "irresistible impulse" to the McNaughtan "knowledge of right and wrong" and awareness of "the nature and quality of the act," as mitigating and exculpating for an otherwise criminal act. But judges and juries have rarely invoked the irresistible impulse clause because they have been unconvinced by it. The concept comes close to evoking a direct confrontation between Western man's paradoxical insistence on his own free will and his eager acceptance of the benefits of science's working hypothesis of determinism. In practice, the legal decision makers have found it virtually impossible to distinguish between the irresistible impulse and the unresisted impulse. The anxious cynicism, which is engendered by this ambiguity,, is typified in the comment of Judge Lidell in Ontario to a defendant: "If you cannot resist an impulse any other way, we will dangle a rope in front of your eyes and perhaps that will help." In this country, Judge Darling succinctly summarized the judicial, if unjudicious, view of this defense: "Impulsive insanity [sic] is the last refuge of a hopeless defense."

From psychoanalytic treatment and from neonatal observation has come persuasive evidence that the milieu of the newborn and his later development are significantly associated with the likelihood of impulsive behavior, and with the probability of social conflict resulting from it. These factors are, however, differently experienced by those with different constitutional endowments. But biologists, the evolutionary theorists, the ethologists, and the physiologists have yet contributed little that is legally relevant to the solution of this problem (Freedman and Roe, 1958). Community-wide studies so far have made some preliminary but helpful observations. For example, we have found that among neurotics bodily malfunction and impulsive acting out are much more frequently diagnosed among lower-class patients (Freedman and Hollingshead, 1957). Subjective psychic states such as depressive reactions, indicating the greater potency of restrictive and self-punitive defense maneuvers against them, are more common in the middle and upper-middle socioeconomic levels (Leavy and Freedman, 1956, 1961). By combining scales of classification within society with classification of symptoms, we were able to detect a configuration that stretched along a continuum from impulsive behavioral difficulties and somatic complaints in the lower-class psychiatric patients to inhibited, subjective, introverted symptoms in the mentally ill of middle and upper-middle socioeconomic levels. A Social Interaction Index (Freedman, 1957), tracing this spectrum with greater precision, revealed that the focus of conflict progressed also through increasingly wider arcs of social dislocation, ranging from intrapersonal symptoms in Classes I and II, the upper and upper-middle socioeconomic levels, to severe social and legal collisions in the lowest Classes, IV and V. We overgeneralized (Freedman and Hollingshead, 1957; Hollingshead and Redlich, 1958), aphoristically, that the psychopathology of neurotics in the most economically endowed and socially privileged Classes I and II expressed dissatisfaction with themselves. The lower-middle Class III patients defended anxiously. The Class IV neurotics ached physically. But disturbed persons in Class V behaved impulsively. These latter, disadvantaged by and disenchanted with our society, express their irreconcilable personal conflicts through an impulsive motor pattern of symptoms that often leads them into social conflict. There is a difference in concept of self as patient, in the different social classes, if he is uncomfortable or unhappy, if his body hurts or functions poorly, if he is unable to be effective in his work, if he is in trouble with his social community, or if he is in difficulty with the law. Alternative to, or coexistent with, impulsive behavior tendencies is the psychosomatic expression of conflict through pain or malfunction, including venereal disease (Freedman, 1948).

Viewed from this perspective, impulsive behavior that provokes legal reaction of men is the concern of psychoanalysts as well as makers of social policy. The successful merchant, bureaucrat, or professional has fulfilled an essential prerequisite for attaining his stake by yielding up or postponing the immediate gratification of numberless wishes. He has set the limits of his expression of spontaneity to the lowest possible tolerance. His conscious desires are vigorously attenuated, his impulses are deflected or submerged. Like the terms of his credit buying, the satisfactions of his biological needs are paid out regularly but fractionally until the postponements within his life merge with eternity at the end of life, still unpaid and unfulfilled. Thus, the middle-class patient avoids social conflicts and social diseases but is afflicted by private anxiety, neurotic syndromes, and semiotic dislocation.

Impulsive behavior as a life style is mainly the prerogative of the very rich and powerful, of the very poor, and of a few others, creative and rebellious, who have opted out of, or have been ejected from, the class system. With its immediate satisfactions, impulsive behavior assaults the middle-class model, the law's model, and the psychoanalyst's model of what is permissible. Of those who can and do act impulsively, those who are both threateningly rebellious and very poor are punished. The law invokes punitive sanctions against the most irritating and the most vulnerable.

Any act, verbal or motor, is set in a matrix of confluent and divergent affects, ideas, and motives at every level of consciousness. The impulsive act, which in the neonate is the immediate response of the individual's biological potential to its stimulating environment, becomes in the adult the eruptive expression of affects, motives, object relationships, and matrix of defenses that is called personality, and that he has accumulated over his span of maturation. For psychoanalysts it is a truism that human behavior involves unconscious and preconscious as well as conscious ideas, emotions, and motives, and that it employs indirect and symbolic as well as direct techniques of expression. This confluence of endogenous, developmental, and exogenous psychic forces makes accurate conceptualization and precise investigation of socially delinquent personalities almost paralyzingly complex. However, the overt act may be taken as the initial unit of observation. From this base, levels of response may then be delineated accurately, scrutinized closely, and studied meaningfully.

A comparative study of social offenders, grouped according to categories of acts rather than legal statutes, offered some answers concerning the behavioral forms of personally adaptive defenses that result in legal discordance (Freedman, 1961). The men had been convicted of offending against the criminal code of the community. The legal ritual that found them guilty resulted as well in publicly stigmatizing them and had penalized them further by confinement in prison. We used the phrases "acquisitive offender," "sexually deviant offender," and "violent offender" to delineate the three major groups of behavior that had evoked the punitive action of law enforcers.

These men had behaved illegally as well as impulsively. In the first group were the common chronic thieves, men who had been intemperate and uncontrolled as well as illegal in their acquisitiveness. In the second group were men who had been indiscreet and uninhibited in their sexual deviation, and those in the third group had been excessive and unchecked in their violence. All had been unhindered by characterological or legal checks from the original expression of their various impulses. All had, after the act, been reacted to with criminal sanctions.

Since any personality, be it stalwartly conformist or outrageously criminal, reflects a persistent life style of characteristic defenses, we treated the form that the delinquency took with the same respect that psychoanalysts accord the symptomatic pattern that different neuroses assume. We predicted that the conformation of legally discordant behavior would be reflected in their infantile and childhood development, in the differential qualities of their adult personalities, as well as in the style of their lives, and that the tiny fraction of their acts that was criminal would be consistent with the predominance of their characteristics that conformed to legal precept. We therefore tested an interlocking set of hypotheses: that repeated behavior of a sexually deviant, violently harmful, or acquisitively illegal nature would be symptomatic of associated dimensions of motivation, of affect, and of personality. As the acts were unmistakably different, so too would be their other traits.[1]

We found that the special characteristics of particular offenses were not random. They were fixed and repetitious. Most criminals are homotropically and monogamously wedded to one form of illegal activity. Men whose illegality took a wide variety of forms we called polytropic or polyphasic. They were a very small minority, made up mainly of psychotic offenders. The overwhelming majority were not only faithful to one of the three categories—acquisitive, sexual, or violent offenders—but each was repetitiously bound to a subgroup of his own offense category. Moreover, his judgment of criminals in offense categories other than his own was extremely condemning and morally critical. Not surprisingly, the specific type of each man's delinquent behavior was a symptomatic syndrome. The internal consistency of his traits and defense systems was as predictable as were the obvious and persistent differences between the categories of his illegal aberrances. Any major category of personality characteristics might be used to examine the validity of these hypotheses as well as the observations that flow from putting them to the test. Psychosexual experience in early childhood and level

---

[1]The men studied lived in the northeastern part of the United States. Their socioeconomic level was predominantly Class IV, the next to the lowest on the five-level socioeconomic continuum. Obviously, application of observations drawn from any single group can be generalized to other strata, periods, and locales only with great caution. To widen the justifiable applicability of knowledge derived from this special group, we developed a set of equipotential hypotheses. Using them, a roughly measurable quanta, or intensity of stress within a defined social and familial environment, might be demonstrably equipotential with an equivalent quanta or intensity of stress in another similarly defined social and familial milieu. Thus, though two factors might appear to be separated by geography or social or legal context, they might be psychically equivalent. To cite a simple example: growing up as a member of one minority group prevalent in one section of the country might have effects similar to or identical with growing up as a member of quite a different minority group that had settled in another part of the country.

of sexual integration achieved as an adult are considered by many psychoanalysts to be at the core of any man's personality. Let us therefore use psychosexual factors as one paradigm of the more inclusive propositions.

The acquisitive offender exceeded by far the other groups in libidinal precosity and promiscuity. The range of his partners, the frequency, and the apparent spontaneity of his sexual expression from his childhood to middle years, his available sexual energy and his polymorphous propensities, were also higher than those of the other groups. He was younger at the time of his first ejaculation. He had initiated masturbation by puberty. He had participated in coital behavior by early adolescence. The thief, in contrast to the sexual deviant, made the transition from masturbation to interpersonal eroticism before his mid-teens. By sixteen his predominant libidinal activity was heterosexual intercourse. If married, he initiated coitus with his wife, just as he did with his numerous extramarital casual pickups and prostitutes. The prevalence, but not the frequency, of his homosexual experiences equaled that of the sexual deviants. He did not tolerate sexual fantasy, however; he rejected and denied erotic daydreams as unpleasant.

The most obvious psychosexual characteristic of the sexual deviant was the damped-down, truncated, abortive, tardy, and joyless quality of his libidinal life. He began masturbation late and continued persistently but infrequently. Inhibited during childhood in initiating autoeroticism, he perseverated through puberty, adolescence, and adult years in this form of self-stimulation. He rarely yielded it entirely for other forms of sexual activity, either conventional or unconventional. His childhood homosexuality had been lower than those who later became thieves. At the onset of puberty, the quickening of sexual interest and activity noted among thieves and violent offenders and common to most boys of their age did not occur among the sexual predeviants. Both heterosexual foreplay and intercourse began late and continued, but with comparatively long intervals between episodes.

The violent offender reflected in his sexual life the greatest intensity of ambivalent flux between libidinal impulse and anxious inhibition. He began masturbation earlier than the sexual deviant but later than the thief. He was least likely to find his autoerotic stimulation either gratifying or satisfying. He rarely experienced or recalled sexual fantasies. For him erotic daydreams were not accompanied by a mood of pleasure; they were disagreeable. The violent offender, then, was as inhibited in his psychic erotic experience as the sexual deviant. His heterosexual behavior reflected equally well his ambivalence of anger and affection, love and hate. Thus, the sexual impulsive behavior of each of the three major categories of men who are in serious legal trouble with society was found to have particular and persistent patterns from their early life onward.

All these men had been defeated, had tried to cope, but unsuccessfully. Publicly stigmatized, castigated, isolated, and restricted, their difference lay not primarily in psychopathology in its traditional sense but in syndromes of socially inappropriate and legally punishable acts. What crucial variables distinguish them from the socially adapted? Repression, as a defense mechanism, is conveniently, conceptually juxtaposed to expression of an affect, idea, motive, or action tendency. I thus far have avoided tackling the tangled skein of the relationship between the concept of impulse and the related constructs of emotions, motives, drives, and cognitive processes. Yet obviously the areas of congruence, difference, and reinforcement between these psychic constructs need to be articulated. The expression or discharge of a compelling cognition, feeling tone, or action tendency is presumably, under "normal circumstances," followed by its disappearance as a dynamic factor in the psychic economy, or its successful incorporation within the consciousness of the person. Its repression, on the other hand, assures its disappearance from consciousness but guarantees it a continuing role in the psychic topography of the person, leading sometimes to its fragmented emergence as mental illness. The particular facet of the personalities of the men whom we are considering reflected disarticulated and differentiated repression of action tendencies. Within the model of adaptation, they suffered from a disequilibrium of motility propensities. If they are considered pathological, their pathology is primarily kinesic. Their deviation from homeostatic balance consisted both of semiotic hypertrophy, which is obvious, and of its atrophy, which is less self-evident.

Any redirection of behavioral tendencies, whether fantasy, hallucination, or any kind of wish-fulfilling inaction that could avoid social conflict while providing adequate, even if partial, gratification of the impulsive action-tendency, seemed to be unavailable to them. While the deflection to alternative objects or victims of compelling action-tendencies was common enough, sublimation appeared not to be within their psychic capacity. The early familial and later community experiences of these men provided some information that helps to explain how and why each selected and persisted in his particular category of illegal response.

The common chronic thief was often, within this population, a transitional person lost between old world parental values and unconcerned, because unidentified, with new world property and personal values. He had never developed a personality capable of forming significant, empathic, personal relationships. With no ego ideal of formidable virtue to measure himself against, and lacking a superego capable of castigating himself to the point of restraint, he was marvelously, but in fact superficially and only apparently, ego-syntonic in his illegal behavior.

The sexual deviant whose familial attachments were stronger and who, in this geographical area, tended to spring from the white indigenous, rural sections of the countryside, in whose cities he later settled, was sexually aberrant for reasons that reflected inner dynamics of his family structure. He was profoundly identified with the dominant values of the community. This identification was reflected partly in the powerful conflictful ego-dystonicity of his impulses.

The violent offender, in contrast to both groups, was likely to be both psychologically and often literally a transient, frequently black, raised within a family constellation that was itself fragmented, fatherless, provocative of wide swings of affect with inadequate identifying figures either in the home or in the larger, threatening and threatened community. Both fearful and feared, he exploded intermittently into action, propelled into violence by anxiety that his poorly structured and inadequate ego was incapable of containing.

Psychosexually and characterologically, the life style of the common chronic thief was the most *impulsive*. He was encumbered least by empathic human object relationships. Correspondingly his impulsivity seemed most ego-syntonic. From his childhood, the common chronic thief appeared to be sexually an impulsive, free-acting, polyfocal man. He was most active, diverse, most transient, and least concerned about his partners. By overt criteria he was the most immediately responsive to endogenous shifts in his physiological and psychological balance, as in puberty. He adjusted readily as well to exogenous, externally imposed variability of available objects, as in prison. He was the most impulsive activist, the least rigid in his forms of sexual expression, and least likely to admit to any feeling of guilt or shame concerning his sexual mode, style, or nature of partner. Neither his heterosexual nor his homosexual prostitution evoked any expression of concern or anxiety. These psychosexual characteristics of the thief bore striking homology to his pattern of objectless, repetitive, illegal acquisition of money and objects. His thefts too were repetitive and guilt free. The interchangeability, the empathic insignificance of his sexual objects combined with the persistence of his sexual aims, was matched by the human objectlessness of his obstinate acquisitive aims. His guiltless sexual promiscuity was matched by a life style characterized by explosive, episodic, angry assault that exceeded in frequency, but not in harmfulness, those of the violent offender.

The sexual deviant, with his low level of sexual activity and general resistance to impulsive behavior during formative years, had nevertheless greater capacity for empathic human relations than the thief. The sex offender as an adult was the least impulsive and therefore most socially compliant in spheres of activity other than sexuality. He therefore might be appropriately described as *compulsive*. This term, with its connotation of tension, reflects acts carried out in spite of conscious reluctance, or conflict, and of ego-dystonicity. More likely to identify with sexual conventions of the larger community, he experienced shame and guilt as he compulsively violated them.

The violent offender was frustrated and goal inhibited rather than unambivalently heterosexual or even overwhelmingly assaultive. He was least likely ever to be sexually deviant. If through drunkenness or seduction or excitement he behaved deviantly, he reacted with guilt, shame, and denial.

In sex as in aggression, he lived a life of ambivalent frustration, intermittently erupting into blindly fierce assault, most often directed against an intimate, a woman. More rarely his victim was a man within his circle of family or friends. In either case his victim had, inadvertently or deliberately, challenged and threatened his tenuous hold on heterosexual balance and masculine identity. Poised precariously between love and hate, lust and destruction emerged sometimes simultaneously, sometimes directed at the same feared and desired partner. This ambivalent dilemma seemed to characterize his sexual as well as his violent acts, which were a reflection and, rarely, a resolution of it. For the violent offender, ambivalence, the fruit of frustration of a life lived on the seesaw of love and hate, of passivity and aggressivity, the assaultive and sometimes murderous act might most accurately be described as *propulsive*, to connote the ego-engulfing nature of its violent resolution.

There are crimes of difference and crimes of dangerousness. Violent offenses are crimes of dangerousness. The sexual deviants commit crimes of difference, with a subcategory of those who combine dangerousness by assault with their unsettling difference. The common chronic thief commits crimes that are nominally different, but his punishment through the lawful apparatus reflects a neutral bureaucratic maneuver designed to maintain social efficiency. Society, through its legal representatives, seems neither appalled by the thief's difference nor frightened by him. His forms of acquisition are simply inconsistent with the tenets of efficient social organization. It is ironic, therefore, that it is the thief who over his life span is penalized most severely, if most routinely.

Conflict between these forms of impulsive, compulsive, and propulsive behavior and socially incorporated inhibition against carrying them out may not be inevitable, but it is ubiquitous. An enormous resonance exists in the general population for impulsive sexual, compulsive acquisitive, and propulsive violent offenses. The criminal and social offender is by no means an isolated phenomenon in our culture. He is a crystallized expression of the omnipresent conflict between private impulse and social structure that is the general concern of psychoanalysis.

Psychoanalysis is based on law. Freud (1895) first attempted to write a value-free theory of human behavior, to create a neuropsychological science. Discouraged, he tried to disentangle functional from organic syndromes of human psychopathology. But it was his discovery of the unconscious, of the bipolar conflict of the pleasure/unpleasure spectrum of hedonism, of the emergence of personality through introjection, imitation, identification, desire, punishment, threat, and reward that were the beginnings of psychoanalysis. All these are intimately related to law. He treats the play of Oedipus, the myth of Moses, the novelistic characters of Alyosha, Dmitri, and Ivan, the atavistic reconstruction of *Totem and Taboo* as dramas of man's social evolution toward a rule of law and of his inner reactions to his own emergent civilization (Freud, 1899, 1912–13, 1928, 1937–39). A now classic exposition of psychoanalysis was written in the form of an imaginary dialogue, a sort of dialectic, between Freud and a government official who was bent on prosecuting one of his brilliant law protégés on the grounds of violation of Vienna's laws prohibiting quackery (Freud, 1926).

The contributions of psychoanalysis to understanding, prediction of delinquency, and the determinants of the law are still primitive, groping, and insufficiently enlightening when we consider that psychoanalysis in its origins and in its models is steeped in law. For psychoanalysts it may be said that in the beginning was the crime, the parricide of the primitive horde, the parricide and incest of Oedipus. No figure haunted the writings of Freud, not even Oedipus, more than Moses. And Moses was preeminently the Giver of the Law. Freud considered that the Jews' selection of abstract monotheism over concrete polytheism was an achievement of profound significance. It predisposed to abstract thinking in areas other than religion, and to the establishment of law based on ethical as well as utilitarian principles. This was a contribution of Freud's hero, Moses.

Freud's literary style of analysis, while graceful and elegant, is also legalistic and talmudic. Concepts are disentangled and clarified from an intuitive and empirical core through progressive analogous, homologous, syllogistic progression to universal laws. Each of them, like the law itself, is contingent on an interlocking meshwork of impinging correlates of laws, mores, and social predispositions. His psychoanalytic detection, based on a virtuoso elucidation of microdetail as reflected, for example, in his "Interpretation of Dreams" (1899), is reminiscent of a similar concern with seemingly minor clues in criminal detection of the great German criminologist, Hans Gross. His emphasis on words as the overly determined, heavily loaded carriers as well as vectors of human desire and guilt is analogous to legal science, which is essentially a system of semantic definitions. Psychoanalysis' concern with motive and need reflects the criminal laws' preoccupation with intent. Its Hobbesian assumption of inherent human aggressivity and perversity is not unlike that of most lawmakers through time. Indeed, if one echoes Freud in saying that religion is an obsessive-compulsive ritual writ large, one must state the reciprocal, that his psychoanalytic theory is the social and legal flux of desire, greed, lust, violence, harm, and punishment writ small in his paradigm of individual human development.

Just as Freud disdained to distinguish between civilization and culture (1930), so he minimized the differences between guilt arising from violations of social mores and guilt aroused by breaking community laws. In his early writings he scarcely distinguished between private and public sources of punishment. Fear of punishment was equally potent as a dynamic element, whether the punishing agent was imposed by parental withholding of love and approval, by condemnation, by alienation from the social group, or by formal sanctions applied by the law.

Yet one of Freud's major scientific as well as personal crises hinged on precisely such distinctions. His early theory of the development of hysteria and obsession was based on his acceptance of his patients' descriptions of their infantile sexual seduction by older members of their own family or other adult intimates of their families. When he realized that these precocious stimulations had in most cases never occurred, that his patients had not been the victims of such premature sexual onslaughts, he was in despair. He believed for a time that this vitiated his empirical method and his theory alike. Out of his despair came his great creative leap. As he had appropriated the language of his earlier efforts to create an anatomical model of psychology, and applied the terms to a mentalistic model, so now he enlarged his complex of hypotheses to include the memory of such early seductions, not as recalled fact but as projected fantasies, as wish fulfillments. This shift from fact to fantasy had profound implications for the development of psychoanalytic theory and method of observation. It represented also a shift from actual overt experience as the preponderant source of a sense of guilt to covert wishes that were incompatible with external reality, or with competing inner drives or defenses. When viewed as fact, the sin, the immoral or illegal act was external, the crime was that of the parent or adult rather than the erstwhile child become patient. In the second instance, the "crime," the psychological sin, is the patient's, a retrograde seduction by the adult patient of his parent.

Thus Freud in middle age swallowed his dismay, saved himself from melancholia by shifting the burden of legal guilt from his patient's childhood family environment to the intrapsychic derivatives of the biological, instinctual imperatives of the patient. This crucial blurring of the actors, of blaming the self rather than others, this psychic burdening of the wish rather than the deed, has had significant, if possibly unintended, effects on the relationship between psychoanalysis and the law. For although Freud was a wry, acerbic, perceptive, and deadly critic of the mores, institutions, and laws of his time, he was no social reformer. He pointed to the soft and often salacious underbelly of the law. He adumbrated the source and the cost of sexual asceticism; he was aware of the corruption of capitalism; he resented the arrogance of power. He traced unerringly the courses of legal self-righteousness and its suppression of crime and civil disobedience through ritual violence to its anlage in social aggression.

Yet Freud never campaigned for change in the economic, sexual, or governmental, political, and power structure in which he lived. His own life was scrupulously moral, lawful. Courageous in adumbrating the dangers of sexual asceticism, he was himself rigidly monogamous. He never seriously challenged the sexual laws of his community, for example, as did Bloch or as did Hirschfeld in his Institute of Sexology. He considered money an ignoble motive, but he valued it as preferable to a naked struggle for power (1930). He abhorred violence between men, yet he was skeptical of outlawing war (1933).

I think it not excessive to assume that for Freud codified law and social mores were psychological realities, as inviolable as privately biologically derived impulses and reaction to them. It seemed hardly to have occurred to him that there were ethical, rational, or psychological reasons for psychoanalysis to serve as anything other than an auxiliary to the law. In his only published paper that related to the uses of psychoanalysis in the courts of law, he discussed experimental techniques of eliciting confessions, or methods of eliciting guilt by word associative techniques and reaction time of Jung, without regard to the nature of the crime or of the law that would thus be served.

The superego is a remarkably faithful reproduction of the body of laws of the legal interdictions of the Western culture of the twentieth century. It is as though psychoanalysis had collapsed the cultural legal incubus of all of the Western Judaeo-Christian tradition. This presumes that the evolutionary phylogenetics of an entire species was incorporated into the law and through introjection of a child's ontogeny, into the psychic homunculus of the human infant (Freedman and Roe, 1958).

The major difficulty of psychoanalysis' present contribution is that while the law is concerned with the act, and with intent as a necessary psychological concomitant, psychoanalysis has become preoccupied with the conflict of motives, and the act has assumed a secondary, corollary significance. Since the unconscious has been shown, through the method of free association, to harbor all manner of illegal wishes, the distinction between the law evader, the law breaker, and the law abider is, within psychoanalysis, less sharp than in the commonsense judgment of the laity or in the decisions of those officially and legally empowered. It is as though the act is not a potent psychological fact at least as significant as the overdetermined psychic vectors that have predisposed to it. So we have arrived at the paradox that the law, with its behavioral and existential sense of the significance of the act, is a more sound and sophisticated psychological sounding board than is the most advanced theory of psychology in the mid-twentieth century. It is within this ironic framework that the radical right of psychoanalysis is able to receive a hearing by denying any legitimate role whatsoever to psychoanalysis within the legal ritual, or indeed, to psychological motivation in the definition of crime, which is a reversal of civilized progress as threatening in its own way as the fascist reversal to feudal structure.[2]

The theoretical implications for the law of psychoanalytic hypotheses and empirical observations must be distinguished from their practical impact. The former are potential, the latter are minimal. It must be fairly said that the impact of psychoanalysis, as a body of clinical observation and as a theory

---

[2]For example, Szasz, having previously denied the reality of mental illness, has advocated that the mentally ill offenders be sent to prison (Szasz, 1963). He considered mental illness to be a myth and declared it nonexistent. For him the conflict of values always implicit in a pluralistic democratic society was easily resolved. In an encounter between law in which he believes and psychopathology in which he disbelieves, prison is the only appropriate solution—an extraordinary detour to a primitive ethic (Szasz, 1965; Freedman, 1964).

of personality, on procedures, attitudes, and the substance of the law is still a rather pale reflection of the diffuse dispersion of psychoanalytic ambience over the surface of American life.

True, the climate of legal response to sexual crimes has changed in the United States in the half century since psychoanalysis was introduced here. But it is not likely that psychoanalysis was the sole, or even the most significant, factor in the progressive mitigation of legal attitudes toward sexual activities that are inconsistent with the Judaeo-Christian model of monogamous heterosexual genital pairing within marriage. Freud has stated that the two great crimes in all social communities in all recorded eras of time and, he speculated, in prehistory as well, have been incest and parricide. But these two primal and universal offenses, slaying the father and copulating with the mother, are quantitatively and qualitatively insignificant in the courtrooms of advanced countries of the world. Such incest cases as reach our courts are almost invariably father-daughter relationships that are legally, but not biologically, incestuous. The man in these cases is most often not the biological parent of the girl but a husband of an older woman who had remarried after the death, divorce, or desertion of the girl's father. It is not unusual for such cases to represent a triangular sexual anaclisis. The mother is at least a tacit participant, tolerating or even approving the sexual relationship between her husband and her daughter, either consciously as a maneuver to maintain the company and affection of a man who she fears might otherwise leave her, or possibly unconsciously as a technique for sharing, by narcissistic projection, the sexual gratifications of her child through a counteridentification and counterintrojection, and occasionally as an intrafamilial mother-daughter example of intense homosexual attraction that can be expressed only by sharing the penis of the same male. Not infrequently, yielding sexual access to her daughter is part of an implicit contract that permits the wife and mother extramarital sexual freedom. The classical Oedipal fantasy and literary theme of son-mother incest is virtually never brought to court, nor frequently seen by analysts. In these few cases, one or both of the participants are likely to be psychotic. Incest, which is a linchpin of psychoanalytic theory, has provided few cases that have been studied in depth.

In most legal codes in the United States, sexual crime is virtually any sexual act outside of genital marital monogamous heterosexual intercourse. Functionally, the law intervenes more discriminatingly. Criminal sanctions are involved when there is a marked age discrepancy between the participants or when sexuality is fused with aggressivity, as when sexual access is gained by violence or its threat. Already the prestigious Model Penal Code of the American Law Institute (1962) has omitted adultery (delightfully labeled criminal correspondence) and homosexuality between consenting adults from its penal sanctions. It is reasonable to assume, although risky to prophesy, that in the next generation the legal codes will more closely approximate the actual practices of the courts. Even the taboo against marked age discrepancy and possibly that against the fusion of aggressivity and sexuality may be discarded. A few years ago the novel *Lolita*, describing the sexual preoccupation of an adult man with a preadolescent girl, became a best seller. One of America's outstanding literary critics described it as one of the few love stories of our time. Nymphet became a word of affirmative currency. Sadistic sexuality, formerly a term of anathema, has achieved the cachet of approval by leading European intellectuals, particularly existentialists such as Sartre and de Beauvoir. Their exegeses, along with the literary works of de Sade himself, are now in vogue and widely circulated in this country.

It can be argued with considerable thrust that the invariant in the patterns of sexual object and aims is not the primacy of genital sexuality nor the goal of maturity. Incest in highly developed cultures such as, for example, the Egypt of the Ptolemies, has been not only socially approved but also the envied prerogative of the elite. The Greeks and other high cultures held homosexuality to be an approved form of relationship and had built into their myths innumerable examples of incestuous loves among their gods, who were far more manlike creatures than our gods. The congruence of aggression and sexuality has been so widespread that no examples need be given.

The one invariant of sexual practices, however, over time and in the mostly widely disparate cultures, is the existence of some accompanying taboo. The nature of the taboo has varied enormously and indeed may, at the same time but in different geographical or culture centers, be quite opposite. In any one locale the form of the taboo may change over time as to the nature of the forbidden person or type of anathemized act. What persists is the potent prohibition. In our time, in our culture, in our civilization there persists, to be sure, a codified and a functioning system of legally defined interdictions concerning deviations from acceptable sexual practices. However, even a cursory perusal of the hundreds of sexual and marital manuals being sold in our bookstores and magazine racks reveals that they advise any and all forms of physical interaction leading to erotic gratification, except those that might seriously injure, or interfere with the sexual gratification of, the sexual partner. Most of these suggestions are illegal, but those who follow them are unpunished.

A taboo nonetheless does attach itself to sexual behavior in our culture. In those communities or subcultures or circles in which religious structuring and legal interdiction and conventional ethical considerations apparently play a feeble role, their place has been taken by what I have called a psychological morality. In a study of "normal sexuality" (Freedman, 1966), we found that men and women who were for the most part highly intellectually endowed individuals from middle-class backgrounds had little reluctance to describe their every form of sexual relatedness, other than those that inflicted physical or psychic harm on their partner. Indeed, the taboo was a reciprocal, a mirror image of the articulate taboo of our popular culture of just a generation ago. These subjects, be it noted, were not psychiatric patients but were selected for their "normality." These persons were concerned that they had violated not the law but the canons of the psychological morality of sexuality. Women who could recall no masturbation apologized, and those who had no sexual affairs to report offered excuses. Women who had not been "fulfilled," who had not experienced a full orgasm, were defensive. Men whose extramarital sexual behavior had been quantitatively deficient explained away this "fault." Most men and women were anxious to know whether they achieved psychological criteria of sexual adequacy as measured by a number of sexual outlets per week. In this country, late marriage also is suspect to the point of a virtual taboo. For both male and female now it subjects most unmarried persons over thirty to the suspicion of at least latent homosexuality, asexuality, or sexual frigidity. Our sexual mores seem to be evolving toward a panhedonism that is at least as unrealistic as were the constricted limits of approved sexuality of recent generations.

Indeed, a numerically small, but culturally significant, minority of our society in late adolescence and early adult age has gone beyond the sexual pleasure principle to the principle of sexual apathy. One of the striking features of what, for a short period, was referred to as the "Beat Movement," was that while subdued sexual aims persisted, the ideal in sex, as in many other aspects in life, was to play it cool, to avoid sweaty passion. This seeming apathy may be ascribed to many causal factors. Possibly it is an expression within this "emancipated" group of the entropic energy loss accompanying the freedom to express impulses without external hindrance.

Be this as it may, the apathy, anhedonism, and unpleasurable quality of sexuality following a generation of desperate experimentation in pansexuality involving all sexes and all anatomical possibilities hints at the adaptive function of the ubiquitous taboo. Apparently, where sexual taboos are minimized, repressed, or denied, sexual expression neither expands the opportunities for pleasure nor leads reactively to pain or unpleasure. Not pleasure but intensity is lost. Sexual gratification apparently requires constraints, not to keep it within limits but to make it worthwhile. The psychological danger of the fulfillment of the extramarital fantasies of the bourgeoisie is not that the family and society will be unable to survive in the competition for sexual access without restriction or introduction but that sexuality as a meaningful human expression as well as a sensual gratification cannot survive the loss of taboo.

The twin dangers to the life of man are derivatives of the core drives of sex and violence. With some exceptions, psychoanalysts describe aggressivity as a multidetermined phenomenon usually evoked by frustrations, generally related to affectional or sexual deprivations. Since the model of psychoanalysis is dynamic, that is, based on conflict, it is assumed that aggression and its derivatives—the affect of hatred, the trait of cruelty and the act of violence—achieve symptomatic expression only when they are components of powerful and unresolved conflicts within the personality.

Unchecked sexuality may yet destroy the species of man on this planet or alter its character in some way now unpredictable. Through overbreeding and overpopulation it may bring into play those competitive, adaptive, evolutionary mechanisms that have in the past eliminated species of animals. Unchecked aggression, not, as in the case of sexuality, by billions of copulating couples, but by a few persons in control of hydrogen and atomic bombs, could end the evolutionary experiment called man. In the mid-twentieth century, psychoanalysts are aware of the technical possibility of species-wide human self-immolation. They have faced parricide without flinching. They have embraced incest. But most have looked at death and denied it. Perhaps they had better look again. The delinquency of sexual dalliance and the sociopathy of seizure of property are important and still unresolved puzzles. But if a man can kill a man, then men can murder all men. And there ought to be a law against that.

Bibliography

Day, C. *This Simian World*. New York: Knopf, 1920.

Durham v. United States, 214 F 2d 862 (D.C. Cir. 1954).

Freedman, L. Z. "Venereal Disease among Naval Prisoners." *United States Naval Medical Bulletin* 48, no. 5 (September–October 1948): 722–28.

———. "Sexual, Aggressive, and Acquisitive Deviates: A Preliminary Note." *Journal of Nervous and Mental Disease* 132, no. 1 (January 1961): 44–49.

———. "Psychiatry and Law." In E. A. Spiegel, ed., *Progress in Neurology and Psychiatry*. New York: Grune & Stratton, 1964.

———. "Social and Legal Considerations of Psychiatric Treatment in a General Hospital." In M. R. Kaufman, ed., *The Psychiatric Unit in a General Hospital*. New York: International Universities Press, 1965.

———. "Sexual, Aggressive, and Anxious Behavior in the 'Normal' Person" (unpublished). Read at Yale Research Seminar, 1958.

Freedman, L. Z. and Hollingshead, A. B. "Neurosis and Social Class I: Social Interaction." *The American Journal of Psychiatry* 113, no. 9 (March 1957): 769–75.

Freedman, L. Z., and Roe, Anne. "Evolution and Human Behavior." A. Roe and G. G. Simpson, eds., *Behavior and Evolution*. New Haven, CT: Yale University Press, 1958.

Freud, S. "Project for a Scientific Psychology, Part I" (1895). In Marie Bonaparte, Anna Freud, and E. Kris, eds., *The Origins of Psychoanalysis: Letters to Wilhelm Fliess, Drafts and Notes: 1887–1902*. 2d ed. New York: Basic Books, 1954.

————. "The Interpretation of Dreams" (1899). *The Standard Edition of the Complete Psychological Works of.* . . . Vols. 4–5. London: Hogarth Press. (Also published as *The Interpretation of Dreams.* New York: Basic Books, 1955.)

————. "Totem and Taboo" (1912–13). *The Standard Edition of the Complete Psychological Works of* . . . Vol. 13. London: Hogarth Press.

————. "The Question of Lay Analysis" (1926). *The Standard Edition of the Complete Psychological Works of.* . . . Vol. 20. London: Hogarth Press.

————."Dostoevsky and Parricide" (1928). *The Standard Edition of the Complete Psychological Works of.* . . . Vol. 21. London: Hogarth Press. (Also in *Collected Papers of* . . . Vol. 5. New York: Basic Books, 1959.)

————. "Civilization and Its Discontents" (1930). *The Standard Edition of the Complete Psychological Works of.* . . . Vol. 21. London: Hogarth Press.

————. "Moses and Monotheism" (1937–39). *The Standard Edition of the Complete Psychological Works of.* . . . Vol. 23. London: Hogarth Press.

————. "Why War?" (1933). *The Standard Edition of the Complete Psychological Works of.* . . . Vol. 22. London: Hogarth Press. (Also in *Collected Papers of.* . . . Vol. 5. New York: Basic Books, 1959.)

Hollingshead, A. B. and Redlich, F. C. *Social Class and Mental Illness.* New York: John Wiley, 1958.

Leavy, S. A., and Freedman, L. Z. "Psychoneurosis and Economic Life." *Social Problems* 4, no. 1 (July 1956): 55–66.

————. "Psychopathology and Occupation. Part I: Economic Insecurity." *Occupational Psychology* 35 (January and April 1961): 1–13.

Miller v. United States, No. 17061. U.S. Court of Appeals (Washington, DC, 15 June 1963), p. 9.

Model Penal Code. The American Law Institute. Philadelphia, 1962.

Szasz, T. S. *Law, Liberty, and Psychiatry.* New York: Macmillan, 1963.

————. *Psychiatric Justice.* New York: Macmillan, 1965.

Psychopathology and Social Offense*

LAWRENCE ZELIC FREEDMAN

A paradox is involved in the category "mentally-ill delinquent." To be mentally ill is to gain from society a defined role that stimulates considerable care and protection, sympathy, and freedom from responsibility to perform the social functions that are required of the healthy. Hidden under this attitude is, of course, masked contempt, but this unconscious attitude is not relevant to our present discussion. The case is quite the contrary with the social offender. The delinquent irritates, vexes, and displeases his community. There is a conscious attitude of contempt toward him. He is held accountable for his acts and he is punishable for them. The phrase mentally-ill offender is thus in a sense paradoxical and incongruous. It epitomizes the social vectors of therapeutic concern for and punitive attack against those who deviate from our sexual habits, deprive us of our property, or threaten our physical well-being.

To describe a boy as a delinquent or a man as an offender is to make a statement that is meaningful, or operational, when we include those who are offended, that is, the socially powerful elite rather than when applied solely to the person himself. These are terms of social opprobrium. They may be misleading and perhaps meaningless when applied simply to the object of this social revulsion. The investigation of the offender must include not only the acting individual but also the responding and reacting society in which the offense occurs. What must be studied is a complex and reciprocal interaction between individuals and the society that they bother and that wishes to hit back or spew them out.[1]

---

*This edition is a slightly revised version of the original article reprinted from Slovenko, ed., *Crime, Law and Corrections* (Springfield, IL: Charles C. Thomas, 1966). By permission of the publisher. The preparation of this paper was aided by the Otho S. A. Sprague Memorial Institute and the Foundations' Fund for Research in Psychiatry.

[1]A young and unhappy boy I was treating in a juvenile court, in trouble with the law and in trouble with himself, was speculating whether, when he grew up, he would want to become a lawyer or a psychiatrist. "Which," he wondered, "would do the most to get the world rid of people like myself. If I could make the world over, so that there would be nobody in the world like me left then I would like to become a lawyer. But that is impossible, when I say nobody in the world like me, I mean what I represent in me, all that is bad in everybody out there, they all are selfish and rotten. This is a terrible world. When I walk down the street and I see the

Let us assume that there is a society in which prestige-seeking drives of the normal individual are typically expressed through striving for wealth. His overwhelming goal is to achieve the status of the top rung of this social and economic ladder in any way possible. In addition to wealth, he requires a high-status ancestry; acquiescent genealogists will supply this. Wealth is defined as having more than the person needs to sustain his family so that he may conspicuously give evidence of leisure and money. Let us suppose, too, that the avenues toward these ends are restricted to a few exceptionally able, ruthless, or privileged individuals. This combination, as you can see, may lead to what is called crime. Perhaps you know the culture that I am talking about and perhaps you can predict the sociolegal response to anyone caught violating the acquisitive mores of such a culture.

Do not be too sure. You may be wrong. I am not referring to the American urban complex but to the Ifugao, a primitive tribe. The Ifugaos have no concept of crime or any public system of punishments. All offenses are private or civil wrongs or injuries. The prosecution is initiated, not by the state, but by the aggrieved, and any damages, penal assessments, or physical punishment inflicted upon the defendants are imposed by the plaintiff and his kinsmen.[2]

Perhaps this false analogy will highlight the habit of thought that has led us not only to accept our criminal law as the crystalized code of our social mores, as in fact it is, but also and more unfortunately as the structure within which not only therapeutic efforts, but our theory and scientific investigation are carried out. This may mislead us. We cannot investigate the nature and problem of the delinquent without an awareness of whom he is offending and why and the customary techniques utilized by them to respond to him.

Research into the causes and the treatment of mental illness has different but nonetheless equally potent traditional and disciplinary stereotypes to

---

way people act and the rottenness of everything, I just want to go off. The first law is the law of self-preservation. If I wanted to, I could study hard and with my brains and background and with enough education I could be a great lawyer or the president of the United States. But the amount of good that I could do would be so small and the changes would be so unimportant that it would not be worth it."

There was also a fatal flaw in psychiatry. It was the psychiatrists' depressingly middle-class values concerning sex and love. "What," he protested, "is love? Just wanting to have something.

"You see a beautiful girl and you want her for your own, so you say you love her, which simply means that you want to possess her, and if our laws allowed you to have ten wives, the greatest lovers today would have ten, because they would see someone else they would want to possess.

"I'm a case, aren't I? I say I am a case simply because I don't fit into the normal pattern. People say they have built up a way of living that makes them almost happy. At least they get along in it, and they are not going to let me come along and interfere with them."

This paper was prompted by the challenge of this "mentally-ill delinquent" and his battle with his "rotten world."

[2]Hoebel, *The Law of Primitive Man* (1954).

overcome before it can become effective. The concept of mental illness springs directly from the derivatives of the Linnean classification in which the psychiatrist as a physician has been trained.

Mental illness, too, is classified in terms that are analogous to anatomical and physiological changes. This has proved helpful, but there are areas of psychiatric deviation—particularly when it manifests itself in behavior which arouses the concern of the community—when it is inappropriate.

MENTAL ILLNESS, DELINQUENCY, AND SOCIETY

The relationship between mental illness and delinquency requires that we somehow coordinate both concepts in our minds and in our methods simultaneously and seek to study their interaction, rather than to investigate one, pretending that the other is a vacuum.

The psychiatric patient lives in a constant reciprocal interaction with the legal structure of his society. Psychiatrists are zealous in pointing out to the lawyers how often their clients' reactions are reflections of essentially psychiatric problems. Psychiatrists sometimes go so far as to say that the lawyer's rituals are evidences of unconscious impulses far removed from the rational jurisprudence that they profess.

Perhaps the psychiatrist might be more sensitive to what he sees in his everyday practice; his patients live within a legal system that potentiates and inhibits the structure of conflict and of behavior with which he is concerned. He might also wonder whether his own aversion to becoming involved in such social processes does not similarly owe its origins to irrational sources. Every experienced clinician has listened to patients, not criminals, describe sexual adventures, illegal acquisitions, and aggressive attacks, which luckily for them were undetected. Had they been caught they would have been labeled criminals.

For the economically depressed and socially underprivileged, the most-traveled path to the psychiatrist passes through police stations, court rooms, and prison cells. We found that, of the total number of neurotic patients seen by psychiatrists in a New England city, at least one out of five of the lowest social class were in psychiatric treatment as a direct outcome of legal difficulties. Moreover, when the psychological symptomatology was correlated with what we called a social interaction index, we found that in this group (classes four and five) almost one-half (42 percent) of these psychiatric patients had behavioral disorders. That is to say, their psychopathology, which involved social offenses, community and legal collisions, was expressed in deviant or provocative interaction with the community. These patients acted out their psychopathology; many were caught and labeled criminals.[3]

The preconscious and unconscious antisocial tendencies of the more socially favored patients invade the social fabric insidiously but more effectively. The significance of this frontier for research in sociolegal problems is obvious.[4]

The dominant, articulate value in American psychiatric culture is the medical concern with health and preservation of life of individuals or defined, relatively small, groups of individuals. Most psychiatrists have not hitherto concerned themselves with social tensions and conflicts. Such involvement violated their private identity as doctors and their social image of psychiatry.

Nevertheless, the epidemiology of social contagion, the pathogenic impact of the transitional family structure, the punitive response of the community to those whom it considers to be irritants, whether because they are deviants or criminals—these are psychic vectors, the focal point of which is the psychiatric patient. If, as has been the case in most other branches of medicine, the major contribution of psychiatry to the promotion of health within its defined sphere will be preventive, then surely psychiatrists must concern themselves with the impact of the institutionally reinforced mores of our communities—expressed through law.

A criminal is a man who has violated the criminal code of a particular community at a stated time, and he must have been detected, apprehended, judged, convicted, and sentenced before he is designated a criminal. A criminal, therefore, is the outcome of a very complicated sequence of sociolegal ritual. He may be socially conditioned; he certainly is socially selected. He has so irritated society that it has taken counterpunitive action against him, and he has been vulnerable to this counterpunitive action. Delinquency, thus, is a dynamically complementary relationship between society and the individual. Moreover, as several studies of sexual delinquency have shown, it is also in some instances a symbiosis of the victim-seducer and the aggressor-victim.

In conducting our studies of the subcategory of nonconformist behavior, which is labeled delinquent, we tried first to observe the social process leading to the labeling, indicting, judging, and convicting; and, secondly, to achieve greater specificity within the modal concept of delinquency of forms of such behavior as well as their psychological characteristics.

Sociologists have demonstrated the malignant role of slums in breeding crime. Shaw mapped specific areas where delinquency could be anticipated.[5]

---

[3]Freedman and Hollingshead, "Neurosis and Social Class," *American Journal of Psychiatry* 113 (1957): 769; Hollingshead and Freedman, *Social Class and the Treatment of Neurotics* (Social Welfare Forum, 1955).

[4]Freedman, "Saints or Sinners?" *Context* 2, no. 4 (Winter 1964).

[5]Shaw, *Delinquency Areas* (1929); Shaw and McKay, *Juvenile Delinquency and Urban Areas* (1942).

Thrasher traced the web of relationships within the gangs of these neighborhoods that predispose to delinquent behavior.[6] Sellin hypothesized the role of culture conflict as precipitating delinquent behavior.[7] Cohen ingeniously propounded what is essentially a class-conflict thesis of delinquent behavior—that lower-class youngsters act out their frustrated social ambitions in aggression and crime, against one dominant middle class.[8] Durkheim's concept of the role of anomie in our Western culture has been applied by Merton to the American scene.[9] Our culture, like the Ifugao, holds out glittering rewards, but it denies access to the prescribed paths to achieve them. Thus, the structure itself creates the conditions that force the so-called delinquent outside the system anomically to achieve his goal. Sociologists, then, have shown that severely frustrating circumstances will lead to criminality and, as Sutherland has said, different associations between criminals will predispose to more criminality.

It is true that deprived, conflictful, and rapidly transitional communities have higher criminal rates. It is also true that these individuals represent only a percentage of such communities. However, causality cannot be ascribed to the association of these factors, rather correlation or at most contiguity. More careful analyses of these factors lead to the microsociology of the family. Healy and Alexander carried the insights of psychoanalysis to those whose maladaptiveness offends the community.[10] Szurek and Johnson described the process by which parents unwittingly may transmit their own unconscious pathological potential toward delinquency through what they called the superego lacuna.[11] In a quarter-of-a-century's work, the Gluecks had isolated family cohesiveness and the balance of parental affection and discipline as crucial predictive factors in delinquency.[12]

Nonetheless, no study so far does justice to factors of community selection as well as psychogenesis and to act-specific delinquency. Some years ago, we undertook such an interdisciplinary study of delinquent behavior. I shall sketch broadly our approach and problems and something of our results.

Since crime is a social judgment as well as an individual act, we made some pilot observations concerning the nature of that social judgment. As a preliminary, we tried to find out how children who misbehaved were labeled.

---

[6]Thrasher, *The Gang* (1936).

[7]Sellin, *Culture, Conflict and Crime* (New York: Social Science Research Council Report, 1938).

[8]Cohen, *Delinquent Boys: The Culture of the Gang* (1955).

[9]Durkheim, *Suicide* (1951); Merton, "Social Structure and Anomie," *American Sociological Review* 3 (1938).

[10]Healy and Alexander, *Roots of Crime* (1935).

[11]Szurek, "Some Impressions from Clinical Experience with Delinquents," in *Searchlights on Delinquency*, ed. Eissler (1955); Johnson, "Sanctions for Superego Lacunae of Adolescents," ibid.

[12]S. and E. Glueck, *Unraveling Juvenile Delinquency* (1951).

Two groups of children, between five and ten years old, of comparable age, sex, ethnicity, geographical residence, and socioeconomic status, were matched for socially condemned behavior. One group came from the juvenile court and the other from the community psychiatric clinic. They had stolen, broken windows, set fires or truanted. After studying their case records, we successively interviewed those responsible for their care and referral.

We found, first, that chance determined who might make the referral, but the direction of referral depended upon the social, vocational, and professional referent points of that agent. For example, policemen invariably sent the child to juvenile court; social workers always and school teachers almost always sent the child to child guidance clinics. This significant secondary social learning process in identifying himself as a bad child to be sent to court or as a sick child to be treated by the doctor was based on the external artifact of the professional identification of the agent of the community.[13]

We asked the school teachers to indicate which were their good children and which were bad children. We independently evaluated the children. In general, the teachers' desirable children were those whose characteristics were conformist even when autistic or schizoid. Undesirable children were those whose characteristics were likely to be vigorous, boisterous, and outgoing. This is consistent with the Gluecks' findings that delinquent children were more athletic, active, and, in Sheldon's term, mesomorphic.[14] The judgments made by the teachers were to a degree predictable on the basis of the class derivation and orientation of the teacher and the degree and kind of anxieties with which she approached her work. In fact, the apprehensive teacher was usually able to satisfy herself that her forebodings were justified since the amount of aggressive, destructive, and even chaotic behavior that characterized her classroom exceeded that of less apprehensive instructors.[15]

We tried to assess community response to types of offenders by random sampling of newspaper reports of offenses about which we had some information: how much space, what size headlines, what selection of data was reported. We found significant skewing with regard to kinds of offenses. But no intelligent American reader needs information concerning newspaper selection and distortion.

We went into courtrooms to ascertain the patterns of response of the district attorney, the defense attorney, and the judges. We found predictable unevenness of judicial response. Judges reacted differently to sexual crimes, to aggressive crimes, and to acquisitive crimes.

---

[13]Freedman, "Referral Mechanisms in Juvenile Asocial Behavior" (unpublished).

[14]Sheldon, Stevens, and Tucker, *The Varieties of Human Physique* (1940); Glueck, *Unraveling Juvenile Delinquency.*

[15]Freedman, "Referral Mechanisms in Juvenile Asocial Behavior."

Like Kinsey,[16] we found a class distinction in the response of officers and judges with regard to concepts of sexual deviation. Most judges were anxious and shocked at sexual perversion. If their anxiety was not too great, they were likely to make a psychiatric referral. If the anxiety was excessive, they responded with punishment.[17]

Case: A mild and meek man of twenty-seven had married an older woman with a fourteen-year-old daughter by a previous marriage. The police found the daughter having sexual intercourse with some boys. In the course of their investigation she told the officers that three years previously she had had sex play with her stepfather. He was then arrested for "incest," later changed to "injury to a child." In response to her seductive maneuvers, he had held her close until he had an orgasm and had played with her genitalia. He was, as is not unusual in such cases, a passive, dependent, anxious man, who was guilt-ridden and confused. He tried in a fumbling way to defend himself.

This infuriated the judge: "That is the stuff that is taught in some institutions of learning. Some writers and professors believe that there should be no inhibitions in sex life. They think there is no wrong, no sin, do as you please, that is what these teachings amount to, to anyone who has done any reading. You have a man up for sentence and he has given vent to these thoughts and, as I have said before, there are those who hold such opinions as mighty dangerous. If you ask me the question, it is coming from the kind of teaching. I happen to know something about it. I have done a little reading myself. That is why he has succumbed to that kind of teaching."

His lawyer pleaded that the culprit be allowed to have psychiatric treatment. The court replied, "You think you say something of advantage to him in that this has not occurred in the last three years and that he needs psychiatric treatment. Why, that is the standard defense. They always run to psychiatrists when they are in trouble. . . . Don't you think that he started this child on her way? . . . Sure he did. He practically admits it in his statement. The way to handle these fellows is to put them out of circulation. . . . It is revolting, monkeying around with a child. I can see a boy of her own age, or a boy a couple years older, that is, it is a temptation and his passion was aroused, but not a man thirty years old. I am not trying to be holier than thou, but something has to be done with these fellows to put them out of circulation. Furthermore, when he gets away from that kind of teaching, if he can get away from it, he ought to have remorse and do penance. These fellows do not want to be punished. They have to be punished. Why do they not take the rap like men? I see some instances of it when they do and they say, 'Do with

[16]Kinsey, Pomeroy, and Martin, *Sexual Behavior in the Human Male* (1948).
[17]Freedman, *The Sexual, Aggressive and Acquisitive Offender—A Comparative Study: The Mentally Ill Offender* (Sacramento, CA: Department of Mental Hygiene, 1960).

me what you will. It is wrong. I will take the rap.' " He then sentenced
the man to four years in prison.

The judicial evidence of anti-intellectualism, anxiety, confusion, ignorance of
what in analytic terms might be called an identification in a negative of the
oedipal relationship is, I think, obvious from the quote. I saw this offender
later in prison. He had become a punk, the homosexual partner of a wolf—an
aggressive psychopath—and psychiatrically he was very sick.

Aggressive offenses are more likely to occur among blacks than among
the white population in comparable neighborhoods. This is generally studied
from the viewpoint of community and individual pathology. In addition to
community pathology, however, blacks are in most communities arrested by
white officers, almost invariably prosecuted by white district attorneys, judged
by white judges, and sent to prison where there are virtually no black guards.

One of our subjects had got into an argument over a gambling debt and
shot a man. He was arrested and charged with assault with intent to kill. The
judge said to him, "When did you come North?" His answer was that it had
been some thirty years previously. The judge then replied:

> That's the trouble. These people come up here from the South,
> they are welcomed, they are aided. They are given every opportunity
> that can be given to them and they misuse the freedom that they get. We
> have a whole lot of crimes here that are committed by that very class of
> people. When they get up here, they seem to misconstrue freedom for
> license, and when they get up here they commit all sorts of crimes. They
> have to be educated or indoctrinated somehow with the notion that
> freedom in the North and respect for their rights does not mean that they
> must think that this is an invitation to do as they please and commit any
> kind of crime that they want.

The irony, the irrelevance, the unfairness of this judge's statement is of course
obvious. The man was sentenced to five-to-eight years' imprisonment. By
contrast, the acquisitive offenses were judged and sentenced without such
moralistic homilies.

So much for distortions in the social-selection process.

PSYCHOLOGICAL SURVEYS OF INMATE POPULATION

Criminal identity results from an act and a sequence of social-selective
and judgmental steps. When these are completed, the criminal sometimes
becomes a prisoner.

The first part of our study was devoted to familiarizing ourselves with
the prison, conducting psychological surveys of the inmate population, and
with specifically focused inductive psychiatric observations and consultation

treatment. There are special problems in dealing with prisoners. They live in a tension-ridden totalitarian garrison. They are dominated by other men; they are resentful and rebellious. Without women, they are enmeshed in endemic homoerotic and homosexual seduction and challenge. Because they are isolated from and rejected by the community at large, their self-esteem is low and, reactively, assertive. Their constant goal is to escape the restriction of the walls and of sexual deprivation and the frustrations of personal expression. They want out. Any non-inmate, particularly one who is presumed to be powerful, is viewed with an unstable compound of fearful suspicion lest he somehow injure them (most feel that society has in fact injured them) and the hope that he will assist them toward their freedom. The inmate is likely to be both seductive and defiant, disarmingly frank and deliberately misleading.

When the administrative impotence of the clinicians and the researchers becomes obvious, negativistic silence, complaints, and abuse may ensue. In this case, it also revealed our autonomy from the administration and helped establish confidence in us. We were able, I think, to acquire intimate information as well as to achieve certain therapeutic successes. We treated this information with absolute confidentiality.

We made preliminary observations on the impact of the duration of the prison stay. We divided our subjects into those who had arrived recently and were in the indoctrination period, those who were mid-term in their prison sentence, and those who were anticipating their discharge. Our overall impression was that newly examined prisoners were relatively open, ingenuous, cooperative, and, to a degree, hopeful. Very quickly this attitude yielded to cynicism, fatalism, nihilism, and a burning, defiant, smoldering resentment that characterized the middle-termers. Men interviewed toward the end of their sentences were likely to be apprehensive or angry. If their sentences had been long, they seemed to feel that they were less fitted to adjust to a competitive society than before.

Again, we were interested in the reliability of the psychiatrist as a diagnostician. We divided the men who came to see us into three groups: those who came voluntarily because of overwhelming subjective anxiety or disabling symptomatology, those who were referred by the administration because they had been excessively disturbing to others in the prison, and those who scored high in psychopathology according to our rating device in the psychological tests. We scored them as: in no need of psychiatric attention, manifesting an elective or nonacute need, and in need of immediate psychiatric attention. (We found a high correlation between the self and administration referrals and psychopathology as scored on the group test.) Scored independently by our psychiatrists, need for psychiatric attention correlated significantly with the results of the group projective tests. All the men for practical purposes labeled as in need of psychiatric attention by the psychologist were also found by the psychiatrists to be severely emotionally disturbed.

Use of group psychological tests proved to be effective not only in the generally accepted psychometric functions such as intelligence but in distinguishing group characteristics in the sexual deviants and aggressive offenders. Using several psychological parameters, we compared the sex-offender group to a control group and found that sex offenders showed greater passivity and greater feminine identification, to a statistical probability far beyond chance.[18]

We attempted to find out to what degree we could relate the content of the Rorschach responses to overaggressive verbal behavior. Inhibitory content was significantly and inversely related to aggressive behavior when total self-expression was used in obtaining the proportion. We thus found that we could use a projective device also to relate aggressivity with observed behavior.[19]

The results of this prestudy largely determined the research design and postulates of our final two years. We constructed hypotheses and designed an integrated interdisciplinary research project utilizing sociological, psychological, psychiatric, and legal approaches. The most meaningful *a priori* unifying concept seemed to be behavioral rather than clinical or motivational entities, and so we divided our research subjects into sexual, aggressive, and acquisitive offenders. Our overriding hypothesis was that repetitive behavior within each of these categories would be consistent with a definable, developmental, and characterological entity. We assumed that by starting with the act we could study motivation and character, and this indeed has turned out to be the case.[20]

Our method consisted basically of structured and therapeutic psychiatric interviews, participant observation in group psychotherapy sessions, sociological interviews, psychological testing and study of all case records, all conceived and analyzed within a psychoanalytic model of personality and culture. Psychological tests included the Rorschach, Blacky, Picture-Frustration Study, Bender Gestalt Technique, a specially adapted Aptitude Scale and the Army Beta, a nonverbal group intelligence test.[21]

A total of 150 men, 50 in each category, were studied. Subjects were selected from a population of 800 men by a random stratified sampling

---

[18]Preliminary analysis of the Thematic Apperception Tests revealed that the sexual offender reported the woman rejected by the man. Conversely, themes in which the woman attempts to restrain the man from committing some unusually aggressive act were more frequent in the case of aggressive and acquisitive prisoners. Thus, projective studies permit some substantive predictions between our groups. Freedman and Kaswan, "Polistaraxis Behavior and Projective Techniques" (paper presented at annual meeting of the American Orthopsychiatric Association, 9 March 1963).

[19]Ibid.

[20]Roebuck, "Criminal Typology," in *Crime Law and Corrections*, ed. Slovenko (1966), p. 257.

[21]Freedman, "Sexual, Aggressive, and Acquisitive Deviates: A Preliminary Note," *Journal of Nervous and Mental Diseases* 132 (1961): 44.

technique. For each of the three classifications, we first computed the distribution of ten variables determined in the course of our prestudy: age, race, marital status, religion, education, intelligence quotient, psychological disturbance rating, minimum sentence, time in prison and type of previous offenses. We then randomly selected fifty subjects from each of the groups so that their distribution on each of the ten variables matched as closely as possible the distribution of the offense group from which the sample was drawn. Each of our sample groups was therefore representative of the total population of sexual, aggressive, or acquisitive offenders in the institution at the time.

Representative Observation on Psychosexual Behavior of Subjects

I shall now present some representative observations concerning the psychosexual behavior of subjects in all three groups. We have proved to a high degree of statistical probability the existence of these groups on a number of clinically identifying and significant variables. Here, however, I am presenting a selective comparison of certain related factors and clinical impressions derived from them, presented out of the context of the complex of interlocking psychosocial phenomena.

Our subjects came from the lowest socioeconomic classes, IV and V, but there were nonetheless socioethnic differences between them; as, for example, the preponderance of geographically mobile blacks in the aggressive group, contrasted with the white, indigenous, rural New Englander in the sexual group. The consistently low socioeconomic status and preponderant minority group origin indicates socially imposed vulnerability, and certain characteristics of their ease of detection points toward self-imposed amenability to punishment. In addition to demographic differences, interfamilial relationships with father, mother, and siblings showed characteristic and possibly clinically significant variations, as did the kind and quality of peer group and community interaction.

The kind and quality of these finds was reflected to a remarkable degree in the psychosexual lives of our subjects. We might summarize these data by describing our sexual group as deviate, our aggressive group as ambivalent, and our acquisitive group as resilient. We divide our psychosexual data chronologically between experiences before the age of sixteen and those after sixteen; that is, we distinguish psychosexual phenomena occurring during the preoedipal, oedipal, and latency periods and the first thrust of puberty, from those occurring in early adult and adult life when genital maturity, in the ordinary course of events, should have been well established.

The most statistically significant and clinically striking contrasts and similarities in our comparative analysis of psychosexuality occurred between the sexual and acquisitive subjects; this was also the case in other parameters of behavior. The aggressives were in most variables intermediate between these extremes, but were far from the stereotype of virile masculinity that one might expect of the self-assertive attacker of other persons.

The overwhelming majority of men who later became sex deviates were deeply inhibited during early childhood and especially during the crucial pubertal stage from all forms of manifest sexual outlet. They had had a significantly lower level of overt sexual behavior of all kinds than any other group. As might be expected, they had far less heterosexual play and coitus with girls than the others. Their childhood practice of homosexuality was surprisingly low, in fact, somewhat lower than those who later became thieves. Their incidence of masturbation was also far less than these acquisitives. They tended to be the oldest at the time they achieved their first ejaculation, which in turn was likely to be attained by masturbation rather than through any physical or psychical relationship with another person. Those sexual deviates who did have homosexual activities before sixteen were likely to have done so with boys younger or their own age, while those aggressives and acquisitives who engaged in homosexuality did so generally with older men.

Early History of Sexual Deviates

There was a curious and possibly significant dichotomy in the early history of the sexual deviates. As a group, they were inadequate or inferior in the overall vitality of overt sexuality, but in a small but definite minority (about 10 percent) just the opposite was true. These had started masturbating and, indeed, had attempted heterosexual coitus before the age of eleven; thus, they had somehow been prematurely stimulated during the latency period. This intrusion into what is commonly experienced as years of sexual quiescence may help us to understand the predisposition and the direction that their perversion assumed in later years. None of our acquisitives, and only a single aggressive subject, reported such early coitus. Those deviates who started early activities had a greater frequency of such activity than the comparative groups. At the level of clinical observation, those who had been stimulated to premature coitus were sexually aggressive toward women; those who had indulged in early autoerotic behavior were more likely to become homosexual pedophiles.

The aggressive and acquisitive subjects experienced a sharp and dramatic upsurge of phallic sexual activity that was chronologically coincident with the onset of the pubertal libidinal thrust. Most of our acquisitive, and almost half of our aggressive subjects, had their first coital experience between their eleventh and sixteenth birthdays. For the sexual deviate, heterosexual intercourse was postponed to far later into adolescence or to adulthood. Again, the majority of the acquisitive group began masturbating during their earliest adolescent surge between eleven and fourteen; among the sexual group, however, only about one in five responded in either of these ways. For them both private masturbatory as well as interpersonal coital behavior occurred late in adolescence or early or middle adulthood. Nor was homosexuality used as an alternative outlet. Only about 10 percent had such relationships with any frequency before the age of sixteen, and an additional 4 percent had very infrequent homosexual interaction.

However, in adult life the overall picture is that of bisexuality or ambisexuality rather than uniformity in selection of sexual object.[22] The sexual deviates were just as apt to be married as the others. Moreover, compared to the aggressives, they had intercourse with their wives more frequently, and were twice as likely to initiate it.

Aggressive Behavior and Sexual History

If there is any single quality that may be said to characterize our aggressive offenders, it is their ambivalent approach to their sexual life. In general, the heterosexual profile of this group is intermediate between the sexual and acquisitive groups. They resemble the acquisitives in some ways, but there are areas where their sexual inhibition and timidity approaches and even exceeds that of the sexual deviates. They had the least homosexual activity of any group, both in childhood and adult years, but their masturbation pattern closely parallels that of the sexual deviates. They tended to be more ambivalent in their feelings about heterosexual relations, were less likely to take sole initiative in marital relations, and engaged in less intercourse with their wives than sexual and acquisitive offenders. They were the most inhibited in fantasying during masturbation, and fewer expressed gratification or relief, while more gave evidence of ambivalence after masturbation than any other group. Feelings concerning sexual daydreams were most likely to be blocked and not articulated. Of those who responded, most regarded them as unpleasant.

Sexual History of Acquisitive Offenders

Acquisitive offenders showed, in general, a significantly higher level of overt sexual behavior of all kinds than any other group. They had a higher

---

[22]This impression of a melding of sexual drives and objects in adult life (within the pattern of their psychosexual diversity) is enhanced by our observation that while in prison, in the absence of appropriate objects, approximately the same percentage of all groups reported homo-erotic activity.

incidence and frequency of heterosexual activity; more of them had had homosexual relationships than the aggressive and about the same percentage as the sexual groups. Almost all started masturbation in their early teens. They tended to be younger at the time of their first ejaculation than any of the others and were far more likely to have participated in coital activity the earliest. Possibly because of their other outlets, the frequency of masturbation before puberty was the lowest of all and they were most likely to have ceased by the age of seventeen. They were most likely to have engaged in coital intercourse both in and out of marriage, to have initiated sexual relationships with their wives, and, for their nonmarital partners, were most likely to have used either prostitutes or women with whom they had had casual and transient relationships. Fewer, indeed, were married than in the other groups. Sexually they were the most active, least rigid of all the groups and, superficially at least, the most accepting of their own sexual proclivities. They accepted their homosexual experience without noticeable upset as compared to the aggressives. They were, however, activists and realists, apparently able to tolerate sexual activity far more easily than sexual imagery or fantasy. Most of them rejected sexual daydreams as being unpleasant.

Several impressions emerge from these findings. There is the early onset of peculiar and persisting patterns of behavior. There is a remarkable unity of seemingly disparate parameters of behavior. For example, from his earliest history, the acquisitive offender is sexually a free-acting, polyfocal being. Although he is most active, his tend to be the most transitory sexual relationships. He is most diverse in his objects, with fewest obvious indications of negative reactions to his sexual experiences. He is most directly responsive to physiological alterations of motivation and adjusts easily to externally imposed variability of available objects. These psychosexual characteristics take on significance when correlated with his pattern of objectless, repetitive illegal acquisition of material goods. There is a parallelism between his sexual relationships and the sociopsychological qualities of the acquisitive acts themselves. Here too he is, we might almost say compulsively and promiscuously, repetitive and reveals least concern about them. The interchangeability and relative personal insignificance of his sexual objects as compared to the persistence of his sexual aims is matched by the human objectlessness of his persistently acquisitive aims.

To cite another example of apparent identity between private-sexual mores and the type of antisocial act, the aggressive is the most heterosexual of all, if we take absence of homosexuality as our criterion. However, we have evidence to justify the assumption that he is goal inhibited rather than overwhelmingly heterosexual. His marital life is more passive and less active than the other groups. It is striking also that the acquisitives reported more fighting and less control of anger than the aggressives. (Since this is self-judgment, it may reveal differences in evaluation of what constitutes control.) In fact, many of these aggressives were clinically passive people who had lashed out during a passive-aggressive crisis in their lives. The aggressive behavior might therefore be a reaction to the active-passive conflict, which seems to be reflected also in their sexual history.

Thus, certain aspects of sexual behavior may be revealing leads to an understanding of seemingly disparate aggressive and acquisitive activity. We have found other comparably significant parallels in the developmental and adult patterns not only in sexual, but in the aggressive and acquisitive spheres as well. That is, we have been able to relate certain repetitive elements in each of these phases of personality to their characteristic modes of antisocial behavior.

Psychiatry and the Law: An Overview

LAWRENCE ZELIC FREEDMAN

Psychiatry and the law are coextensive in the problems they face and in many facets of their history. Neither is wholly intelligible without some awareness of the corresponding development of the other. In broad areas their influence is reciprocal and complementary. Both concern themselves with people who are different, who are in trouble, who may behave in a way that is often a nuisance, usually an irritant, and sometimes a danger to those around them. Each discipline functions as a pragmatic technology based on empirical observations made in the course of experience. Apparent conflicts between them that remain unresolved are frequently legacies of their common background. More, perhaps, than many psychiatrists and lawyers realize the methods of the sources of information of the two fields have resembled or paralleled each other, even after each had emerged from its smothering incorporation within the church.

When Oliver Wendell Holmes stated that "the life of the law has not been logic but experience," he was not sparking a revolt against rational, logic-tight spirals of reasoning from legal precedent. Holmes rested his case on Darwinian evolution, comparative anthropology, and the comparative study of laws in different times, locales, and cultures. It was no revolution but a revelation, a simple statement of observed history. The law has always been a natural science, reflecting the biological characteristics of its human victims, villains, heroes, and chorus, no less than their social values.

There are today differing schools of law, just as there are differing schools of psychiatry, and for essentially the same reasons. Each discipline exists because of the imperative needs of society and its victims rather than by virtue of its acquired knowledge, demonstrated validity, and proven effectiveness. Each is indispensable, not because of its excellence of learning and skills but rather because each must perform as well as it can despite a lamentable, still insurmountable, deficiency in its information, skills, and tools.

You perhaps already have heard the aphorism that the law exists for the protection of the many, for the preservation of the state, and that the goal of psychiatry is to aid the individual in his struggles to adjust to the society within the structure of that state. This neat apposition of the one and the many, while superficially plausible, is a specious sophistry. A primary function of democratic government is the protection of minorities against unjust and

117

gratuitous harm that might be inflicted on them by more powerful and more numerous members of their society. The phrase, "the law," conveys a sense of monolithic solidarity, of constancy, of impersonality, of predictability that sounds persuasive but belies the self-evident fact that all law is initiated and administered by individuals. In this country laws are introduced in legislature by representatives, voted by citizens, and approved by a single executive. The decision to arrest is made by a policeman; particular attorneys employed by the state must decide whether to seek indictments or to ignore the police evidence. Judges and juries, like all these other legal actors, bring much that is idiosyncratic to their sense of the immediate environment. First and finally is the accused person, and with him the attorney whose task it is to defend him. At every stage therefore the law is created, approved, and invoked by individual decision or act that must express one man's values, springing not only from his environment but also his personality, including his unique characteristics and sometimes his psychopathology. "A government of laws, not of men" is a pious reaction against tyrannical despotism rather than an accurate reflection of legal reality.

In countless statues of varying artistic merit the law is allegorically represented as a woman dressed in a Roman palla, her eyes blindfolded, one arm holding a set of scales. Her sightless eyes symbolize a disregard for the station, power, and wealth of, or empathy or sympathy for, either legal contestant. Unlike the stone woman, however, all participants in the legal process have their eyes open; their blindfolds lie within them. The personality, station, power, and wealth of the accused and the political and journalistic reactions to the accused provide intrapsychic impediments to seeing when the scales are in balance. The private desires, ambitions, fears, and vulnerabilities of each participant play their role in the weighing of the scales.

Justice is, I hasten to add, a reality because the structure of the law and the will of most of its participants seek it. It is this seeking that gives the law vitality and meaning. The myth that the corpus of laws, written and unwritten, operates free of ordinary human bias may in the past have given the faith in legal procedure that it required. I see no hazard, however, in viewing the law today as an imperfect social process, a continuing ideal rather than an accomplished fact. A person is an emergent process toward one or another ego-ideal that he never achieves. So in a social framework is the law. Justice may be aspired to but is never completely realized because law implementers, like offenders and psychiatric patients, are people and not automata. From birth the human creature is inextricably part of a meshwork of human related-ness, of which the law is the most formal but neither exclusively nor prepotently the most restrictive. The official framework within which his personality evolves and matures, and within which he must live out his life, is the law.

Law, blended into religious ritual, was the earliest response by the organized group to aberrant personalities, whether they were evil or mad. In theocratic societies, legal restrictions were administered by religious leaders, shamans, and priests who exorcised those diabolic spirits that had invaded the bodies of human beings and caused all sorts of mischief, frequently sexual but often violent and avaricious as well.

The dichotomy between mind and body, which has dominated psychiatric and legal thought since Descartes, is itself an anachronism springing from this prehistory. The mind and the body are basic tenets of law as they are of psychiatric and psychoanalytic thinking. Philosophically, the main psychological theory of our time is monist; it holds that mind and body are one. Psychiatrists, for the most part theoretical monists (e.g., the mind is the instrument of the brain and body), are practical dualists since the psychoanalytic model of personality most common among them is a mentalistic one. Within the past few decades the success of some of the psychopharmacological agents for the cure of mental illness, the discoveries and developing technology of neuroanatomy and neurophysiology, have tended to move psychiatry closer to a monist practice as well as faith. Today, psychological parallelism, or convergence of the physical and somatic factors, are more accurately descriptive of the psychiatric viewpoint than earlier monism or dualism.

The sacred writings of the early Jews instructed the priest how to treat the mad as well as the sick and the sinful. By ritual he was to transform the profanity they shared to its preexisting holy sanctity. When Christ adjured his fellows to cast out devils, he meant to cure the mad no less than the lame, the blind, and the halt. Early monasteries sheltered the physically ill, the psychically and spiritually possessed madmen, and the impoverished together. This tradition of lumping the varieties of misfits together was never given up. By statute it permeated the United States in the last century. It has not yet been entirely abandoned in psychiatric state hospitals or jails all over this country.

SOCIAL VALUES, THE LAW, AND PSYCHIATRY

The law has been consistently empirical, pragmatic, utilitarian in reaction to socially obnoxious, harmful, and dangerous persons. But it has not been exclusively preoccupied with their behavior. The Old and New Testaments describe religious sanctuaries for those who through accident or incapacity, but not by design, had incurred the wrath of their fellows or the state.

Lawyers have distinguished between an illegal act, which they term *malum in se* (evil in itself) and illegal acts, which are *malum prohibitum* (things that are crimes because they have been prohibited by law). The former may be roughly equated with social values, which through court decisions, have become part of the common law; the latter, through administrative decree or legislative decision. To this day there is no universal definition of crime other than, as the word's semantic derivation hints, simply a judgment according to law. The legal definition of crime is an act that violates the law of the community in which it was carried out and for which an individual has been convicted by a properly conducted trial or by a decision of an authorized person. But identical acts may be judged as criminal in one time and place but not in another. Individuals may be judged differently according to their social class and context of their offense.

The social values that laws are intended to reflect may change, but the laws themselves often remain. This seeming inconsistency is an example of cultural adaptation at work over time. Because the law is conceived of as a stabilizing system, the form, however anachronistic, is retained. But by reinterpretation and selective use it finds new employment in implementing values that may vary greatly from those which it was originally intended to reinforce. Such laws, like certain anatomical structures that have developed in the course of adaptive evolution, have become functionless over time or have fallen into disuse. Consequently, one cannot now understand how a community lives by studying its laws. Instead, we must observe which laws are effectively invoked and which tiny fraction of people is arrested, convicted, and imprisoned under them.

Dead-letter laws might be compared to the human appendix, which remains attached to our digestive apparatus with no known function but is susceptible to infection requiring surgical removal to save the life of its human host. Often, however, legal appendices that appeared to be vestigial and useless are like the pineal and thymus glands, which have been revealed to play crucial roles in the body politic, or like the old rhinencephalon brain that has assumed the emotional "gut" responses of a "visceral" brain. Seemingly ineffectual, rarely or never invoked laws may play a crucial, if ineffable, role in maintaining the smooth functioning of the society and its government. More obscurely, strange ancient laws may reflect residual roles derived from our prehistory. So, for example, the two great crimes of the history of mankind—patricide and maternal incest, killing the father and having sexual congress with the mother—are potentially active but statistically minuscule in the operation of legal sanction. As laws, however, they stand as concrete evidence of socially articulated reactions against a deeply repressed psychic propensity, which while possibly common at the earliest stages of the emergence of man as a species, are now aberrations mainly of psychically disturbed social isolates.

HISTORY

Johannes Weyer, a sixteenth-century doctor, was one of the first to apply a naturalistic clinical perspective to the behavior of witches. He sought the explanation in the personality of the "bewitched" rather than in the agency of supernatural intervention. In that century only Paracelsus treated mental illness as a form of disease rather than as a willful evil or as demonic possession. But diabolism died hard. A century after Weyer the Saxony codes denied the validity of his clinical demonstrations and recommended that they be ignored because Weyer was not a lawyer but a physician.

The men of the Renaissance and their descendants expressed explosive creativity in the service of the mentally ill and the criminal, as well as in the rediscovery of Greek rationalism and in the production of their own aesthetic classics. From Italy, heart of the intellectual revival, have come leaders too in criminology. They experimented with rehabilitative penology a century before the famed Quaker penitentiary was in existence in Philadelphia. Later, Lombroso studied criminals with precision and concern for clinical detail. He found their common traits to be impulsivity, relative moral insensitivity to harm done to other individuals, and poorly developed or nonexistent social values. Using an anthropometric method, reminiscent of phrenology, he demonstrated facial and head characteristics which, he judged, distinguished them physically from law-abiding folk. Influenced by Darwin's theory, he concluded that criminals represented an early stage of human evolutionary growth. They had been fixated at, or had genetically regressed to, an atavistic stage of mankind's adaptive emergence. Lombroso's anatomical speculations have been widely rejected, but studies continue of physical correlates of antisocial behavior. Lombroso was, moreover, a careful clinician and an astute sociological observer.

Ferri, Lombroso's contemporary and countryman, was an articulate positivist, urging that the primary legitimate goal of law was to diminish the social ill of crime rather than to assign blame and affix guilt. He denied, as others have since, that there was empirical justification for the belief that the traditional punitive methods of detection, conviction, and detention accomplished the goal of deterrence. They neither lowered the social cost of delinquency nor prevented the human waste of the lives and the agony of the delinquents. Ferri held that social defense, in a rational society, would implement whatever methods served to prevent the initiation of the first criminal act, or aided in restoring the already convicted offender to lawful behavior before an irreversible recidivism became fixed. If kindly rather than harsh social responses could best accomplish these goals, then logic and humanity argued for a helpful rather than punitive reaction to such persons. (Only recently have we begun to treat our juveniles in legal trouble in this way. With rare exceptions, traditional punishments are the unimaginative and usually inadequate legal response to criminal behavior.) From Italy too came early reform of court procedure. Where formerly the presiding judge was expected to intuitively sort out the truth from the evidence presented, important steps were taken to objectify the evidence according to more generally valid rules than the judge's hunch or homemade psychology.

The emancipation of the French Revolution was followed soon by the unlocking of the manacled madmen by Citizen Pinel at Bicêtre. This was one of the most important steps toward our still unrealized goal of free and voluntary hospitalization of the psychiatrically disabled. The influence of such men as Pinel and Esquirol affected not only the spread of humanitarian and libertarian reforms to the mentally ill but also contributed to establishing the psychiatric practice of maintaining comprehensive clinical records, and the careful systemizing of psychiatric disability into defined clinical syndromes. For good or ill, these in turn affected judicial responses to the mentally ill offender. Esquirol categorized monomanias in which a preoccupation with a single idea was associated with feelings and action tendencies. Among these manias were some that led to legal consequences such as kleptomania, the repetitive compulsion to steal. Esquirol described as well the patient who suffered from the *manie sans délire* (mania without delirium).

The direct sociological descendant of this psychiatric syndrome is the personality type now variously described as neurotic character, sociopathic personality, and psychopathic personality. Janet's concept of split consciousness and Charcot's work with hysteria, along with that of Liebeult and Bernheim on hypnosis, brought back into medicine the original observations of the transplanted Viennese, Mesmer, on "animal magnetism." The checkered history of hypnotism typified the still unresolved dilemma of how to eliminate charlatanry without penalizing legitimate scientific innovation, however strange. It also anticipated the yet disputed question of whether a medical degree is necessary to practice forms of therapy that do not call for somatic intervention. In France, too, Comte established his "queen discipline" of sociology, of which criminology is a branch; and Durkheim's contributions to our understanding of suicide and his construct of *anomie* paralleled to a remarkable degree those clinical models of Freud, which are of special interest to psychiatry and law.

Esdaile and Elliotson, through careful study and sober reports, were pioneers in introducing hypnosis (neurohypnology) to the English-reading medical public. Tuke established in England a model of considerate care of the mentally ill, using kindliness and "moral treatment"—the meaning of "moral" at that time being very close to our modern use of "mental" or "psychic." This benign humanity was a marked advance over the wild bedlam of Bethlehem Asylum, where psychotics, along with criminals and other undesirables, were kept in chains and where they made a wild racket for the benefit of sightseers who were admitted for a fee to view them, rather as we once viewed freaks at a circus. The reactive din was so great that the word "bedlam" remains a semantic fossil, a reminder of the noisy uncontrol that excessive inhuman control provokes.

In 1835, Prichard, influenced by the *manie sans délire* of Esquirol, described the psychopathic personality as an amoral man who behaves impulsively and sometimes criminally to satisfy his immediate impulse. The psychopathic personality learned little from experience and was unable to restrain himself from his present temptation, even when he had promise of richer gratification by waiting just a short while, and although he incurred risks of punishment and danger disproportionately great compared to his possible immediate reward. This psychopathic personality fellow, under various names, remains one of the great obstacles to agreement on the issue of responsibility between legal and psychiatric scholars and practitioners. Maudsley, a distinguished English psychiatrist, was convinced that the mind was the instrument of the brain, and thus that a deranged mind was symptomatic of a deranged brain. He conceded that techniques then available were unable to detect the anatomic defect. One hundred years later we are still unable to detect the neurophysical laws of criminality, or of neurosis.

In Germany and in German-speaking cantons, particularly in the nineteenth century, the relationship between psychiatry and law was intimate and important. Kraff-Ebing described clinical syndromes of sexual aberrations with encyclopedic thoroughness. Wagner-Jauregg's malaria treatment and Ehrlich's Salvarsan injections began the assault on general paresis, then a major medicolegal problem. Kraepelin so comprehensively catalogued the varieties of mental disease that it had the possibly unlooked-for effect of equating severe mental disease syndromes, which he called dementia praecox and manic-depressive psychoses, with legal irresponsibility. Bleuler developed Kraepelin's dementia praecox into the more finely wrought diagnosis of the schizophrenias, which for all practical purposes frequently, but equally mistakenly, have been used medicolegally as the equivalent of "legal insanity." In Switzerland, Forel, superintendent at Berghölz, led the fight against alcoholism and other sociolegal ills, relying strongly on moral persuasion. The contemporary Swiss, Piaget, has made important observations on the development of the child's moral sense, from the concrete and general to the abstract and specific.

In Austria, Freud described the unconscious and delineated the psychic defense mechanisms of the developing child and in the character structure of the adult. He proposed a tripartite personality construct, with an instinctual id, a reality-testing and integrating ego, and a self-judging superego. He advanced a hypothesis of the evolutionary development of a sense of justice, based on the shared guilty reaction to primal parricide, resulting in the belief that all (brothers) should be treated equally and impartially according to predictable rules called laws. He suggested that the sense of "guilt" might itself precede rather than follow the crime, and consequently that the prospect of punishment could predispose toward rather than deter illegal acts. To the traditional triumvirate of the legal rationale for punishment—deterrence, retaliation, and rehabilitation—psychoanalysis added a fourth: the need for punishment. Inspired by psychoanalysis, Alchorn applied techniques for the treatment of "wayward boys" who were responsive to their own psychological needs rather than to the repressive punishments of conventional law.

Alexander, a psychoanalyst, and Staub, a jurist, described the range of criminal types in psychoanalytic terms. Those whose acts were in harmony with their delinquent subculture and their egos were "normal criminals." Those whose illegality sprang from deeply repressed impulses, of which they themselves were unaware, were labeled alloplastic neurotic characters, in contrast to autoplastic psychoneurotics. The crucial difference seemed to be that the psychoneurotic suffered from his symptoms and the criminal acted out his conflicts on the community, and at its expense.

In the United States, Benjamin Rush of Philadelphia, influential revolutionist and foremost alienist, helped establish the first mental asylum here and introduced care for the mentally ill in a general hospital. He also invented a ducking stool that dipped agitated patients into a cold-water tub, and he favored leechings, bleedings, and purgations. Rush's influence in stabilizing a democratic government and in improving the institutional conditions of the mentally ill has stood the test of time better than his treatment procedures. In 1832, Isaac Ray, a young general practitioner practicing in Eastport, Maine, published a remarkable book, *Insanity and Jurisprudence*. The most significant work in medical jurisprudence written in English, it was cited a decade later in the crucial McNaughtan case, which has influenced the legal concept of responsibility to this day in our country as well as in England.

RESPONSIBILITY

When in England in 1843, McNaughtan, a deluded young man, killed the secretary to Sir Robert Peel, the English prime minister, he was acquitted by reason of insanity. After the trial, England's law lords were asked to answer a set of questions that would aid in defining the limits for legal responsibility in future cases of a similar nature. The responses to a few of these queries have become known as the McNaughtan formula, and until recently they have controlled the determination of legal responsibility in England and in most of the United States. The word "responsibility" as generally used denotes personality traits, trustworthiness, and dependability. However, these subjective characteristics are not identical with legal responsibility. In law, responsibility means culpability and hence punishability. Criminal law does not designate socially harmful acts alone as crimes. The perpetrator of that objectionable behavior must have intended to do it; he must have had a *mens rea*, an evil intent. Nor can there be a *mens rea* if the quality of mind of the offending person is so deficient, so abnormal, so diseased as to have deprived him of the capacity for rational intent.

It is frequently but mistakenly assumed that modern psychiatrists are attempting to intrude their professional and social values into the procedures of the law. This is incorrect. The ascertaining of the mental state of the accused derives from ancient legal precedent, not modern psychiatric evangelism. In psychotherapy the patient's wishes and intentions are at least as important as his acts. In religious morality, an evil intention may be the sinful equivalent of the act. But the law is invoked only when an illegal act is carried out. Behavior, however harmful, is not criminal unless accompanied by the mental state of intent as described in the law.

The McNaughtan formula, therefore, attempted to prescribe what criteria the court, judge, and jury should apply in exculpating a person accused of crime from punishment, in declaring him irresponsible. A man should be considered irresponsible, the law lords said, when he was unaware of the nature and consequences of his act or when he was unable to know that the act was wrong. McNaughtan himself was suffering from a delusion. The lords also declared that a delusion to exculpate a man from punishment had to be one that *if true* would be an adequate defense. If the *deluded idea* did not justify the crime, then presumably the man was to be held responsible, guilty, and punishable. It was under this formula that Jack Ruby, the slayer of Lee Harvey Oswald, President John Kennedy's assassin, was tried and found guilty. Several weeks after Ruby's trial, when his "guilt" was no longer in question, he was diagnosed as psychotic by the doctors who, less than six weeks previously, had testified that he had fulfilled the criteria of legal responsibility.

Alienists have protested ever since 1843 that these criteria are exclusively intellectual, that separation of the cognitive faculty of personality was at best misleading, and worse, meaningless. They complained that they could not testify competently under such arbitrary legal restrictions. The lawyers, however, replied that these were not medical standards of insanity but legal standards of responsibility. And so the debate has continued for more than a century.

In 1869, New Hampshire adopted a rule of responsibility that placed psychopathology in the same category as physical pathology and other scientific and technical problems that required expert assessment and diagnosis. Psychiatric experts were to testify to the best of their ability in accordance with their highest level of professional competence concerning the mental state of the person they had clinically studied. Their data and opinions, like all information obtained from experts on technical questions, then become part of the sum of facts available to the jury. The expert's testimony, treated as one set of facts among many, was then to be evaluated by the judge or jury to ascertain its proper relationship to the legal requirements of *mens rea* and responsibility. This straightforward, sensible solution, however, remained an isolated oasis of rationality in northern New England. The rest of the country and England have pursued the tortured and confusing requirements of the McNaughtan formula. The sensible Scots added an intermediate state of partial responsibility to the rigid dichotomy of the all-or-nothing decisions of responsibility or irresponsibility. Certain American states have added the "irresistible impulse" to the criteria of knowledge and awareness. An accused may be held not responsible if he was affected by impulses that were sudden, immediate, and overwhelmingly powerful so that they were, in fact, irresistible at the time of the crime.

These irresistible impulses, in practice, have proven to be generally unprovable, or at least unpersuasive in our courts. Judges and juries have found themselves unable to distinguish between the unrestricted impulse where, possessing "free will," the culprit had chosen not to resist, and the irresistible impulse where the defendant's "free will" was incapable of restraining his irresistible impulse. This skepticism was most explicitly and succinctly expressed by an Ontario judge who said to a defendant claiming irresistible impulse: "We shall dangle a rope in front of you and see whether your impulses are irresistible." The social philosophy behind this cynical aphorism goes back to one of the many legal criteria that have marked the progress of English tests for responsibility of earlier centuries. Before McNaughtan, the "police-man-at-the-elbow" test was an important criterion of responsibility. The trial attempted to ascertain whether the defendant would have carried out his act with a policeman at his elbow. Presumably, if this immediate prospect of detection, arrest, and punishment failed as a deterrent, then the man was legally irresponsible, incapable of controlling himself. In vain did alienists of the nineteenth century and psychiatrists of the twentieth point out that even psychotically deteriorated patients in institutions were often secretive in carrying out acts that they knew to be forbidden. Their argument that the dangerous paranoiac might be the most cunning of all in planning objectionable and harmful behavior so as to escape detection and punishment was without effect.

In 1963, Oswald assassinated the president without witnesses; this secrecy does not by itself prove that he was a sane man. Ruby shot Oswald in the midst of a host of policemen and before millions of television eyewitnesses, but this killing before a myriad of policing eyes was held to be an act of a legally responsible man. For a Ruby, there is no evidence that dangling a rope before his eyes or the presence of a policeman at his elbow had any inhibiting effect. For an Oswald, the attempt at secrecy tells us little about the severity of his psychopathology. It is reasonable psychological conjecture that in Ruby's case public exposure may have contributed toward, rather than mitigated against, his tragic, impulsive homicide. He could thus openly rectify a terrible wrong, demonstrate that he had guts, and identify himself with the law enforcement officers whom he so admired and envied. In 1881, Guiteau assassinated President James Garfield in the presence of police but was found guilty and hanged in spite of psychiatric testimony of his psychopathologically erratic, eccentric life history of meaningless wanderings. In 1901, Czolgosz killed President William McKinley within inches of his guards. Czolgosz was whisked off to trial and executed before he could be adequately studied by alienists, in spite of evidence that he too was a rootless, confused wanderer, possibly deeply disturbed emotionally, who also killed with many policemen at his own and his victim's elbow. In 1933, Zangara shot at Franklin Roosevelt in public, surrounded by witnesses and within easy reach of policemen.

In 1954 the appellate court in Washington, DC, district held, in the case of Monte Durham, that a man should not be held responsible for an otherwise criminal act when his behavior was the "product of mental disease or deficiency." This decision resembles the policy of New Hampshire, promulgated a century earlier. The American Law Institute also has included a formula for legal responsibility in its monumental Model Penal Code, prepared by leading American scholars and legal authorities over a ten-year period. This would free from responsibility anyone who, because of mental defect or deficiency, had been incapable of appreciating the criminality of his act, or if he had appreciated its criminality and had been nevertheless unable to control his behavior. The code cautions, however, that mere repetition of harmful antisocial behavior would not by itself free a malefactor from responsibility for his crime. The reason for this exclusion of the repetitive criminal is to prevent the psychopathic personality from escaping punishment. Another federal appellate court decision, during the 1950s in the Currens case, frees from responsibility those who were unable to control their behavior. It makes the ability to control one's behavior the crucial distinguishing factor rather than perceptual, intellectual, or emotional traits. A California decision, in the case of Gorshen, introduced into American jurisprudence something resembling the century-old partial responsibility clause of the Scots. Mental disability may serve as a mitigating circumstance, affecting not so much the decision as to guilt or innocence as the nature and duration of disposition, whether penal incarceration or therapeutic treatment as an outpatient or inpatient. California has two separate trials in criminal cases where the question of mental illness is raised. The first trial seeks to ascertain whether the accused person carried out the illegal act. If so, the second trial seeks to determine how his state of mind at the time related to the legal criteria for responsibility.

These several variants in legal procedures affect, however, only a small fraction of the criminally accused. A few states have so far followed the legislative example of the Model Penal Code, but the impact of the Durham, Currens, and Gorshen decisions thus far have been mainly confined to the jurisdictions of the courts that pronounced them. By and large, therefore, the question of criminal responsibility remains approximately where it was when promulgated by the legal lords in the age of Queen Victoria. But coming as they do within a single decade after a century of neglect, these defections from the McNaughtan formula reflect widespread dissatisfaction, and presage a legal consensus certain to be more harmoniously adapted to contemporary social values and social science than the century-old answer of the English lords has been.

Words, whether wrought with marvelous elegance or crudely and awkwardly phrased, are not the final or even necessarily the prepotent determinants
of how the law of responsibility operates. Empirically, the language of legal
formulas for determining legal responsibility is probably less important in
determining guilty responsibility than is commonly believed. The nature of
the offense, the defendant's personality, the competence of the attorneys, and
the emotional reaction of the jury seem to affect the outcome of criminal trials
more effectively than the particular words of the responsibility formula.

There has been an excessive emphasis on the topic of responsibility and
criminal behavior as the point of interaction between law and psychiatry. For
many, it has become an emotion-charged *idée fixe*, and for others a preoccupying moral question. For most, it leaves very little time or energy for other
equally significant and quantitatively more extensive joint problems of law
and psychiatry. But we cannot escape this redundant dialogue until we resolve
it. When there is individualization in imprisonment, probation, and parole;
when the psychiatrist becomes the diagnostician before and the therapist after
the trial, rather than the instrument of social arbitration during it; when
deterrability by punishment and amenability to treatment are sensibly assessed
in human individuals and not in hypothetical statistical entities, this repetitious
colloquy may end.

COMPETENCE TO STAND TRIAL

In the Anglo-American jurisprudential system, an accused person must
have not only the right to a speedy trial but also the competence to consult
with his counsel if he is to get fair treatment in a basically adversarial system.
Supreme Court decisions have attempted to rectify the fact that many indigent
defendants cannot afford to pay counsel and have reversed convictions of
men who were unable to obtain counsel because of poverty. However, even
when a competent defense attorney is available, he cannot provide an adequate
defense unless the defendant is intellectually and emotionally capable of
cooperating with him by providing relevant information and by discussing
alternative courses of action in order to decide which is optimal for his legal
defense and most likely to protect his rights. When an accused man, because
of intellectual deficiency or serious psychopathology, cannot advise, inform,
discuss, and consult with his attorney, he is, by definition, precluded from
having his day in court, according to Anglo-American tenets of justice.

This crucial pretrial determination of competency to stand trial is the
least understood by psychiatrists. It is a hidden shoal that has probably caused
more hardship and injustice than the more highly visible and frequently
acrimoniously disputed issue of responsibility. There is generally greater
latitude and range of discretion available to the judge in this determination

of competence to stand trial than for the hotly challenged and highly articulated responsibility formula, where the court proceedings are carried on before spectators and reporters. The judge's instructions to the examining psychiatrists are more diffuse and ambiguous. Most psychiatrists and not a few judges confuse the defendant's competence to consult with counsel with his legal responsibility.

Even when such pretrial commitment does not suffer from these artificial impediments it is, at best, unresolved and unpredictable in its effects. Although they have been arrested and may have been indicted, these defendants have not been found guilty of any crime. They presumably will one day stand trial to determine whether they did carry out the illegal act of which they are accused. In addition, that trial will have to ascertain whether at the time of the alleged crime their psychological state satisfied the legal criteria of intent and *mens rea*, as to make them responsible, punishable, and culpable.

Quantitatively, the congruence and range of legal and psychiatric concerns has far greater representation in civil issues of mental competence than in the more dramatic criminal questions. Evaluation of mental states may be necessary for purposes stretching from contracts, deeds and wills to marriage, divorce, annulment, and guardianship of minors, from citizenship to military service. Wisely, therefore, the law zealously guards its precedents, which always presume such competence unless there is strong evidence not only of incapacity but also that this incapacity affects the particular issue and is potentially harmful to the person himself.

PSYCHIATRY AND LAW: AN OVERVIEW

The phrase "forensic psychiatry" is an old one, and it connotes the rhetorical tactics of the courtroom. But the concern of psychiatry with the law is far wider, for whether he acknowledges it or not every physician is constantly dealing with patients whose feelings of guilt, shame, dependence, or unresolved conflict are significantly affected by the legal environment in which he lives and in which he grew up. The law's concern with the state of mind of those accused of offenses against society preoccupied its practitioners for centuries, and there is still no final solution. From this wider perspective it seems self-evident that there can be no ultimate resolution. Forms of human social organization are the products of cultural evolution, just as the form of human anatomy has emerged from biological evolution. Cultural evolution, of which legal codes are a part, is a never-ending process. So, the role of the psychiatrist during a criminal trial may become less significant than his function in helping to prevent harmful social maladjustments.

There is no forensic psychiatry, no psychiatry of rhetoric of law or of debate in the courtroom. There is only the psychiatry of the psychically sick, or healthy man, who has aroused the anxiety, anger, and revenge of aggregate man, who in turn has reacted through the rituals of law. There is an urgent need for this sort of psychiatric concern. The sense of urgency does not arise from an increase in man's destructive, greedy, and polymorphous promiscuous tendencies. We are not more erotic, brutal, or thieving than our biological and historical ancestors. Rather, the capacity and range of the disturbed person to act beyond the boundaries of his family and community has extended to wider spheres of human impact. His biosphere is enlarged. Meanwhile, the technology of our sociosphere has increased its ability to permeate our environment and our inner selves.

There is a social contagion of delinquency as well as an epidemiology of mental illness with which physicians and psychiatrists are, or ought to be, concerned. Disorganized communities and fragmented families predispose to emotional distress. An environment in turmoil will find its chaos reflected in the inner conflicts and delinquent acts of its inhabitants. More hopeful than the psychiatrist's role in ascertaining the mental state of offenders is his potential contribution toward preventing those outward manifestations of personal conflict that may damage the life of the delinquent as well as the community in which he lives. Positive legal evolution promotes not only social stability but also psychic health because a shared sense of justice is an essential prerequisite for both. Harmful legal experiments degrade politics and government as well as the personal psychological integrity of their citizens.

In this discussion our concepts have come mainly from psychiatry. The goals of psychiatry are therapeutic. But psychiatry is biological in its origins, scientific in its method, and individual in its concern. Some of these criteria apply to other specialties, but all apply only to psychiatry. Like religion it has values; like politics it is concerned with the role of power and the management of men; like law it concerns itself with the structure, rituals, and functions of serious dislocations between the individual and the group; like psychology and sociology it has methods of study; and finally, like education its goals are growth, change, individuation of personality, and generalization of major values. Psychiatry combines the humanistic and healing traditions of medicine and the disciplined empiricism of biology. It shares the awareness of both fields that the anatomy and physiology of the human animal are the primary data of his being, whether he is viewed as an individually reacting organism or as part of social patterns of interaction.

In recent years the pattern of diverse and often discrepant studies of crime in the mass by sociologists, in comparative law by lawyers, and of individual psychodynamic and semantic factors by psychiatrists, has shifted somewhat toward halting but hopeful advances in collaborative efforts and language. We seem to be moving away from an era of separate and disparate studies of the purely sociological examination of deviancy, of comparative law, and of individual psychodynamics. The past decades have seen the development of a rapprochement among these disciplines. There are now institutes set in academic environments in which social scientists, lawyers, and psychiatrists are grappling with, if not solving, common sociopsychological problems.

American universities are in the midst of rapidly expanding programs of collaborative undertakings between psychiatry and law. The psychiatrist is being called upon to play an increasingly important part in every phase of community deliberation and action. The Institute of Social and Behavioral Pathology is devoted to a comprehensive attack on all phases of strategic problems common to psychiatry and law and is responsive to the scope of these social problems. Many of the techniques and areas of psychiatric and behavioral science research lend themselves to investigation of compelling legal as well as psychopathological questions. These include studies of the participants in the legal process, of the sanctioning methods employed by the community to accomplish its objectives, of the factors that affect the degree of conformity or nonconformity to legislative policies, of the process of struggle and agreement in this community, of professional education and development. Detailed knowledge of the formal and effective decision-making institutions of the community is essential to uncover pertinent information about the degree to which legal arrangements increase or decrease mental disease, or affect its form and content. Psychiatric findings and methods of clinical study can be of far-reaching importance in explaining the consequences of community decision.

The American Medical Association has recommended increased interdisciplinary training in law and medical schools and in governmental facilities, as one of several efforts toward improved medicolegal communication. It has urged that the psychiatrically deviant offender, including the alcoholic and the drug addict, be treated with adequate medical facilities rather than punitively. It emphasized the urgency of freeing psychiatric patients from legal restrictions. Neither voluntary procedures nor those that require temporary commitment need rob the patient of his civil rights any more than do comparable practices in the treatment of infectious and contagious disease. The AMA also recommended making legal criteria for responsibility and the psychiatrist's courtroom testimony more responsive to contemporary knowledge than hitherto has been the case.

The Model Penal Code, sponsored by the American Law Institute, is a major document for those concerned with mental health. As all of these plans are models for action, lacking as yet the force of official power, their effect depends upon their proper implementation. If they are carried out, the psychiatric, medical, and ethical level of justice in the United States will be elevated.

Common Frontiers of Psychiatry and the Law*

HAROLD D. LASSWELL
LAWRENCE ZELIC FREEDMAN

We want to discuss those regions of personal distress and public disorganization that lie within the necessary and legitimate boundaries of both psychiatry and law and that are not yet fully explored. In the spirit of our title we will seek to identify and corral some of the common problems now ranging tantalizingly outside the borders of scientific law and social order. Finally, we will suggest a structure within which this initial foray may be extended in time and in legal, psychiatric, and political significance.

In an earlier symposium with us,[1] our late colleague, Professor George Dession, a pioneer in the collaboration of psychiatry and law, succinctly epitomized our common interests as being concerned with the "two areas of social process in which individuals seem to experience exceptional difficulties in the pursuit of their objectives."[2]

After tentative and rather slow beginnings American universities are in the midst of rapidly expanding programs of collaborative undertakings between psychiatry and law. Mainly, these are concerned with the initiation and development of courses for the training of law students in the elements of psychiatry and behavioral science as they apply to the law. Several law schools including Yale,[3] the University of Pennsylvania,[4] the University of Chicago,[5]

---

*This paper was written with the assistance of the Foundations' Fund for Research in Psychiatry. Presented at the annual meeting of the American Psychiatric Association held in March 1959 at Philadelphia. This edition is a slightly revised version of the original article reprinted from the *American Journal of Psychiatry* 117, no. 6 (December 1960): 490–98; 117, no. 8 (February 1961): 692–94; 117, no. 9 (March 1961): 847–48. Copyright 1960, 1961 American Psychiatric Association. Reprinted by permission.

[1]H. D. Lasswell, "Legislative Policy, Conformity, and Psychiatry," in Hoch and Zubin, eds., *Psychiatry and Law* (New York, 1955), pp. 13–14.

[2]G. H. Dession, "Deviation and Community Sanctions," ibid., pp. 1–12.

[3]L. Z. Freedman, "Experiments in Legal Education at Yale," *Yale Law Alumni Newsletter* 8, no. 3 (May 1951): 4–5.

[4]See symposium on "The Law and Behavioral Science Project of the University of Pennsylvania," *Journal of Legal Education* 2, no. 1 (1958): 73–99.

[5]Participating members of the faculty were A. S. Watson, A. L. Levin, and C. Foote. H. Kalven, Jr., commented in the perspective of experience at Chicago.

Temple University,[6] and other academic centers are now experimenting with teaching methods and preparing teaching material for this purpose.[7] Less advanced are plans for programs of joint research. Already, however, a few research units in psychiatry and law have been organized and new ones are in prospect.[8] Our emphasis will be on implementation of this phase of their collaborative efforts.

It is our thesis that, hopeful as are the beginnings which have been made in law schools and departments of psychiatry in this country, even in anticipation of their future contributions, no program thus far undertaken or planned is responsive to the range, significance, and urgency of the problems involved. We therefore propose that this national problem, affecting as it does society's most essential personal and community interests and values, must be approached on a commensurate scale.

No plan less ambitious than a national institute devoted to an integrated and comprehensive attack, simultaneously carried out on all phases of strategic problems common to psychiatry and law, is responsive to the scope of these social dilemmae.[9] It is our intention to consider some of the basic desiderata for such an institution, including its structure and function, the training and disciplinary background of its chief participants.

It is appropriate, therefore, to review some of the experience we already have gained in joint ventures of this kind and to propose a map that provides a sketch of what appears to be the lines of special promise. In so doing we shall perforce give some attention to the value assumptions and goals of the professional groups involved and consider the proposed alternatives in the light of developing trends and projections as well as behavioral and psychiatric findings to date. We will suggest how these trends may be fused in a research institute for carefully planned and integrated long-range investigation into these common problems.

Although the range of challenging questions is enormous, it is encouraging to be able to say that some collaborative work already has led to discernible results. The new intermingling of research-minded lawyers and psychiatrists is producing a common frame of reference whose potential significance for mental health and community policy is far-reaching. We shall presently refer

---

[6]The active interest in Temple is reflected in the special issue on "Law and Psychiatry," *Temple Law Quarterly* 29, no. 3 (Spring 1956): 233–408.

[7]At Northwestern University Howard Sachs is adapting the methods of small group therapy to the needs of law students. See his "Human-Relations Training for Law Students and Lawyers," *Journal of Legal Education* 11, no. 3 (1959): 316–45.

[8]The Psychiatry and Law Unit at Yale was organized to further research as well as teaching. One aim of the present report is to indicate some of the orientations and results that developed during the time when the late Professor Dession was the principal law school collaborator.

[9]For an earlier suggestion made over a quarter of a century ago see Jerome Michael and Mortimer J. Adler, *An Institute of Criminal Law and Criminal Justice* (New York, 1932).

to some representative bits of research, but it would give a distorted image of these developments to lay too much stress upon present contributions.

The psychiatrist is rare who does not very soon discover after he undertakes treatment a not insignificant range of undetected illegal activity, not merely fantasied or anticipated but actually carried out by his patients, including those who come mainly from ostensibly conformist middle- and upper-class groups. Indeed, only the most insensitive lawyers and counselors remain unaware for long that legal actions undertaken by or against many of their clients are reflections of essentially psychiatric problems. These could be treated most efficiently and justly with a proper and adequate understanding of the sublegal and subrational conflicting motivations expressed by them. Legal organizations may be the principal recruiting agency of psychiatric patients from the depressed socioeconomic groups. In an eastern state about one-quarter of the patients from the most socially and economically deprived groups, who had been seen by psychiatrists, had arrived there through the intervention of police or the courts. Further, the psychopathological symptomatology of this group was likely to be expressed in deviant or provocative interaction within the community.[10] If we thus combine the social impact of lower-class patients who act out their psychopathology so as to be caught and labeled "criminals" with our more socially favored patients whose preconscious antisocial tendencies invade the social fabric more insidiously but more effectively, the significance of this frontier of common legal-psychiatric concern becomes self-evident.[11]

The broad scope of research in the field of psychiatry does not need to be dwelt upon. All manifestations of mental disease are its province, and its investigation probes into the problems of individual and collective diagnosis, prognosis, and therapy, searching in particular for the factors affecting the etiology and course of the disease process. As a physician the psychiatrist's dominant articulate values are life and health. There are, however, social demands upon him, with which the profession is far from one mind or comfortable. These range from the question of the use of his knowledge for purposes of crime detection (e.g., narcosis, hypnosis)[12] to its use for internation

---

[10]L. Z. Freedman and A. B. Hollingshead, "Neurosis and Social Class," *American Journal of Psychiatry* 113, no. 9 (March 1957); Hollingshead and Freedman, "Social Class and the Treatment of Neurosis," *The Social Welfare Forum* (1955): 194–205.

[11]H. D. Lasswell, *Psychopathology and Politics* (Chicago, 1930); and Lasswell, *Power and Personality* (New York, 1948). [T. W. Salmon Memorial Lectures, New York Academy of Medicine.] For a succinct statement of present views and evidence see Marie Jahoda, "Environment and Mental Health," *International Social Science Journal* 11, no. 1 (1959): 14–23.

[12]L. Z. Freedman, "Pharmacodynamics and Psychiatric Investigation," *International Journal of Medicine* 172, no. 10 (October 1959); L. Z. Freedman, " 'Truth' Drugs," *Scientific American* 202, no. 3 (March 1960); G. H. Dession, L. Z. Freedman, R. C. Donnelly et al., "Drug-induced Revelation and Criminal Investigation," *Yale Law Review* 62, no. 3 (February 1953): 315–46.

destructive purposes, for example, psychological and biological warfare. Somewhere intermediate is the problem of their implementation with the aim of promoting or achieving less debatable social or national political goals.

Several psychiatric projects already are engaged in gathering data about the frequency of occurrence in communities of various size and composition, not only of neurotics, psychosomatic cases, and psychotics but also of psychopathic characters—the recidivist criminals of our culture.[13] Until the present, psychiatrists have participated to a very limited extent in the study of the first steps that often lead to full-scale court action in juveniles and adults. As a biologist and medical specialist the psychiatrist was early concerned with those organic changes that might catapult an individual into psychopathology of a personally distressful or socially harmful nature. Organic causes range from feeblemindedness on an anatomic or physiological basis to brain disease, toxicities, physical degenerative changes, and psychosomatic illness arising from predominantly psychic stimuli. Certain tentative studies would seem to indicate that there are empirically observable and measurable correlations between physical illness and social delinquency.[14] Reports of those careful and able investigators, the Gluecks, indicate a positive correlation between particular body types and incidence of juvenile delinquency.[15] Intensive and specialized investigation into these somatosocial delinquencies would therefore appear to be one of the proper functions of the psychiatric member of a research team concerned with antisocial behavior.

Many of the conventional techniques and areas of psychiatric research lend themselves with little distortion to investigation of these compelling social psychiatric questions. For example, the wards of a mental hospital can provide rich opportunities for the investigation of power operations, loci of decision making, and factors affecting those decisions that may have profoundly deprivational impacts. Not only learning and rewarding techniques but also retribution, imposition of deterrents, and efforts at rehabilitation—the classical triad of criminal law—are applied daily in large mental hospitals. On the side of the patients, this interaction involves a wide variety of character types and of symptomatic deviation. On the side of the doctors, who act as judging and decision-making figures in these hospitals, there is a comparably broad range of personalities, motives, and objectives. Stanton, Schwartz, Caudill, and others already have made important preliminary observations; thus, enough empirical data exist for the development of relevant and heuristically

[13]A. H. Leighton, "A Proposal for Research in the Epidemiology of Psychiatric Disorders," *Epidemiology of Mental Disorder* (Milbank Memorial Fund, 1950).
[14]T. A. C. Rennie, "The Yorkville Community Mental Health Study," *Interrelationships Between the Social Environment and Psychiatric Disorders* (Milbank Memorial Fund, 1953).
[15]S. Glueck and E. Glueck, *Unraveling Juvenile Delinquency* (Cambridge, MA, 1950); S. Glueck and E. Glueck, *Physique and Delinquency* (New York, 1955).

promising hypotheses.[16] There are sufficient opportunities in the course of the daily hospital activities for experimental observations of the effect upon future behavior of decisions that implement either punitive or rewarding responses.

The focus of legal research is the community-wide process of authoritative decision. For argumentative purposes research has the relatively modest role of discovering precedents or facts likely to influence the judgment of tribunals. For scientific purposes the arguments and the facts become part of the phenomena to be explained. What factors account for the acceptance or rejection of proposed statutory prescriptions by the legislature or the electorate (e.g., fluoridation)?[17] For the invocation or failure to invoke a provision in the formal code on the part of law enforcement officers (e.g., blue laws)? For the acceptance or rejection of interpretations by administrators, courts, juries (e.g., the doctrine of the Durham case)?[18] The effect of formal requirements upon conduct, and especially of sanctioning measures (e.g., recidivism)?

Within traditional legal court and pedagogical procedures, there exists ready-made opportunity for research. For example, law schools frequently adopt a role-playing procedure as a training device which, to a remarkable degree, succeeds in integrating the factual context of an actual or hypothetical case with freedom of interpersonal interplay. Such so-called "moot court cases," properly studied by qualified teams of psychiatrists, social scientists, and lawyers, may provide data to improve judgment about the most efficient way to permit the presentation to the court of the total relevant picture of personality stress and social strain. Indeed, a comparable technique is proving its effectiveness in the University of Chicago's study of small group interaction in a jury trial.[19] Additional experiments may be designed to explore the effectiveness of memory under these trial conditions and to test procedural changes in which the psychiatrist is able to communicate his best factual estimates without attempting to transmute them into terminology employed in legal doctrine.

Even these brief and inadequate reminders of the distinctive frames of research reference among psychiatrists and lawyers suffice to identify many areas of overlapping interests. On the one hand, a detailed knowledge of the formal and effective decision institutions of the community is essential if

[16]A. H. Stanton and M. S. Schwartz, *The Mental Hospital* (New York, 1954); W. Caudill, F. C. Redlich, H. R. Gilmore et al., "Social Structure and Interaction Processes on a Psychiatric Ward," *American Journal of Orthopsychiatry* 22 (1952): 314–34.

[17]See B. M. Gross, *The Legislative Struggle: A Study in Social Combat* (New York, 1953).

[18]A valuable case study is C. E. Vose, "NAACP Strategy in the Covenant Cases," *Western Reserve Law Review* 6 (Winter 1955): 101–45.

[19]F. Strodtbeck, Rita M. James, and Charles Hawkins, "Social Status in Jury Deliberation," *American Sociological Review* 22, no. 6 (December 1957): 713–19.

society is to uncover pertinent information about the degree in which legal arrangements increase or decrease mental disease or affect its form and content. On the other hand, psychiatric findings and methods of clinical study may be of far-reaching importance in explaining, or considering, the consequences of community decision on general issues or concrete cases.

The impact of legal process upon mental health—the established practices of arrest, detention, arraignment, provision of counsel, handling of release on bail, investigation, assigning of judge, fixing of trial date, demeanor of judge, mode of examination—may, upon combined psychiatric and sociological inquiry, prove to be unnecessarily anxiety producing. These practices may be so disruptive to crucial family relationships, so damaging to self-esteem, and so shocking to standards of justice embodied in the superego that they inflict the precipitating and necessary cause for severe and irreversible psychic damage. Within a wider community framework, if these practices are demonstrated to be relatively confusing and hence unenlightening to the reading public, demoralizing to the livelihood and competence, and disillusioning to faith in democracy, it may become clear that their deterrent effect is the reverse of that intended.

In a word, if we examine the total "value impact" of legal practices with the armory of psychiatric and behavioral instruments now available for the study of any detail in context, it is practicable to discover the degree to which legal practices have positive or negative impacts upon the psychiatric health (well-being) and other values of individuals and institutions. This means that society samples how legislators, executives, administrators, police, judges, and other officials (and official doctrines and operations) affect the emotional integrity and the total value position of others, thereby in turn affecting itself.[20]

More specifically, we turn to the promising lines of collaborative research, hoping to amplify and modify the conceptions touched upon thus far. For convenience, the proposed lines of study have been classified into six groups: 1) studies of the participants in the legal process, 2) procedures by which legal administrative decisions are arrived at, 3) sanctioning and corrective methods employed by the community to accomplish its objectives, 4) factors that affect the degree of conformity or nonconformity to legislative policies (authoritative prescriptions) of the community, 5) process of struggle and agreement, especially in the world community, and 6) professional

---

[20]The allusion here is to the "indulgent" or "deprivational" analysis of every interaction constituting the social process of any context, however large or small. If we think of men as seeking to maximize future value outcomes by the use of the values at their disposal (their base values), we can examine the who, what, how, and whom of interaction. For the value-institution analysis with special reference to the political and legal process see H. D. Lasswell and A. Kaplan, *Power and Society* (New Haven, CT, 1950); and more recently M. S. McDougal, "The Comparative Study of Law: Value Clarification as an Instrument of Democratic World Order," *Yale Law Journal* 61 (1952): 915–46.

education and development. Each individual and group that plays a role in the decision process of every community is a potential subject of investigation by the use of the hypotheses and methods of psychiatry and the social sciences and oriented toward the principal questions pertinent to the legal inquiry. We concentrate briefly upon two groups—the "recommenders" and the "invokers"—in order to provide a somewhat specific picture of the possibilities.[21]

Not much is known about the psychological identity of persons who take the lead in demanding legislation whose primary or sanction provisions stand out, in terms of community norms, as either remarkably coercive or restrictive, or as notably tolerant or permissive. Society is almost ignorant of the epidemiology of pressure groups and individuals who are strikingly coercive or permissive on sanctioning measures such as capital punishment, prolonged imprisonment, deportation, or sterilization, and who are active in support of extreme and violent policies on such topics as school and social segregation, intermarriage among ethnically distinct individuals, divorce, obscenity in the contents of mass media of communication, religious worship in the public schools, loyalty oaths, regulation of trade unions and business monopolies, and alcohol consumption. These issues are all controversial at various times and places in our civilization, and psychiatrists have come to realize that they may provide congenial forms of ego-syntonic role taking as defenses against expressions of the inner tension of the mentally ill, or may be social reflections of ego-dystonic conflicts and compulsions.

It is obvious that even if these psychic realities are better studied they do not necessarily determine the social validity of the conflicting opinions themselves. Even an extreme position, or willingness to play an active agitational part in public life, does not warrant an insinuation of disease. However, it cannot be denied that the accumulation of psychiatric knowledge has often connected the different with the pathological. Enough miscellaneous data, amply augmented by a steady stream of innuendo, is now in circulation to justify a serious attempt to place the entire problem in balanced perspective. It may even diminish somewhat the alleged tendency, for example, to assume that whatever is not conservative is crazy.

Such an enterprise is peculiarly suitable to the joint efforts of lawyers and psychiatrists. This is especially true when not only the recommenders but also the invokers of existing statutes, doctrines, and other formally authoritative prescriptions are studied. What motivations energize public officials who are extraordinarily zealous in "carrying out the law?" What are the motives and characteristics of unofficial members of the community who

---

[21]We speak of "recommenders" and "invokers" in reference to a seven-phase classification of the process of decision—intelligence, recommending, prescribing, invoking, applying, appraising, and terminating. For details consult H. D. Lasswell, *The Decision Process: Seven Categories of Functional Analysis* (College Park, MD, 1956).

formally take the initiative in alleging, whether falsely or accurately, the criminal violation of which sorts of community rules? There already has been psychiatric concern and clinical research directed at the so-called litigious, frequently paranoid, personality. How many of these complaints, when investigated by competent teams, would prove to have a factual basis, whether or not the complainants press them? There is also the converse problem: What are the qualities of those considerable numbers of passive, possibly masochistic, individuals who suffer undoubtedly illegal deprivations (e.g., assaults) without invoking legal protection?

The way that judges or juries solve the problems with which they are presented depends in no small degree not only upon what comes to their conscious focus of attention during the litigation but also the myriad preconscious stimuli that unknowingly impinge upon the unconscious (endogenous) factors to which they respond but do not attend. And not all that is brought into the conscious attention field is successfully guided by the procedures that bear this label in legal language. In general, there has been insufficient concern and hence knowledge about the psychological effect of the procedures that relate to the persons permitted to be present in the courtroom, or that formulate limits upon how the parties present their claims and justifications through counsel (including arguments and evidence), or that seek to determine as to how the final acts of deliberation and commitment are arrived.

It is essential to realize that in terms of effect any given decision is oriented toward the future and toward the community as a whole. The immediate response of judge or jury has an equally immediate effect upon the total value position and especially the emotional well-being of the immediate parties. But the conspicuousness of this impact should not distract us from recognizing that all other participants are similarly affected. This is not only true of counsel for the defense and prosecution but also for the witnesses, the judge, the jury, the immediate spectators, and the community outside the courtroom.[22] These immediate effects, however, are only some of those that follow a decision outcome; hence they are presumably brought to the notice of decision makers when they allow themselves to be guided by the comprehensive value-objectives of a body politic. Relevant considerations include: 1) longer range as well as immediate effects upon the offender, 2) deterrent impacts upon potential deviants from prescribed norms, and 3) impacts upon other members of the public. The problem that challenges joint research is how to bring psychiatric knowledge to its optimum place in the predecision sequence.

---

[22]The outcome indulges or deprives the value position of those affected in all values, although with varying emphasis among them in degree of intensity as well as in the specific value practice through which the change occurs. The mental and physical well-being of the conscientious judge is not to be overlooked any more than the possible significance of the result for the defendant's health or his moral and respect position, political prospects, economic welfare, skill opportunities, family life, and access to inside information.

Clinical data derived from representative psychiatric cases, supplemented by psychiatric interview and psychological projective material, need to be studied step by step in order to develop more explicit criteria for the total involvement of psychiatrists in the case from its inception. It is abundantly evident from experience to date that lawyers and psychiatrists have been insufficiently informed of the considerations that enter into their distinctive approaches. Hence, very few new procedural proposals have thus far emerged. It would be valuable to have other disciplines represented in these case studies, notably sociologists and psychologists.[23] Still another feature of these case studies could be the making of estimates of the future result of the entire range of alternatives open to the community decision makers (police, prosecutors, court, etc.) at each step of the way. This could be especially productive when teams composed of several disciplines are included, both in the investigation of past cases and in the concurrent examination of pending cases.

Some of the estimates of future alternatives will relate almost entirely to the defendant. What is the probability that he will repeat the same act that he is believed to have committed in the past? For example, what is the likelihood that a molester of children will turn into a rapist within the next five years if released without therapy of a particular kind? Or, on the contrary, with therapy what are the chances that he will abstain from any sexual offense? If the assumptions made about the future are less contingent upon estimates of present psychopathology than upon exposure to specific environmental circumstances, the critical question becomes that of judging the likelihood that the defendant, if released under various conditions, will be confronted by an upsetting environment. We use the term "upsetting" only to imply that the situation will favor the occurrence of an act that violates a norm of conduct. In our capacity as scientists, it is relevant to consider another possibility, although this is formally excluded from the scope of the court, although appropriate to other public order officials. Is it likely that the defendant who is performing a mild sex offense today will turn into another type of offender, a murderer, for instance, tomorrow?[24] Such questions arouse the uneasiness of lawyers since they appear to contain an element of prior judgment; they ought therefore to be considered in detail as part of the agenda of research.

We have been referring to the specific defendant before the court and the range of psychiatric testimony that can be brought to the notice of the court by procedures. Another body of psychiatric and social science investigation can relate to potential offenders other than the defendants. What will

---

[23]L. Z. Freedman, and J. W. Kaswan, "Polistaraxic Behavior and Projective Studies," read at annual meeting of American Orthopsychiatry Society, 1958, New York; L. Z. Freedman, "Sexual, Aggressive and Acquisitive Behavior: A Study in Polistaraxic Psychiatry," summary of scientific papers given at annual meeting of American Psychiatric Association, 1959.

[24]G. H. Dession, "Psychiatry and Public Policy," *Psychiatry: Journal for the Study of Interpersonal Processes* 18, no. 1 (February 1955): 1–8.

be the effect upon potential offenders of adopting any specific alternative in dealing with individual defendants of various categories? Deterrence is a recognized aim of public policy in these matters, and it is plausible to believe that court procedures can be adapted to the simple presentation of expert estimates of collective results.

For purposes of systematic analysis it is convenient to add a third category to be covered by estimates referring to the future. We include all members of the public other than defendants or potential performers of a given offense. Under various circumstances members of the public are likely to respond to a court action in ways that affect public order and psychic health. Hence, experts on public response may be asked to estimate the reception likely to be given a range of specified decision outcomes. For example, if the court deals with an offender in ways that are regarded as outrageously lenient by influential and active members of the public, how will this affect the treatment received by a released defendant as well as the status of the officials and organs responsible for public order? One outcome may be a strong demand that the legislature change the criminal code in directions that restrict the individuation of the court's treatment of offenders. Here again we are touching a topic that occasions uneasiness among lawyers. No one need deny that estimates of public response probably enter into the judgment of courts. But there is reluctance to face such matters directly for fear of undermining the degree to which courts operate independently of political factors, or are reputed so to operate. Clearly a borderline topic of this kind is peculiarly suitable for careful, long-term, joint research. Eventually it may be regarded as practical to experiment with rules of procedures that permit estimates of public response to be made by experts.

Psychiatry and the behavioral sciences as yet have contributed little to many questions of trial process such as proof in the adversary setting, the meaning and efficacy of traditional devices like the oath, and of the validity of newer information-gathering methods such as the polygraph "lie detector," and "truth serum" drugs.[25] Still broader inquiry is needed into the dynamic interaction of the trial participants, the accused, the judge, the contending attorneys, the public, and the mass media of communication.

A further major line of joint research relates to measures relied upon by community decision makers to cope with deviational conduct.[26] It is more obvious than ever that ordinary sanctioning arrangements, when they are not

---

[25]Dession, Freedman, Donnelly et al., "Drug-induced Revelation and Criminal Investigation." For newer techniques of communication research see R. Arens and A. Meadow, "Psycholinguistics and the Confession Dilemma," *Columbia Law Review* 56 (January 1956): 19–46. See also G. H. Dession, "The Technique of Public Order: Evolving Concepts of Criminal Law," *Buffalo Law Review* 5, no. 1 (Fall 1955): 22–47.

[26]H. D. Lasswell and R. C. Donnelly, "The Continuing Debate Over Responsibility: An Introduction to Isolating the Condemnation Sanction," *Yale Law Journal* 68, no. 5 (April 1959): 869–99.

purely punitive, are primarily educative. They presuppose that an individual knows enough about the appropriate culture to learn when he is confronted by a contingent threat of negative sanction, or when he is exposed to the sanction if he takes a deliberate risk and loses. The presupposition that an individual is educated or educatable, in this sense, does not apply to some categories of people. It is one of the continuing contributions of psychiatry that it is improving the criteria by which it can estimate the future conduct of individuals under specified conditions, helping thus to identify the defendant who is not at a given time amenable to the educative impact of sanctions and hence not deterrable by them. Besides the unassimilated, who have not acquired the culture in the first place, are certain categories of psychological illness and mental defect. These are not sanction but corrective problems, and the aim of corrective measures insofar as the defendant is concerned is to reconstruct the individual's mastery of himself and the culture to a level that makes it possible for him to learn from sanctioning measures. This is consonant with the psychiatric therapeutic goals of reestablishing an effective function by balance of ego-superego control of psychic functions.[27]

Further research is needed to provide firmer bases for the prediction of the relative efficacy of various alternative deterring and sanctioning methods on the individual and his community. Not enough is known about the dynamics and effectiveness of retributive, deterrent, and rehabilitative techniques in response to behavior that offends the social group. Although absolutist and often contradictory assertions are reiterated in the literature of the two professions, we have little evidence concerning whether punitive sanctions deter potential malefactors. More specifically, it is not known which legal sanctions deter what kinds of individuals from committing what kinds of antisocial acts. There is, as yet, practically no body of valid information to draw upon in selecting candidates for probation and parole, or in abetting the success of those who have been selected.[28] Perhaps most important is the tentative nature of our information regarding the relationship between the informal processes of social sanctioning and the formal legal procedures, especially of the reincorporation into the community of the released offender.

In modern America the psychiatrist is being called upon to play an increasingly important part in every phase of community deliberation and action. While it is common knowledge that the psychiatrist is drawn into many criminal and civil cases and is continually involved in the activities of agencies of correction and custody, it is necessary also to recognize that he

[27]If technique is yet too poor to carry through the reconstruction the subject will presumably be withdrawn from full participation in the life of the community. Today the difference between an educational (a sanction) problem and a reconstruction (a corrective) problem is being more generally understood and hence becoming operational.

[28]G. Hughes, L. Z. Freedman, and L. Michaels, "Differential Prediction of Parole Successes in Sexual, Aggressive, and Acquisitive Offenders."

is now likely to be asked to appear before administrative boards and commissions and, speaking for himself or for an association of professional colleagues, to testify before committees of the legislature at all levels of our governmental system. Properly organized research teams are in a position to explore for the first time the total impact of a given kind and magnitude of psychiatric difficulty upon conformity and nonconformity to community norms. It is possible that one result of this research will be to suggest that some of the norms of conduct prescribed in community codes are unenforced and in fact may be unenforceable due to ambivalent community responses to them.[29] Scientific teams may provide the factual inventory on the basis of which codes may be kept in harmony with the fundamental objectives of public order. For instance, we suspect that revisions are likely to be indicated in some of the statutes relating to sexual conduct.[30] The attempt in writing criminal codes to stigmatize as "criminal" certain forms of behavior may fail because the particular sanction fails to correspond to the moral judgment of the community.[31] It is at least possible that psychiatric problems may be precipitated in these cases by the individual conflict, which in turn is a reflection of paradoxical and inconsistent community expectations and sanction.[32]

In view of the urgency of world affairs, we feel a special sense of the importance of the field of international law and relations insofar as the problems connected with these difficult issues can be given factual study. Psychiatrists have traditionally fought shy of the study of factors contributing to war and crisis, to revolutionary conflict, rebellion, and riot. Yet, it is obvious that our professional concern for mental health goes much further than the case-by-case care of individuals. We do in fact explore the collective impact of various factors upon the incidence of mental difficulty. Before the last war physicians of the Netherlands issued a declaration concerning war as a medical problem of research and therapy. And it must be admitted that insofar as collective, no less than individual, living is responsive to unconscious factors the psychiatrist (and psychoanalyst) is professionally involved. The crucial issue is whether we are equipped with research methods and conceptual categories capable of being fruitfully applied to the gigantic issues at stake.

---

[29]This ambivalence may be manifested by such maneuvers as appropriating inadequate funds or manpower or by confining the choice of sanctioning targets to a single socioeconomic unit within the community.

[30]See G.A.P. Report No. 9, "Psychiatrically Deviated Sex Offenders" (May 1949; rev. February 1950).

[31]A pioneer field study of community norms in relation to legal norms is J. Cohen, R. A. H. Robson, and A. Bates, *Parental Authority: The Community and the Law* (New Brunswick, NJ, 1958). For a keen evaluation of the issues that arise in utilizing such data see W. J. Blum and H. Kalven, Jr., "The Art of Opinion Research: A Lawyer's Appraisal of an Emerging Science," *University of Chicago Law Review* 24, no. 1 (Autumn 1956): 1–69.

[32]G. H. Dession and H. D. Lasswell, "Public Order Under Law: The Role of the Advisor Draftsman in the Formation of Code or Constitution," *Yale Law Journal* 65, no. 2 (December 1955): 174–95.

Our view is that we are in position to make a beginning and that exploratory research can be productively directed to certain problems. Can we aid in identifying the situation, for example, in which the rival leaderships in a community situation, or in an institution, move toward a breaking point? Published studies of such community situations probably would serve as objective reminders to leaderships everywhere of the explosion points in human affairs, and they might exercise a deterring influence upon risk taking under hazardous conditions. At any rate, we can hope by means of joint researches to learn more about the propensities to coerce, lawfully or unlawfully, that are found in the relations among national states as well as social classes, interest groups, and individuals. We believe that whatever we can contribute, however modest, is worth the effort.[33]

The study of the selection and training of physicians has made rapid strides forward in recent years. The psychiatric profession in all its branches is a beneficiary of this redoubling of concern for the recruitment and formation of the profession. It cannot be said that research upon the legal profession is as far advanced.[34] We shall forego the temptation to deal in detail with the sophistication of the lawyer in psychiatric conceptions and methods, and of the psychiatrist in legal concepts and techniques.[35] Perhaps it is enough to reiterate the importance of the problems involved, and to select for emphasis four topics of high importance for the future of creative working relations between psychiatrists and lawyers. We focus upon problems of 1) communication, 2) professional values, 3) subjective stresses of collaboration, and 4) competency on the part of collaborators.

PROBLEMS OF COMMUNICATION

Not enough attention has been given to the study of one of the principal tools at the command of both professions, namely, language. More investigation is needed to bring out the subtle influence of categories upon perceptions of relevance. Modern instruments of communication (and information) research are available to cast into high relief the categories and problem-solving

---

[33]For the current state of research see H. D. Lasswell, "The Scientific Study of International Relations," *Yearbook of World Affairs* (London, 1958), pp. 1–28.

[34]Nothing is as valuable as R. K. Merton, G. Reader, and P. L. Kendall, eds., *The Student Physician: Introductory Studies in the Sociology of Medical Education* (Cambridge, MA, 1957).

[35]For an example of joint activity see the seminar on "Psychiatry and Psychology as a Tool for Lawyers," organized by Judge A. H. Schwartz, in *Bar Bulletin* 16, no. 4, pp. 131–57. Note especially the suggestions made by Doctors L. S. Kubie and H. C. Modlin, and Harriet F. Pilpel of the New York Bar.

processes appropriate to legislator, advocate, judge, and jury; and the categories and problem-solving processes appropriate to the psychiatric physician. The community's official decision makers are authorized to decide, in the name of the body politic, what preferred forms of human relationships are to be protected by his decisions. This is the basic job of the decision makers who formulate constitutional charters that provide the framework of goal and method within which legislators, executives, administrators, and judges work. The language of the legal formula refers to the institutional arrangements that are to be protected by authority; in a word, to the public order.[36] The decision makers are authorized to use the terms and prescriptions of the legal formula, as embellished by proper authorities, to guide their problem-solving activities when confronted by a broad problem of legislation or a question involving the fate of an accused person.

The physician is not able to make his best contribution if he is bound by this language. The Durham decision in the District of Columbia has been a landmark in clarifying this point, in making it evident that the appropriate language of the physician is that of his own profession, and in illuminating synonyms in ordinary speech. Communications are most usefully studied in situations in which we can identify who with what intentions and capabilities is saying what in what channel to which audience with what effects. It is entirely feasible to observe and record the professional situations in which lawyers and psychiatrists operate and to bring out significant likenesses and differences. For instance, the psychiatrist interviews patients, relatives of patients, physicians, and other staff members; the lawyer interviews clients, opposing and cooperating counsel, and witnesses. The psychiatrist testifies as an expert in the decision-making processes of the community. The lawyer's advocacy role in official proceedings is to examine witnesses and argue the claims of the parties whom he represents. These reminders are sufficient both to suggest that much can be done in providing a common body of objective material about language in action and to suggest the possibility of principles of effective communication.[37]

PROBLEMS OF PROFESSIONAL VALUES

It is apparent that professional education does not now clarify the professional standards of lawyers and psychiatrists where their activities

---

[36]For detail see M. S. McDougal and H. D. Lasswell, "The Identification and Appraisal of Diverse Systems of Public Order," *American Journal of International Law* 53, no. 1 (January 1959): 1–29.

[37]See the symposium of "The Language of Law," organized by Walter Probert, in *Western Reserve Law Review* 9, no. 2 (March 1958): 115–98. See also H. D. Lasswell, "The Value Analysis of Legal Discourse," ibid., pp. 188–98.

overlap. For instance, privilege and confidentiality of communications and records, as well as evaluation of capacity and competence to perform certain legal acts, involves the psychiatrist in making legally pertinent judgments. Experience shows that psychiatrists and jurists often misunderstand the basic assumptions of the other in protecting the rights of individuals and of groups. The psychiatrist thinks primarily in terms of his responsibility for the health of the patient and interprets his license from the community as a recognition of his competence to defend the medical rights of a patient. The lawyer is accustomed to emphasize the fundamental importance of providing procedural safeguards by means of which all rights can be given effective protection by the community. Accustomed to view himself as the benign, therapeutic protector of his patient, the psychiatrist often cannot understand the lawyer's concern with the rights of the patient while under his care. The psychiatrist sees impartial, court-appointed testimony concerning mental states, commitment to mental hospitals and psychiatrically ill people, and medically determined dates of discharge as essential medical prerogatives for the optimal psychiatric welfare of emotionally disturbed persons whether or not they have violated legal codes. He finds it difficult to comprehend the lawyer's assumption that adversary experts, court procedures for admission to hospitals, and legally imposed limits for treatment within them constitute essential protection of the rights of the patient.

This illustration serves to point up the necessity for clearer conceptualization by each of his professional body image and social posture. It has become apparent that recruitment, self-selection, and acceptance for training by the prospective professional schools may favor certain motivations and personality types within each profession. If we are to remove these misunderstandings that so often arise, we need joint research teams to investigate specific cases and to subject them to mutual discussion and evaluation. A clear delineation of their respective roles, values, and semantics is probably best carried out by disinterested social scientists with the active cooperation, as subjects, of adequate samplings of lawyers and psychiatrists representative of differing schools of thought, status level, backgrounds, and age groups. In the course of these studies workable arrangements may be suggested and explored that provide guidance for the psychiatric hospital, the private physician, and the public officials involved in typical dilemmas.

PROBLEMS OF SUBJECTIVE STRESSES OF COLLABORATION

Perhaps equal in importance to the considerations just made are the personal motives and social qualities of the lawyers and psychiatrists who work together on research tasks. At present little attention is given these matters in the course of professional preparation. It may be diplomatic and strategic to deny the irrational strivings, rivalries, anxieties, and conflicts that inhere to a project bringing together men of varying professional backgrounds, personal values, and characteristics. But it is not realistic or constructive. While it would be sanguine to assume that the mere delineation of anticipated pitfalls at a personal level will eliminate them, certainly it is essential that they be delineated and anticipated if precious time, manpower, and financial support be not dissipated. Worse still, the original energy may be supplanted by frustration and disillusionment, not as a result of difficulties inherent in the social challenge but as an artifact springing from the human dislocations within the collaborative team.

Professionally the lawyer and the psychiatrist have much in common with each other as shared experience, which could facilitate the preliminary stages of research collaboration. For example, both professions have perforce learned to conduct their observations on human behavior under conditions permitting maximum spontaneity of response of their subjects. Neither is hampered by the illusion the laboratory is the only place to study the activities of man. Against this is the much reiterated therapeutic ambition of the psychiatrist, leading him to identify with his single patient as against the threatening and oppressive community, and the social concern of the lawyer, leading him to think in terms of the maximum good to the maximum numbers while trying to do least harm to its individual members.

Lawyers and psychiatrists belong to prestigeful professions, which offer them successful, status-occupying positions within the community. This maximizes their tendency to maintain identity and minimizes the likelihood of their yielding autonomy and sovereignty. When the opportunities for success within one's own profession, using one's own language, sharing one's values with fellows are great, only a very particular subgroup selects itself out for collaborative enterprises with skeptical and alien brother disciplines. The ambivalences inherent in this situation are sharpened by the skepticism encountered by these interdisciplinary pioneers on both sides—members of their own professional group and members of the collaborating group.

PROBLEMS OF COMPETENCY ON THE
PART OF COLLABORATORS

Intellectual preparation for collaborative work doubtless calls for realistic modesty about competence. It would be overoptimistic to assume that it is practicable to bring together an effective group, each member of which has sufficient information to encompass and incorporate even the basic principles of the collaborating disciplines. Another requirement for such a research team, therefore, is that the members are capable and willing to devote the time and manifest the humility necessary to educate one another. As a corollary to this, the participants must be willing to eschew the defensive maneuver of claiming for themselves and their own disciplines "expertness" in all fields that fall within their professional prerogatives. For even within any given discipline, it is unlikely that a single man encompasses the knowledge available to his entire specialty. Psychiatrists, for example, while medically and biologically trained, are hardly in a position to speak for medicine and biology except vis-à-vis their nonmedical collaborators. Similarly, lawyers specializing in one or another subcategory of this massive field should not feel forced to pretend to a range of expertness beyond it.

A PLAN FOR A NATIONAL INSTITUTE

Our discussion of research areas in this paper, far from exhaustive though it is, nevertheless has indicated how vast the field of psychiatry and law is now perceived to be. The map of common problems of social and behavioral pathology has unfolded gradually through the years. In our view the moment is opportune to provide a national center of investigation designed to provide a continuing stream of initiative, an integrating focus, and a place of work entirely devoted to the study of social and behavioral pathology.

Such an institute should be geographically inclusive in the sense that it should take intellectual responsibility for examining the problems in the national context. It will naturally assume some special responsibility for the locality where it may be situated. Preoccupation with national trends and potential developments would not blind the institute's investigators to the world context or to the importance of comparative research studies that seek the significant phenomena regardless of political boundaries. A national institute of social and behavioral pathology would be a natural participant in the work of similar establishments at every level—personal, local, national, and international. A broad responsibility of the institute would be to aid in the clarification of national achievement objectives in the fields of law and mental health. It would undoubtedly operate within the fundamental assumptions of human dignity, which are incorporated in the aspirations of American society and partially articulated in such instruments as the Universal Declaration of Human Rights. Goal clarification calls for the presentation of long-range, middle-range, and more immediate objectives.

The clarification of goal called for above must be conducted in the light of dependable information about the remote and recent past and the projection of the future. Since existing machinery for obtaining essential statistics is wholly inadequate, one prime task of the institute would be to establish procedures for the collection, evaluation, and publication of needed information concerning the incidence and prevalence of various forms of crime and alleged crime, their disposition by the social, police, prosecutory, judging, and incarcerating agencies including probation and parole. It is hoped that these initiatives would lead to the development and dissemination of more psychologically illuminating data.

The core of the institute's work is the discovery and verification of social and behavioral hypotheses that explain the individual and social dislocations that concern us. Thinking nationally, it is evident that the varied circumstances among the several states permit us to design experiments in nature, using states as "controls" for each other, comparing by field studies factors—demographic, economic, ethnic, for instance—that predispose to high rates of crime in some areas and to greater conformity in others. Investigative methods would be in no wise restricted to this pattern. As our review of promising lines of attack has suggested, there is room for much versatility, which it will be one of the principal aims of the institute to encourage. It is of fundamental importance to provide a hospitable environment for the pursuit of every promising lead and to guard against the domination of inquiry by advocates of any one set of factors, whether economic, political, or professional.

Besides the broad definition of the overriding objectives of American society, the problem will be to study a limited array of sociolegal possibilities in terms that bring out the social costs as well as the probable gains of following a particular sequence of change. In terms of culture, social class, interest group, and personality form these costs (and gains) need to be brought into the clear light of rational assessment. In a word, we are affirming that the many common frontiers of psychiatry and law involving social and behavioral pathology now justify a national effort at joint exploration, settlement, and incorporation into the fraternity of organized intellectual states.

PART II
CRIMINAL RESPONSIBILITY AND SOCIAL REACTION

Psychiatry and the Law:
Historical Relevance to Today*

JACQUES M. QUEN

In reviewing some of the history of the insanity defense in Anglo-American law, it is hoped that certain myths that cloud appreciation of the deficiencies and the strengths of what we have done and what we are doing in this field will be dispelled. It is also hoped to demonstrate that there is something to be learned from the experiences of the law, psychiatry, and of society in struggling with the complicated and difficult problems of attempting to provide justice for the insane and for society.

There is one myth that should be dealt with immediately, and that is that insanity is a legal and not a medical term. In 1844 at the time of the founding of the organization that was to become the American Psychiatric Association, the original thirteen members chose the name the Association of Medical Superintendents of American Institutions for the Insane. The organization did not change that name until 1892 when it became the American Medico-Psychological Association. From 1844 to 1921 the name of their journal was the *American Journal of Insanity*, at which time it became the *American Journal of Psychiatry*. By 1923, William Alanson White already had declared that insanity was not a medical term but a legal one. That is how that myth appears to have started. Insanity, like dropsy or consumption, was a medical term that was used originally as a description and that cut across several modern diagnostic categories. During the course of the nineteenth century, it was applied to idiocy, senility, mania, melancholy, alcoholism, compulsive theft, and compulsive fire setting.

Although insanity previously had been considered to involve a derangement of intellectual powers, as early as the late eighteenth century Benjamin Rush had described a condition, which he called "moral derangement," and Philippe Pinel described a similar one, independently, which he labeled "*manie sans délire.*" In 1835 the British psychiatrist James Cowles Prichard described a condition he termed "moral insanity." All of these shared the element of

*The original version of this paper was prepared for delivery at the conference entitled "Psychiatry and the Law: Reaching for a Consensus," held in Chicago on 12–13 October 1979 under the sponsorship of the University of Chicago Medical Center Department of Psychiatry and the Institute of Social and Behavioral Pathology.

excluding hallucinations, delusions, or deterioration of the intellect. "Moral" referred to affective and volitional mentation. This diagnosis was the most controversial one in American psychiatry throughout the nineteenth century. Today it would include such conditions as severe depressions, compulsive disorders, episodic dyscontrol, and some functional psychoses.

In 1955, Judge John Biggs, Jr., in his Isaac Ray Award Lecture, referred to his effort to locate a legal definition of insanity:

> But the legal definition of insanity is almost impossible to come upon. Bouvier states it as 'the prolonged departure, without any adequate cause from the states of feeling and modes of thinking usual to the individual in health.' This authority then follows with some eleven printed pages of what may or may not constitute insanity. The resulting confusion is in large part due to the application of the M'Naghten Rules which, supplying hard and fast definitions, are a fruitful source of confusion.[1]

The judge identified his source for the above definition as Rawle's third edition of *Bouvier's Law Dictionary*. Biggs was unaware that he was quoting the definition that first appeared in Bouvier's twelfth edition in 1868, when Ray was the contributing author for the definitions of idiocy, imbecility, insanity, and the articles relating to insanity throughout the work. The judge spoke more truly than he knew by stating that a legal definition of insanity was almost impossible.

Some years ago a psychiatrist published an article in which he expressed his anger, claiming that "our courts had never considered that a man was innocent by virtue of insanity until psychiatry convinced them it was so."[2] It is this kind of ignorance of the law that leads some psychiatrists into impassioned debates that obscure the real problem. Common law crimes consist of a material element (the *actus reus*, or the criminal act) and a mental element (the *mens rea*, or a criminal intent). This principle apparently dates back to early biblical days. In the Old Testament there are references to "the manslayer that killeth any person unwittingly,"[3] with the assertion that such a one is "not worthy of death inasmuch as he hated [the victim] not in time past."[4] In the legal code of the ancient Hebrews, known as the *Mishnah*, repeated reference is found to the nonliability of the infant, the imbecile, and the deaf-mute. For example, "if the ox of a man of sound senses gored the ox of a deaf-mute, an imbecile, or a minor, the owner is culpable; but if the ox of a deaf mute, an imbecile, or a minor gored the ox of a man of sound senses, the owner is not culpable."[5] (One might say the applicable law

---

[1]John Biggs, Jr., *The Guilty Mind* (Baltimore, 1955; pbk. 1967), p. 117.

[2]Karl K. Lewin, "Insanity in the Courtroom—WHOSE?" *Journal of Legal Medicine* 2 (1972): 19–21.

[3]*The Bible* (King James version), Num. 35:11.

[4]Ibid., Deut. 19:6.

[5]H. Danby, trans., *The Mishnah* (London, 1933), chap. 8, sec. 4, pp. 342–49.

depended on whose ox was gored!) This applied equally to the law of religious ritual cleanliness, a most stringent area of ancient Hebrew life.[6]

The last words of Jesus, as recorded in *Luke* 23:34, were: "Forgive them, Father, for they know not what they do." Here too we find a concern with the question of intent and the mental state of the actor. This tradition persisted in many aspects of criminal law through Anglo-Saxon times, while in civil law in early England strict liability was the standard. In such cases the person causing the damage, regardless of knowledge or intent, was held legally responsible for the actual damage done and responsible for restoration or reparation. Even here, however, in cases of mental incompetence (minors and the insane) the families were held liable for damages.

In the thirteenth century Henri de Bracton, the renowned British jurist, in his treaties on the laws and customs of England, wrote:

> We must consider with what mind or with what intent a thing is done . . . in order that it may be determined accordingly what action should follow and what punishment. For take away the will and every act will be indifferent because your state of mind gives meaning to your act, and a crime is not committed unless the intent to injure intervene, nor is a theft committed except with the intent to steal. . . . And this is in accordance with what might be said of the infant or madman, since the innocence of design protects the one and the lack of reason in committing the act excuses the other.[7]

In the sixteenth century yet another legal commentator, William Lambarde, wrote: "If a madman or a natural fool, or a lunatic in the time of his lunacy, or a child that apparently hath no knowledge of good nor evil do kill a man, this is no felonious act, nor anything forfeited by it . . . for they cannot be said to have an understanding will."[8] This constitutes an expansion of the lack of reason concept. The primary reason that they are not punished is not lack of knowledge of good or evil but what this lack of knowledge signifies, that is, lack of an understanding will. An understanding will implies several mental elements, including knowledge, ability to weigh competing factors and values differentially, an ability to make a choice or form an intention, and a freedom of will or freedom from coercion.

Still further legal authority was provided in the seventeenth century when Edward Coke defined the four classes of *non compos mentis* for legal purposes:

> 1) an idiot, who from his nativity by a perpetual infirmity is *non compos*;
> 2) He that by sickness, grief, or other accident, wholly loseth his memory

---

[6]Ibid., chap. 3, sec. 6, p. 719.

[7]Henri de Bracton, *De Legibus Consuetudinibus Angliae*, as quoted in F. B. Sayre, "Mens Rea," *Harvard Law Review* 45 (1932): 985.

[8]W. Lambarde, *Eirenarcha or of the Office of the Justices of the Peace* (1581), as quoted in Biggs, *Guilty Mind*, pp. 83–84.

and understanding; 3) a lunatic that hath sometime his understanding, and sometimes not . . . and therefore he is called *non compos mentis*, so long as he hath not understanding; 4) He that by his own vicious act [i.e., vice] for a time depriveth himself of his memory and understanding, as he that is drunken. But that kind of *non compos mentis* shall give no privilege to him or his heirs.[9]

Coke goes on to refer to a drunkard as a *voluntarius daemon*. Involuntary intoxication, however, would confer the protection of *non compos mentis*.

Mathew Hale was probably the most learned and accomplished of the early English judges. In his *History of the Pleas of the Crown*, written toward the end of his life, Hale observed:

Man is naturally endowed with these two great faculties, *understanding and liberty of will*, and therefore is a subject properly capable of a law. . . . The consent of the will is that which renders human actions either commendable or culpable; as where there is no law, there is no transgression, so regularly, where there is no will to commit an offense, there can be no transgression, or just reason to incur the penalty or sanction of that law instituted for the punishment of crimes or offenses. And because the liberty or choice of the will presupposeth an act of the *understanding* to know the thing or action chosen . . . it follows that where there is a total defect of the *understanding* there is no free act of the will in the choice of things or actions[10] (emphases added).

Hale went on to say:

Some persons that have a competent use of reason in respect of some subjects, are yet under a partial *dementia* in respect of some particular discourses, subjects or applications; or else it is partial in respect of degrees; and this is the condition of very many, especially melancholy persons, who for the most part discover their defect in excessive fears and griefs, and yet are not wholly destitute of the use of reason; and this partial insanity seems not to excuse them in the committing of any offense . . . for doubtless most persons, that are felons of themselves . . . are under a degree of partial insanity, when they commit these offenses: It is very difficult to divide the indivisible line that divides perfect and partial insanity, but it must rest upon circumstances duly to be weighed and considered both by the judge and the jury, lest there be a kind of inhumanity towards the defects of human nature, or on the other side too great an indulgence given to great crimes: the best measure I can think is this; such a person as labouring under melancholy distempers hath yet ordinarily as great understanding, as ordinarily a child of fourteen years hath, is such a person as may be guilty of treason or felony.[11]

---

[9]Edward Coke, *Institutes of the Laws of England* (London, 1853), 2:246b, as quoted in Biggs, *Guilty Mind*, p. 117.

[10]Mathew Hale, *The History of the Pleas of the Crown* (London, 1736), pp. 14–15.

[11]Ibid., p. 30.

What are we to make of Hale's measure? In that period, English law provided an absolute freedom from any charge of felony for an infant under the age of seven, while a child between the ages of seven and fourteen could be found guilty of a felony, according to Blackstone, if the child understood he was doing wrong. A child with the understanding of an eleven year old, but who is otherwise normal, might be capable of a felony; however, Hale's standard would rule this capability out for anyone who had the understanding of an eleven year old because of insanity. This is a remarkably liberal definition of exculpable insanity. It means that Hale's references to "a total defect of understanding" and to "perfect insanity" do not mean what they initially convey to the modern American mind. He clearly was trying to ensure that there would not be "a kind of inhumanity towards the defects of human nature, or on the other side, too great an indulgence given to great crimes."

Blackstone seems to have had no disagreement with Hale, although he offers no standard of his own. He does quote Coke as saying "the execution of an offender is for example . . . but so it is not when a madman is executed; but should be a miserable spectacle, both against law, and of extreme inhumanity and cruelty, and can be no example to others."[12]

Before leaving these legal commentators, it should be pointed out that Bracton speaks of intent and reason; Lambarde focuses on an understanding will. Coke speaks of understanding only and mentions neither knowledge, reason nor wrong. For Hale, "understanding" is the critical word, while he also speaks of "the use of reason." However, judges either through laziness or ignorance avoided using the understanding as an essential aspect of determining exculpable insanity. Up to this point there is no indication that the jurists were using anything other than the knowledge possessed by students of law. There is neither reference to nor indication that medical opinion was consulted for judicial definitions of insanity. Hale's and Blackstone's discussions are based on the legal concepts of the psychological capabilities and thus competencies of minors at different ages for legal purposes. These concepts, with similar age-related capabilities, are found in European medieval codes as well. For those who insist that the insanity defense is the illegitimate offspring of incompetent judges and uninformed, naive and theorizing psychiatrists, the time has come to realize and to acknowledge that the insanity defense was conceived and promulgated solely by the outstanding leaders of the legal profession over a period of centuries. Medicine played no direct role in this development until the 1840s.

In 1724, Edward Arnold, known locally as "Crazy Ned," was tried for attempted murder of Lord Onslow. In a carefully considered charge to the jury regarding exculpable insanity, the presiding Justice Tracy said: "It must

---

[12]William Blackstone, *Commentaries on the Laws of England: Of Public Wrongs,* vol. 4 (Boston, 1962), p. 22.

be a man that is totally deprived of his understanding and memory, and doth not know what he is doing, no more than an infant, than a brute, or a wild beast."[13] Unfortunately, this became known as the "wild beast test."

In 1800, James Hadfield, an ex-soldier discharged from the British army because of insanity secondary to skull and brain wounds received in battle, fired a loaded pistol in the direction of King George III. Hadfield had the delusion that God was going to destroy the world but that he, Hadfield, could save it by sacrificing his life. However, despite the selfless nobility of his cause, Hadfield did not want to commit the moral crime of suicide. Knowing that attempted regicide was a capital offense, he believed that he could accomplish his purpose by having the state execute him.

The brilliant young lawyer Thomas Erskine was assigned to defend Hadfield. In his opening remarks Erskine responded to the prosecutor's comments on the standard of exculpable insanity, being that of perfect or total insanity. Behaving as if he did not know of Hale's definition of perfect insanity as less understanding than that possessed by an ordinary fourteen year old, Erskine said that if this meant "such a state of prostrated intellect as not to know his name, nor his condition, nor his relation to others—that if a husband, he should not know he was married, or if a father, could not remember that he had children; nor know the road to his house . . . then no such insanity ever existed in the world." He went on to say that in his experience with the insane "they have not only had the most perfect knowledge and recollection of all the relations they have stood in towards others, and of the acts and circumstances of their lives, but have, in general, been remarkable for subtlety and acuteness. . . ."[14]

Erskine explained that "delusion where there is no frenzy or raving madness, is the true character of insanity. . . . I must convince you, not only that the unhappy prisoner was a lunatic, within my definition of lunacy, but that the act in question was the immediate offspring of disease." Here is yet another instance of insanity, its definition and its pathognomonic symptom, announced by a lawyer with no reference to any physician or medical authority, although they were available. It should be added that Hadfield had quite visible scars and missing parts of his skull, which demonstrated to the jury he had unequivocal organic disease. Hadfield was acquitted explicitly on the ground of insanity. It would be well to point out that this occurred in a case where no material damage had been done to anybody.

The presiding Chief Justice Kenyon apparently was not aware that he was writing new law when he told the jury: "If a man is in a deranged state of mind at the time, he is not criminally answerable for his acts." He told

---

[13]T. B. Howell, comp., *A Complete Collection of State Trials etc. 1722–1725,* vol. 15: *The Trial of Edward Arnold* (London, 1812), no. 465, cols. 695–766.

[14]T. B. Howell and T. J. Howell, comps., *A Complete Collection of State Trials etc. 1798–1800,* vol. 20: *The Trial of James Hadfield* (London, 1812), no. 646, cols. 1281–1356.

them that to find Hadfield criminally responsible "his sanity has to be made out to the satisfaction of a moral man . . . yet if the scales hang anything like even, throwing a certain proportion of mercy to the party."[15] In essence, Kenyon was saying that once a reasonable doubt had been raised as to Hadfield's sanity, the prosecution must prove the *mens rea* as well as the *actus reus*.

On 11 May 1812, John Bellingham, an insane British businessman, shot and killed Sir Spencer Percival, the prime minister of England. On 14 May his court-appointed attorneys were notified that they had been assigned to defend him at the trial scheduled to begin the following morning. A request for postponement to allow witnesses from his home town to come to London to testify as to his mental condition was denied. The trial ended in the early afternoon and went to the jury with a "knowledge of good and evil" charge by Chief Justice Mansfield that is rivaled only by Marc Antony's speech for covert inflammatory intent, including, according to one reporter, the judge pausing to wipe tears from his eyes as he referred to the noble character of the victim. The jury returned that same afternoon with a verdict of guilty. Judge Mansfield pronounced sentence immediately, and on 18 May, eight days after the homicide, Bellingham was hanged and dissected. This was a blatant instance of judicial murder.[16] In the course of this trial no reference was made to the Hadfield trial nor to any of the principles mentioned in it. In fact, from the transcript of the trial, it would not even be possible to conclude that the Hadfield trial had ever taken place.

While this case was explicitly renounced for any precedential authority in a high treason trial in 1840 and again in the debate in the House of Lords in 1843, Justice Benjamin N. Cardozo, an outstanding judicial scholar, cited it as authority for his classic opinion in *People* v. *Schmidt* (1915) in which he attempted to analyze the meaning of "wrong" in the McNaughtan rules.[17] One would almost prefer to believe that Justice Cardozo did not read the charge or the case in its entirety and was ignorant of the denunciation of the case in the British court and Parliament, although that too is somewhat frightening for a mere private citizen to contemplate.

In 1840, Edward Oxford, a delusional eighteen year old, made an unsuccessful attempt to assassinate Queen Victoria and Prince Albert. He was acquitted on the ground of insanity after Chief Justice Denman told the jury: "If some controlling disease was, in truth, the acting power within him which he could not resist, then he will not be responsible. . . . The question is, whether the prisoner was labouring under that species of insanity which

---

[15]Ibid. See also J.M. Quen, "James Hadfield and Medical Jurisprudence of Insanity," *New York State Journal of Medicine* 69 (1969): 1221–26.

[16]G. D. Collinson, *A Treatise on the Law Concerning Idiots, Lunatics, and Other Persons Non Compotes Mentis*, vol. 1 (London, 1812), pp. 636–74.

[17]People v. Schmidt, 110 N.E. 945 (1915).

satisfies you that he was quite unaware of the nature, character, and consequences of the act he was committing, or, in other words, whether he was
under the influence of a diseased mind, and was really unconscious at the
time he was committing the act, that it was a crime."[18] This charge, unlike
that in *Bellingham*, was in keeping with the legal philosophy implicit in
Hadfield. It should be noted that here too no material harm or damage was
done to anybody.

The most famous insanity trial in the Western world resulted from an
assassination on 20 January 1843. Edward Drummond, private secretary to
Prime Minister Sir Robert Peel, had just left his brother's bank at Charing
Cross when a young man walked up behind him, placed a pistol against his
back, and fatally shot him. Except for a short struggle to fire a second shot,
no resistance to arrest was offered. Upon arraignment the following day the
prisoner, a Scotsman named Daniel McNaughtan, said that "the Tories in my
native city have compelled me to do this; they follow and persecute me
wherever I go, and have entirely destroyed my peace of mind. . . . I can get
no rest from them night or day. . . . They have accused me of crimes of
which I am not guilty; and they have [done] everything in their power to
harass and persecute me, in fact they wish to murder me. It can be proved
by evidence."[19] Nowhere in this statement is reference or allusion made to
Peel. Nothing to indicate, as some have said, that he thought Peel was involved
in his persecution.

In that trial, which took place on 3–4 March, the attorney appointed to
represent McNaughtan was Alexander Cockburn, later solicitor general of
England. For his information and the rationale of his defense strategy,
Cockburn relied primarily on *A Treatise on the Medical Jurisprudence of
Insanity* by Isaac Ray, a thirty-one-year-old general practitioner in Eastport,
Maine, who later became one of the thirteen founders of the Association of
Medical Superintendents of American Institutions for the Insane. This book
remains a classic of forensic psychiatry, although it seems to have had far
less impact on the jury and the court than did the unanimity of the testimony
of the eight physicians that McNaughtan was undoubtedly insane. Part of the
judge's charge to the jury was that "if he was not sensible at the time that he
committed the act that it was a violation of the law of God or man, undoubtedly
he was not responsible . . . or liable to any punishment flowing from that
act."[20] No reference was made to delusion, monomania, moral insanity, or
lack of control over one's behavior because of a diseased will or mind. In

---

[18]Regina v. Oxford in *The English Reports. Vol. 173. Nisi Prius IV Containing Carrington
& Payne 7–9; Moody and Malkin* (Edinburgh, 1928), pp. 941–52.
[19]J. M. Quen, "An Historical View of the M'Naghten Trial," *Bulletin of Historical
Medicine* 42 (1968): 43–51.
[20]Ibid.

short, none of the points argued from Ray's *Treatise*, nor those in the medical testimony, were in any way acknowledged by the judge.

It is part of the mythology of the McNaughtan trial that the jury returned a directed verdict. What actually happened was that Lord Chief Justice Nicholas Tindal asked the solicitor general if he had any testimony to refute that of the eight physicians. He did not. At that point the chief justice said, "we feel the evidence . . . to be very strong, and sufficient to induce my learned brother[s] and myself to stop the case . . . but if on balancing the evidence in your minds, you [the jury] think the prisoner capable of distinguishing between right and wrong, then he was a responsible agent and liable to all of the penalties the law imposes." This was not a charge for a directed verdict.[21]

A strong angry reaction from the public ensued. The House of Lords asked the fifteen judges of the Queen's Bench to answer five questions in order to clarify the law regarding insanity "to operate in all time, for the guidance of the courts of justice, and to direct, with more force than is attained by the influence of a single judge, the verdicts of justice."[22] The first question related to the status of persons committing criminal acts while under the influence of partial delusions; the second and third were combined into one question: What should be the charge to the jury in an insanity defense case? The fourth was "if a person under an insane delusion as to existing facts, commits an offense in consequence thereof, is he thereby excused?" And finally, "can a medical man conversant with the disease of insanity, who never saw the prisoner previously to the trial, but who was present during the whole trial and the examination of all the witnesses, be asked his opinion as to the state of the prisoner's mind at the time of the commission of the alleged act?"

Of the fifteen judges, one dissented and the other fourteen spoke through Lord Chief Justice Tindal who had presided at McNaughtan's trial. Their answers were advisory only and did not have the force of law. The answer to the first question was that a person is "punishable according to the nature of the crime committed, if he knew at the time of committing such crime that he was acting contrary to the law, by which expression we take your lordships to mean the law of the land." This response was greeted with hoots by many, since the judges were ignoring a basic tenet of English law—that all are presumed to know the law and that ignorance of the law is no excuse.

The second and third questions were answered with what is generally known as the McNaughtan rule, that is:

---

[21]R. M. Bousefield and R. Merrett, *Report of the Trial of Daniel M'Naughton, at the Central Criminal Court, Old Bailey (on Friday, the 3rd, and Saturday, the 4th of March, 1843) for the Wilful Murder of Edward Drummond, Esq.* (London, 1843).

[22]*The English Reports*, vol. 8: *House of Lords Containing Clark & Finnelly 8–12* (Edinburgh, 1901), pp. 718–24.

the jurors ought to be told that every man is presumed to be sane, and to possess a sufficient degree of reason to be responsible for his crimes, until the contrary be proved to their satisfaction; and that to establish a defense on the ground of insanity, it must be clearly proved that at the time of the committing of the act, the party accused was labouring under such a defect of reason, from disease of the mind, as not to know the nature and quality of the act he was doing; or if he did know it, that he did not know he was doing what was wrong.

Present in the common law before the judges' answers had been an understanding will; delusion in the presence of reason; mind or will overwhelmed by disease; ungovernable delusions; controlling disease, the acting power of which could not be resisted; or an understanding less than that of the ordinary fourteen year old. All that remained was "knowledge of the nature and quality of the act" and knowledge of "wrong." Furthermore, and perhaps more destructively, gone was the flexibility of prior common law and the freedom for the common law of criminal insanity to continue to evolve gradually from the accumulation of different cases and decisions.

To the fourth question regarding an insane delusion under existing facts, the judges answered that the individual must be judged as if the facts respecting the delusion were true and then held to the same standard as a sane man in his actions and culpability. Ray observed:

This is certainly very plain and it must be the fault of the lunatic, if he do[es] not understand it. It is very reasonable, too, *if insane men would but listen to reason. . . .* This is virtually saying to a man, 'you are allowed to be insane; the disease is a visitation of Providence, and you cannot help it; but have a care how you manifest your insanity; there must be method in your madness. Having once adopted your delusion, all the subsequent steps connected with it must be conformed to the strictest requirements of reason and propriety. If you are caught tripping in your logic; if in the disturbance of your moral and intellectual perceptions you take a step for which a sane man would be punished, insanity will be no bar to your punishment. In short, having become fairly enveloped in the clouds of mental disorder, the law expects you will move as discreetly and circumspectly as if the undimmed light of reason were shining on your path.[23]

Somewhat later British psychiatrist Henry Maudsley said of this answer: "Here is an unhesitating assumption that a man, having an insane delusion, has the power to think and act in regard to it *reasonably*; that, at the time of the offense . . . he is, in fact, bound to be reasonable in his unreason, sane in his insanity."[24] That jurists had a similar criticism of this answer is attested

---

[23]Isaac Ray, *A Treatise on the Medical Jurisprudence of Insanity*, 3d ed. (Boston, 1853), p. 46.

[24]Henry Maudsley, *Responsibility in Mental Disease* (New York, 1897), p. 104.

to by the statement of Judge Ladd of the New Hampshire Supreme Court: "It is probable that no ingenuous student of the law ever read it for the first time without being shocked by its exquisite inhumanity."[25] However, in fairness to the judges it must be recalled that they did not solicit or consult any expert on the nature of insanity. Their answer was purely a legally determined one, unencumbered by experience with the insane or even a particularly impressive appreciation of the origin, rationale, and developmental history of the insanity defense in law.

The fifth question was answered by stating that ". . . the medical man, under the circumstances supposed, cannot . . . be asked his opinion in the terms stated above, because each of those questions involves the determination of the truth of the facts deposed to, which it is for the jury to decide, and the questions are not mere questions upon a matter of science, in which case such testimony is admissible." This answer is particularly significant because in the trial the last two physicians to testify had never examined McNaughtan personally but testified on the basis of knowledge obtained as observers of the trial. In fact, in his charge Justice Tindal had said: "We feel the evidence, especially that of the last two medical gentlemen . . . who are strangers to both sides and only observers of the case, to be very strong, and sufficient to induce my learned brother[s] and myself to stop the case."

Not only had Chief Justice Tindal changed his interpretation of the law between the time of the McNaughtan trial and the answers, but Justice Denman, who had presided at the trial of Oxford in 1840, also had undergone a radical change of view. What accounts for these judges providing a regressive and simplistic interpretation of the common law of England? One must look at the political and social background in which these events took place. England was in a state of political, social, and economic turmoil. There were the Chartists and the Anti-Corn Law Leagues, agitation for extending suffrage to all men, demands for reform of abusive child labor practices, and various schemes for what was then considered irresponsible expansion of welfare relief. Radicals were rife and appeared to be threatening the structure of England. It was a time of violent ideas, violent feelings, and violent acts. McNaughtan had killed someone close to the prime minister (while the prosecution tried to make it a political case of attempted assassination of the prime minister) and had been acquitted. The anxiety over lawless violence found a target in the McNaughtan verdict. It focused attention on the violent criminally insane and on the protection the law offered to society. The effectiveness of that protection probably was perceived as being directly proportional to the stringency of the law. The two cases, which had what I have characterized as liberal interpretations of the law, were ones in which

[25]*Reports of Cases Argued and Determined in the Supreme Judicial Court of New Hampshire*, vol. 50 (Concord, 1872), p. 37.

no actual damage had been done, and it is suggested that in this McNaughtan rule the judges were responding to the political, social, and economic unrest that was threatening England.

Looking at subsequent events in America, whose common law was based on English common law, perhaps the most scholarly discussion of the evolution and vicissitudes of the insanity defense in the English language can be found in Judge Doe's dissenting opinion in *Boardman* v. *Woodman*. In 1853, Isaac Ray published a third edition of his *Treatise*. The following year a young lawyer, Charles Doe, purchased it, read it, and remembered it. In 1868, Doe, who was then an associate justice of the New Hampshire Supreme Court, began corresponding with Ray in an effort to gain a better understanding of insanity for a dissenting opinion he was writing in a testamentary capacity case, *Boardman* v. *Woodman*. Through his opinion in this case and his participation in two homicide trials and appeals, Doe was able to establish the New Hampshire doctrine.[26] As he characterized it later, it states "not that the common law prescribes a test of any disease, physical or mental, but that an act caused by a mental disease is not a crime, a contract, or a will."[27] Furthermore, it restored the whole question of insanity—its definition, its existence, and its relation to the act in question—to the realm of fact, and therefore a matter for determination by the jury.

In 1954 the U.S. Court of Appeals of the District of Columbia promulgated a new rule called the Durham rule, which it declared was not unlike the New Hampshire doctrine. It was greeted with great enthusiasm by many psychiatrists but by somewhat fewer lawyers. The Durham rule was not adopted by any other federal district court, and the state of Maine was the only one to adopt it by statute. In 1972 the originating court abandoned the Durham rule in favor of the American Law Institute (ALI) rule. A scholarly study of the birth, career, and death of the Durham rule should make it clear that the cause of its short life lay in the differences of the philosophical foundations between it and the New Hampshire doctrine. This difference in rationale led to excessive interference in the functioning of Durham by the court of appeals, which destroyed any value that Durham had. The Durham rule is dead and the McNaughtan rule is moribund. It is the ALI rule that is now in the ascendancy: "A person is not responsible for criminal conduct if at the time of such conduct as a result of mental disease or defect he lacks substantial capacity either to appreciate the criminality of his conduct or to conform his conduct to the requirements of the law. The terms 'mental disease

---

[26]L. E. Reik, "The Doe-Ray Correspondence: A Pioneer Collaboration in the Jurisprudence of Mental Disease," *Yale Law Journal* 63 (1953): 183–96. See also J. M. Quen, "Isaac Ray and Charles Doe: Responsibility and Justice," in W. E. Barton and C. J. Sanborn, eds., *Law and the Mental Health Professions: Friction at the Interface* (New York, 1978).

[27]C. Bell, "Editorial: The Right and Wrong Test in Cases of Homicide by the Insane," *Medico-Legal Journal* 16, no. 1 [1896]: 260–67.

or defect' do not include an abnormality manifested only by repeated criminal or otherwise antisocial conduct."[28]

Just as the McNaughtan rule brought with it interminable debate on the meaning of "nature and quality . . . know . . . [and] wrong," one may wonder whether the ALI rule will bring with it equally interminable discussions on the meanings of "substantial," "capacity," "appreciate," or "conform." Unfortunately, past efforts to deal with the problems raised by the insanity defense seem to have been characterized by a pathological obsessional concern with the magic of words on the part of both the legal and the psychiatric professions. In 1953 the British Royal Commission on Capital Punishment issued its report in which it considered recommending abrogation of the McNaughtan rule and leaving it to the jury to determine whether at the time of the act the accused was suffering from disease of the mind (or mental deficiency) to such a degree that he ought not to be held responsible.[29] This suggestion was considered because of the dissatisfaction with all the various tests proposed in the past, and it is equally relevant to the philosophy behind Judge Doe's interpretation of the common law and the establishment of the New Hampshire doctrine. The British Royal Commission did not finally propose this solution because of three dissenting votes.

For centuries the insanity defense has represented a problem that seemed to have no satisfactory solution. It may be so because it is true. It may be true because the field of psychiatry does not recognize that the insane may require, for purposes of justice, a body of law specifically designed for their unique situation, needs, and vulnerabilities in our society. They may require a separate body of laws, perhaps like maritime law, which has its own due processes adapted for dealing with the unique problems of life at sea and the maritime trade. But society certainly will need judges far better educated in the law of insanity than it has had. There may be a need to have obligatory continuing judicial education legislation. Until judges become conversant enough with the mental realities of the insane, they may continue to stumble, confusing formal diagnoses with the more important evaluations of degree of disability, limitations of competences, and of vulnerabilities. This is equally so for psychiatry; until we arrive at some carefully considered and practicable mode of balancing the need of society to be protected from the destructive or antisocial insane with the need of the insane to be protected from destructive elements in and of our society, we may continue to deal piecemeal with their problems and continue to find that piecemeal solutions are not adequate. Certainly, the use of the criminal law to provide a legal system model for the insane has been unsuccessful, both in civil commitments and competency as

---

[28]American Law Institute, *Model Penal Code*, as quoted in R. Slovenko, *Psychiatry and Law* (Boston, 1973), p. 83.

[29]*Report of Royal Commission on Capital Punishment, 1949–1953* (London, 1953).

well as criminal insanity, but those are histories for other occasions. Today the insanity defense still remains a controversial issue within the legal and psychiatric professions, and between the legal and psychiatric professions, with many in both professions calling for its abolition or its radical modification.

Psychiatry and the Law:
An Old-Fashioned Approach*

GEORGE ANASTAPLO

> . . . . It is clear that the polis is among those things that are by nature, and that man is by nature a political animal. And a man who is without a polis on account of nature, not on account of fortune, is either base or better than a human being like the 'clanless, lawless, and heartless' man reviled by Homer. . . . A man who is incapable of entering into community, or on account of self-sufficiency has need of nothing, is no part of a polis, so then he is either a beast or a god.
>
> Aristotle, *Politics*, 1:2

Practical measures, drawing upon a general intuition of nature, usually precede theoretical discourse about such matters as the relations of law and medicine. Nature is the guide that soundly directs practice before a community truly understands what it is doing. Thus, a man does something that should not have been done. What should be done about it? Should he be held responsible by the community, or at least treated as if responsible? Can psychiatry, as one branch of medicine, help the community determine: 1) whether this man knew right from wrong; 2) whether he knew this particular act was forbidden and hence wrong; or 3) whether, in short, he knew what he was doing?

An action cannot be truly seen unless one also can see whether it is good. In this sense few, if any, know that they are doing something that is bad and hence wrong. But before it holds someone responsible the law does not require the understanding of a philosopher. On the other hand, the law does require some recognition of what one is up to, if only the recognition that one's acts are forbidden. However, some argue that the community should have little to say about right and wrong once certain minimum standards of conduct have been established. There is a certain attraction to this approach, if only because of its simplicity, but it ignores one of the traditional functions of the law, that of reflecting and reinforcing pervasive opinions about good and bad in a decent community.

---

*The original version of this paper was prepared for delivery at the conference entitled "Psychiatry and the Law: Reaching for a Consensus," held in Chicago on 12–13 October 1979 under the sponsorship of the University of Chicago Medical Center Department of Psychiatry and the Institute of Social and Behavioral Pathology. The epigraph for this article is taken from the translation of Aristotle's *Politics* by Laurence Berns, St. John's College.

Certain kinds of people, badly disturbed though they may be, should be quickly and decisively dealt with by the law when they do certain things. Indeed, something is wrong with either the law or psychiatry (if a variation of the insanity defense is involved) when such people are not dealt with quickly and decisively. Notorious instances include Berkowitz, Gacy, Manson, Oswald, Ruby, Sirhan, and Speck. If one can judge by press reports alone, all of these men were competent enough for the purposes of the law—for the purposes both of assigning guilt to them and of their being able to stand trial.[1]

There does not seem to be in these cases just mentioned any serious question about the "facts," in the ordinary sense of that term. For the purpose of the law, not much should be required by way of inquiry or trial, whatever complex problems may intrigue the scientific observer. There should be no serious problem either about pretrial publicity. Indeed, in cases where the notoriety of the crime and the obviousness of the offender are so blatant that only the village idiot could fail to be unaware of what has happened, much of our concern about publicity seems rather silly. Certainly, it is silly to insist that a community cannot be permitted to know what every sensible person knows.

Something is probably dreadfully wrong with each of the men listed and with others like them whose bizarre conduct has happened to be limited to far less notorious acts. The magnitude of the offense, however, should not automatically generate a comparable immunity. None of these men believed themselves to be attacking anyone but another human being; none believed they were using anything but a deadly weapon; and none even had a paranoia that blinded them as to what they were doing. In every instance, the care taken to escape detection or apprehension is revealing. To make it more difficult, if not impossible, for the law to condemn such men promptly is to display a lack of confidence in the perception and judgment of the community at large. It is doubtful that modern psychiatry has taught us anything about the human soul that should properly interfere with what the community would otherwise do in identifying and passing judgment upon such people.

What, then, should the relation be between psychiatry and the law? It depends, in part, on what is thought within the community about 1) the law, which concerns itself primarily with the common good; and 2) about psychiatry, which concerns itself primarily with private interests. Critical here is how psychiatry sees people and why it is, as it often seems, more permissive than either the law or general community opinion. To speak of the relations of psychiatry and the law is to speak, to a considerable degree, of the relationship of the individual to the community, with psychiatry standing for

---

[1]The latter consideration, it has been argued, is secondary. See Robert A. Burt and Norval Morris, "A Proposal for the Abolition of the Incompetency Plea," *University of Chicago Law Review* 40 (1972): 66.

one and the law standing for the other. Moderns do invoke something called "personal autonomy." But is this not an attempt to blend individuality and legality? Is this not an attempt to have the individual lay down, or be guided by, a law to himself? In such a case is not the law subordinated to personal inclinations and therefore not, strictly speaking, a law?

Psychiatry itself cannot do without law. Thus, psychiatrists lay down the law for their patients in the form of rules about appointments, payments, and even therapy. In addition, the psychiatrist, in most cases, depends on the law of the land to legitimize his calling, to define and sometimes to enlarge his powers, and to protect him in various respects.

The individual, to whom psychiatry can be said to be dedicated, is also dependent upon the law. The individual is who he is primarily because of opinions that come from his community. How successful he will be depends, for the most part, on the quality of the opinions his community supports. If that community is fragmented, institutions within the community, such as the family or the church to which he happens to belong, will be the primary sources of the authoritative opinions that shape him. But even these institutions are themselves reflections of earlier communities. Thus, it is not a question of the community or the individual but rather the question of whether the supposedly liberated individual is aware of the community that has shaped him.

Since it is common, upon thinking of the relation of psychiatry to the law, to consider primarily the role of psychiatry in criminal proceedings, it would be useful to touch upon certain underpinnings of the criminal law. The shaping of opinion and not the "control" of criminal behavior is critical to the solution of our crime problem. When opinions (and hence desires) are sound, there is little need for the crime control, of which so much is made today.[2] Vital to the opinions upon which a truly law-abiding people depends is the opinion that insists upon the intrinsic goodness of justice. Thus, people have to be taught that "crime does not pay, really," and that they are harmed by the injustice they perpetrate, whether or not they are detected and apprehended.[3] It is not necessary here to say anything more about the opinions rooted in human nature that promote law-abidingness. It suffices to notice,

---

[2]See Section 4, "Human Nature and the Criminal Law," in Anastaplo, "Human Nature and the First Amendment," *University of Pittsburgh Law Review* 40 (1979): 661, 715. That article includes another section that bears on my discussion of psychiatry and the law, "Prudence and Mortality [in Shakespeare's Tragedies]," which is included in Anastaplo, *The Artist as Thinker: From Shakespeare to Joyce* (Chicago: Swallow Press, 1983), chap. 1. See also "Appendix A: A Primer on the Good, the True and the Beautiful," ibid.

Also bearing on my discussion of psychiatry and the law are essays 4, 6, 7, 10, and 17 in Anastaplo, *Human Being and Citizen: Essays on Virtue, Freedom and the Common Good* (Chicago, Swallow Press, 1975). See also Anastaplo, "The Public Interest in Privacy," *DePaul Law Review* 26 (1977): 767; and "One's Character is One's Fate," *Congressional Record* 125 (15 December 1979): E6162.

[3]See the "Gyges" stories in Herodotus's *History* and Plato's *Republic*.

contrary to what is fashionable to advocate today, that the community should have a good deal to say (and to do) about what is right and wrong.

To be a community means that all, or almost all, are being "judgmental" in much the same way about the same things. If psychiatry should insist upon withholding judgment—if it should go so far as to insist that there is no such thing as right or wrong but that only "thinking," if not "feeling," makes it so—then psychiatry is to that extent alienated from the community, if not even antisocial.

The importance of the community is evident, I have suggested, in the reliance by the well-developed soul upon proper opinions, especially upon those that seem proper because they are, in large part, old opinions. But to speak of "the well-developed soul" is to approach these matters differently from those who prefer to speak of the individual, or of the self. Does not this latter approach appeal more to the psychiatrist? What, indeed, is the view of modern psychiatry with respect to the individual, the community, and the relation of one to the other? Does it not tend to see every person as fully open to the truth, equipped to make his own choices among life-styles and hence obliged to take issue with the inevitable repressiveness of society?

To approach man thus is to pay homage to the presuppositions and aspirations of the Enlightenment. It is to assume, among other things, that there is naturally a self that yearns for expression independent of any community, and that the community (except perhaps at the most primitive level) is bound to confine or otherwise corrupt one. In short, man is born free but is everywhere in chains. This means, among other things, that there is no truly good society and that there can be no enduring harmony between an individual and the community since it is the community that keeps him from his full development as an autonomous person.

But the traditionalist would respond that for most people the particular makes sense only in the context of the general: the typical individual can find solid fulfillment only as a social being and not in rebellion or in self-satisfaction. There must be an overall, prevailing standard by which he must take his bearings or he becomes a nobody going nowhere. Psychiatry, the traditionalist would continue, is but one art among many, taking its place in and being subject to the general order of things. In this respect it is essentially like the ordinary medical art. A number of "medical" decisions, that is, decisions that doctors make, depend on considerations that are not strictly medical. Doctors may be able to explain what this or that measure does— whether it is a "heroic" treatment, a preventive program, or the routine use of a particular remedy—but they often cannot tell us, or we do not want to rely upon them to tell us, whether a measure should be employed. The decision to employ a certain measure often depends on an overall view of human life itself and of the good life. This is reflected, for example, in the decision as to what part or function of the body is to be sacrificed for the sake of preserving another.

The dependence of ordinary medicine (that is, medicine of the body) upon standards and objectives dictated, or at least ratified, by the community is evident. Why is it not also evident with respect to psychiatry, or the medicine of the soul? Indeed, why is it not even more obvious with respect to mental health determinations that community standards and objectives should govern, inasmuch as common opinion affects one's sense of what is one's due, what is good or bad, what is a grievance, all of which intimately bear on one's mental health?

The critical question, therefore, is not whether and how psychiatry is to be used in the law (for example, in the court system) but rather the extent to which psychiatry is to be guided by the law and by that community opinion of which the law itself is an instrument. Related to this are questions concerning both the extent to which psychiatry is to be respectful of common sense and the relative worth within the community of the strong as against the weak, of the good as against the bad.

Although psychiatry can be considered to stand in the same relation to the law as ordinary medicine, it is obvious that there are fewer problems about that relation associated with ordinary medicine. Difficulties will arise from time to time in the practice of ordinary medicine, for example: How should the terminally ill be dealt with, especially the permanently comatose? Such difficulties are made particularly acute because of recent technological developments. But by and large, sound medical practice, including the proper relation between ordinary medicine and the law, has long been established. This practice prescribes the standards of care doctors should exercise in the light of available information, techniques, and equipment.

Why, then, should there be problems for psychiatry in defining the proper relation between it and the law that there are not for ordinary medicine? Is not this partly because the practice of ordinary medicine was well established at a time when an almost instinctive respect for nature still dominated the thinking of Western man? Psychiatry, on the other hand, developed at a time when nature had gone under a cloud. Psychiatry has been deprived thereby of the moderating guidance of the old-fashioned attitude toward nature. And yet psychiatry as a modern intellectual movement has attacked repressive conventions, that is, traditions, regimes, religions, laws, and cultures in the name of nature. Does not this reliance of modernity upon nature, in its condemnation of various longstanding conventions, suggest that it is a mistake to argue that psychiatry has been deprived of the influence upon it of nature?

Curiously enough, the modern attack upon conventions in the name of nature—an attack not by psychiatry alone—has had the effect of undermining the status of nature among moderns. It should be helpful to this inquiry on the relations of psychiatry and the law to review, if only briefly, how it is that this modern attack upon conventions has undermined the status of nature.[4] The following review also suggests things about modernity and hence about the sense of individuality and of community that influence the relations of law and psychiatry:

1) Conventions (sometimes rather arbitrary, sometimes even ridiculous) are needed for proper training, for discipline, and for securing standards. (Consider what is resorted to in basic training or in boot camp in the military services.) Thus, conventions seem to be necessary in order for human beings to learn about nature herself and to maintain control in accordance with nature. This means that conventions can be truly seen for what they are, and in the light of nature only by someone who has been subjected to conventions and who has, in a sense, graduated from or risen above them. But if conventions are repudiated from the outset, the preliminary training that the community provides becomes deficient and a later (higher) development becomes difficult, if not impossible.

2) Related to the first way by which the modern attack on conventions in the name of nature has undermined the status of nature is that it is natural for human beings to have conventions. To rule these out completely is to subvert, at least to that extent, the promptings of nature.

3) Furthermore, the modern attack on conventions in the name of nature was made on the basis of an inadequate view of nature. Nature was seen by these moderns primarily, if not only, as the desiring part of us and not as the rational or moral (self-restraining) part. That is, a certain aspect of nature, seen in the persistent, instinctive physical desires of mankind, was legitimated in the struggle against certain (restraining) conventions, which to some extent reflect the sobriety of nature. This struggle can be said to have gone too far, in that it permitted one aspect of nature to overwhelm other aspects of nature in the human soul.

4) Perhaps critical to this development of the attack on conventions may have been the assumption, for some four or five centuries now, that nature is something to be conquered, to be used, to be exploited. If nature is to be conquered and harnessed, she is difficult to regard as a master or a guide. The conquest, or exploitation, of nature is to be done for the sake of personal desires, including whatever peculiar desires happen to arise from time to time, "natural" desires that begin to sound in their variability like conventions. Thus, enduring conventions are attacked in the name of nature; nature comes to be understood to be in the service of quite changeable desires.

5) A related consideration here is that nature is more apt to be set aside today because the sight of her is easily lost. Manifestations of nature in growing things (woods and meadows, crops and flowers, to say nothing of

---

[4]On what nature means, see Jacob Klein, "The Nature of Nature" (lecture available from St. John's College Bookstore, Annapolis and Santa Fe).

all kinds of animals) are now largely concealed from view. But it goes deeper than this. Nature also is concealed from view in modern science. Ordinary experience no longer can be relied upon in the organized effort to understand the nature of things. In addition, the explanations constructed by modern science cannot be put in terms of everyday observations, even as rough approximations or as crude analogies. Only mathematics can be used to describe what the scientists (especially the physicists) construct, and these descriptions, however ratified they may be in common opinion by astonishing technological marvels, are simply incomprehensible to most of the community. But it is not only in physics that nature is concealed from view. Ideological considerations also have tended to impede our ability to see nature. Thus, for example, the modern emphasis upon equality can mean that what once would have been considered obvious distinctions, say between the sexes or between the bright and the dull, can be dismissed as conventional. In this way, too, we lose sight of natural differences and hence of nature herself; in this way, too, we extend the domain (in our theories, at least) of the conventional and hence of change.

6) Furthermore, art is no longer seen as an imitation of nature but rather as the free expression of the unencumbered soul. Such free expression is seen as natural. Here, too, we can see that it is a less inhibiting aspect of nature that replaces the older understanding. Thus, art no longer teaches or reassures one about nature.

7) Finally, the decline in the status of nature also can be traced to the now prevalent opinion that constant change is good, that there always is something even better that lies ahead, and that perpetual progress is vital to the happiness of mankind. The emphasis here is on the process and not on the goal, which can be dismissed as "static." Thus, there is nothing fixed, no perfection set by or evident in nature by which to take one's bearings.

Related to this eclipse of nature is what has happened to the status of the divine, at least in the public discourse of intellectuals. At one time a useful way to talk about nature was to talk about the divine. Certainly, the divine provided standards, guidance, and goals; it provided a reliable context within which the arts, including medicine, could work. It was once considered natural, even among many skeptics, that the divine should be publicly respected. Certainly, a general respect for the divine, as manifested in various religious practices and commandments, can very much affect conduct in most people. But such respect is considered by all too many intellectuals as repressive, as an illusion, as hypocritical, as a kind of wish fulfillment, or as mere fearfulness. Nevertheless, a respect for nature, in the old-fashioned sense, and a respect for religion do tend to go hand in hand today despite whatever tension and ultimate divergence there may be between students of nature and students of the divine.

No doubt there are other causes for the decline of the status of nature in modernity, since nature is hard to "put down." After all, nature is always there, always powerful. Even when her status is depreciated, she continues to be, however distorted or even perverted she can come to seem, or even to be, because of the opinions people have about her. Ordinary experience continually draws upon nature. Communities instinctively rely upon her, whatever intellectuals may say. Thus, an effort to invoke nature is routinely seen in the criminal law, in the misconduct that the criminal law anticipates, and in the sanctions it provides.

Critical to any consideration of nature's place in the life of a community is the awareness of the significance of natural right teaching. Natural right is that body of principles and ends that invokes a law above the positive law of the land.[5] The innovative community that does not recognize natural right is ultimately subjected to blind obedience, either in the name of laws of history or of the fatherland, or it is ultimately reduced to mere permissiveness, with each individual allowed to gratify himself, or "to do his own thing." The "state," under this latter dispensation, is reduced to the minimal functions of a referee or umpire.[6] Also, under this dispensation the law is little more than a process.

As suggested, however, this is the theory of intellectuals. Various institutions do endure and provide brakes on the pursuit of personal gratification. That is, nature is still there whether she is thought about or not, although things are better when nature is cooperated with rather than left to have her effect without our knowledge, or even against our inclinations. This is especially evident when efforts are made to find a place, the proper place, in a community's life for innovations such as psychiatry.

A depreciation of nature—a depreciation rooted in modern science and its marvelous accomplishments—has had its effect on psychiatry just as it has on political science and on law. But the effects on law and politics of this depreciation of the status of nature have been less since the legal or political practitioner, as distinguished from the legal or political theoretician, must still appeal to unsophisticated multitudes in the forms of juries and electorates. But alas, the theoretician and the practitioner in psychiatry seem much closer together than they are in law or in politics. And so the depreciation of the status of nature means that the tendency of psychiatry is to see people as other than people, that is, it is not truly to see them. In this, psychiatry shares the failings of modern social science.

---

[5]Natural right points ultimately to the best possible regime and to the best possible development of the soul, between which two goals there can be some tension. See Leo Strauss, *Natural Right and History* (Chicago: University of Chicago Press, 1953); and Harry V. Jaffa, "Aristotle," in L. Strauss and J. Cropsey, eds., *History of Political Philosophy* (Chicago: Rand McNally, 1972).

[6]On the emergence in modernity of "state" see Leo Paul S. De Alvarez, ed., *Machiavelli's Prince* (Irving, TX: University of Dallas Press, 1980), pp. iv–x.

It already has been suggested that if one cannot see certain things as either good or bad, as either beautiful or ugly, then one cannot see them properly or in their entirety. In some respects the law, with its rituals and its precedents and with its other restrictions and even blind spots, comes closer to seeing people properly, or in their entirety, than does psychiatry. Perhaps the same can be said of long-established religions, that is, nature has had her effects there also.

Thus, psychiatry has much that is fundamental to learn from the law. Expressed another way, the law is not merely old-fashioned in its venerability, rather it draws upon centuries of experience of mankind with nature and with the natural limits upon self-gratification and innovation. The familiar resistance of the law to the innovations of psychiatry, therefore, may be well grounded, based at the least on a sound instinct.

I have argued that there may be a tendency in psychiatry to see people as other than people. This misconception can take two principal forms. One misleading way that psychiatry sees people is primarily as products of causes of various kinds, just as do physiology, sociology, and economics. Such materialistic causation places an emphasis on people as mere responses to outside stimuli. (These "outside stimuli" include, in effect, chemical processes within the human body. These, too, are outside the soul's consciousness.) This emphasis suggests that our sense of freedom or responsibility is an illusion. (Certainly, it makes much of chance.) In any event, this approach to humanity is to see man as overinfluenced by the "outside." This is probably the most important stage of this analysis, raising as it does questions about free will. But it is also a stage that is more difficult than, and not as immediately relevant to, our concerns as to what is available in the second approach.

The second approach by psychiatry, sometimes pursued concurrently with the first, is to see a man as underinfluenced by the outside. Thus, man is seen as an autonomous being, a self-generated self, with his own standards and goals. At the root of this approach may be an authoritative concern with the desire to avoid anxiety and pain, which can be quite subjective. In fact, it is difficult to see how this approach can be anything but subjective and undisciplined and therefore ultimately unsatisfying. This approach probably dominates psychiatric thought today, at least for the general practitioner. It is an approach that depends on a particular view of society and on the relation of the individual to the community, with the emphasis on the prerogatives of the individual. There is little recognition here of the causes of one's opinions or desires.

Which approach is the sounder, that which stresses outside stimuli, or that which stresses the autonomy of man? Is there not something to be said for both? Indeed, it would be unnatural if either approach could be long adhered to without any basis in fact. One is shaped by stimuli beyond one's control. Thus, chemistry matters, sometimes enough to impede clear thinking, perhaps even to make all thinking impossible. Furthermore, stimuli beyond our control seem to be critical to our instincts and desires. On the other hand, one can become somewhat independent, in a sense autonomous. That is, a person can be so shaped and instructed as to be able to rise above his physiological and social origins, at least so long as health and bodily processes, including those in the brain, hold up.

A third approach is not merely a compromise between the two approaches just sketched. Rather, it combines parts of both and rises above them to a truly human level. When one is properly instructed, one is not only "liberated" but also is enlisted in and disciplined by a new regime. Only when one has the right desires and acts upon them is one really free. Only then is there the ability to know and to pursue what is truly desired.

However, there remains the question: How does one come to have the proper passions? For this, communities rely upon the law, which itself relies in part upon and is influenced by art. Thus, when one talks of public opinion, or of private passions, one looks to the law, to art, and to religion. The artist reaches into the deepest level of our being, or at least appears to do so. What the artist does, which reflects the promptings of nature (properly conceived), is best seen in the works of the greatest poets, who are influential, if not decisive, in shaping our opinions, passions, and to some extent our thoughts.

Particularly critical for the English-speaking peoples has been Shakespeare. He refines—he does not repudiate or simply agitate against—community opinions and generally held standards. His greatest characters reach up to that which the community yearns for from a greater distance. Shakespeare considers enduring community opinion to reflect nature. (That opinion may be seen in the law and certainly in the common law.) In Shakespeare the accountability of the human being for what he does is emphasized. "If your fellow men do not get you for your misdeeds, nature or God will," he seems to say. Excuses for misconduct are at best partial justifications. By and large, people do get what they deserve. In this respect Shakespeare continues to shape us, if only because he has helped shape the language in which we desire and think.

Compare perhaps the most influential modern playwright Ibsen who, despite his supposed realism, is more sentimental than Shakespeare. He is generally critical of community opinion; he does not merely refine it. There is in Ibsen what Malcolm Sharp has called considerable "unnecessary woe." Again and again in Ibsen's work there are examples of how the community goes wrong and how the self-expressive individual is more apt to be right, especially if a female. (An implicit, though confused, reliance on nature may be seen here.) Ibsen makes much of the repressiveness of the society of his day, that is, Norway before the First World War. Yet, are we not entitled to look back upon that community as almost idyllic in many respects?

Has not Ibsen's attitude, rather than Shakespeare's, toward society, toward so-called repression, and toward individual fulfillment become, in large part, the attitude of modern intellectuals and hence of psychiatry? This is especially to be seen in Ibsen's emphasis upon the right and need of each person to express himself at almost all costs to realize what he has within himself. Much can be learned from a comparison of these two playwrights and from a consideration of why the sentiments and attitudes of Ibsen hold out a greater attraction today than does the inspired moderation of Shakespeare with his "instinctive" respect for law and order.[7]

What follows from this analysis is that anyone interested in the relation of psychiatry to the law should consider several questions touched upon in this article: What is the competence in these matters of psychiatry? Can psychiatry know men reliably for social purposes more so than, or even as well as, thoughtful citizens? What are the presuppositions of psychiatry? Should it not have a limited role in the law, especially in trials? Perhaps its principal use in the interest of both humanity and justice should be during the sentencing process and during pardon and parole determinations. The answers to such questions, along with the opinions they depend upon and lead to, affect the incidence and form of mental diseases. They also affect decisions respecting treatment and standards of accountability in everyday life as well as in the courts.

It has been argued here that certain fundamental opinions not only affect how one responds to various kinds of human conduct but also how one sees that conduct. The human being is most apt to see things properly and behave sociably when the fundamental opinions he has are sound, that is, when they are grounded in nature. A healthy soul depends, to a considerable extent, on the doings and sayings of the community. In other words, psychiatry is in many ways subordinate to a decent political order—to that politics which Aristotle spoke of as the master art and to which both medicine and the law are properly instrumental.

---

[7]Thus, Malcolm P. Sharp's father observed that "Shakespeare is nature." Frank Chapman Sharp, *Shakespeare's Portrayal of the Moral Life* (New York: Charles Scribner's Sons, 1902), p. 105. Does not nature tend to promote sensible conduct in well-established communities?

The Relationship of the
Mental Health Power and the
Criminal Law Power of the State*

NORVAL MORRIS

The progress of medicine, now having set aside quarantine as a rare, brief, and relatively inconsequential event, there remain only two grounds for compulsorily separating the citizen from the community: imprisonment and commitment to a mental hospital. Throughout the world, jails and prisons lawfully cage citizens until trial or as a punishment for crime, while mental hospitals lawfully hold secure the mentally abnormal. When the mentally abnormal commit crimes, or when criminals are or become mentally abnormal, the two powers of the state overlap; and in this overlapping, confusion and cruelty proliferate. Four main areas of that overlapping will be discussed and a principle offered that could bring order to what is at present a series of relatively unprincipled expediencies by which the mental health power is related to the criminal law power. If order can be brought to these great powers, then it should not be difficult to do so with the lesser treatments and conditions that society compulsorily imposes.

Consider the broad grounds on which these two powers are invoked to separate the citizen from the community. Leaving aside the many nuances and qualifications that would have to be made if this topic were dealt with at greater length, here are the principles: 1) to imprison: an individual has been convicted of a crime and imprisonment is deserved and socially necessary; and 2) to commit to a mental hospital: an individual is mentally ill or retarded and is dangerous to others or to himself, or is incapable of caring for himself. These are broadly true statements in every legal system. The subjective conditions precedent to the invocation of these powers differ: in one, the commission of a crime; in the other, the presence of a certain mental state. They are conditions precedent to the invocation of the power, but they do not require the power to be invoked. Further, the objective required social conditions differ: the different socially protective purposes of punishment and of compulsory hospitalization.

---

*The original version of this paper was prepared for delivery at the conference entitled "Psychiatry and the Law: Reaching for a Consensus," held in Chicago on 12–13 October 1979 under the sponsorship of the University of Chicago Medical Center Department of Psychiatry and the Institute of Social and Behavioral Pathology.

The concept of the maximum deserved punishment limits the state's criminal law power. The concept of continuing dangerousness or continuing incapacity to care for oneself limits the state's mental health power. And whenever these two distinct powers are confused, as they often are in current law and practice, injustice and inefficiency result.

There are four occasions when that overlapping and confusion occur. First, in inquiring into the capacity of a person to be tried. Second, in inquiring into his responsibility for the crime. Third, in his capacity to be punished for the crime—the appropriate sentence, which is a separate issue from the other two. And fourth, the appropriateness of prisons as a setting for punishment or for treatment of mentally ill criminals. Or, described in single words, there is the *triability* question, the *responsibility* question, the *punishability* question, and the *treatability* question. All are distinct and separate, both analytically and operationally, and enormous confusion has flowed from the failure to preserve their distinction.

My general submission is that caging—to try to use a neutral word— should never be ordered or prolonged under any mixture of these two powers of the state. And that each of these, the mental health power and the criminal law power, is sufficent in itself, without any amplification being drawn from the other, to handle with justice and with balanced protection of society all four situations. There are minor qualifications, but they are few.

Difficulties with the principle of total separation of these two powers have come from an ambivalent attitude toward the mentally ill criminal, and this is what has pervasively corrupted our efforts at clarity, both in practice and in scholarship. The ambivalence stems from society's view that though a person has committed a criminal act, done that which is criminal, being mentally abnormal he is less guilty in moral terms. St. Peter may well hold him faultless, or less blameworthy, and so should we. On the other hand, he is also different from us and in the view of many probably more dangerous. Therefore, since he has committed a crime we had better, for his sake and for ours, separate him from the community. In these areas we are both more forgiving and more fearful, less and more punitive. Society tries to have it both ways.

If my offered principle for separation of the mental health and the criminal law powers in these areas is correct, then the following would be the consequences for the four situations of *triability, responsibility, punishability,* and *treatability*. First, there should be no special plea of incompetency to stand trial, of "unfitness." When socially necessary the mentally ill or retarded should be charged or tried by criminal process. A series of compromises are now made in many states and in much of the literature that moves in this direction. It seems that sometimes it is necessary to try, by criminal process, those who are now classified as incompetent, and that it is neither socially wise nor objectively kind to them to preserve our present uneasy compromises.

Second, there should be no special defense of insanity to a criminal charge. This is an old argument and will be dealt with only briefly. It is constantly stated that there should be no defense of insanity to a criminal charge, which is an erroneous way to state the proposition. There is an irreducible minimum of a defense of insanity that must exist. Mental illness must be relevant to the presence or absence of the *mens rea* of the crime. Mental illness cannot have a lower level of defense capacity than, for instance, voluntary drunkenness. The question is whether there should be a special plea added beyond that, and I think not. We went wrong in McNaughtan, and no form of words, no textual amendments will cure the error. The error is more fundamental than capable of being rectified by choices between tests like the ALI formula, Durham, McNaughtan, or modified McNaughtan.

Third, with regard to the sentencing question, mental abnormality would remain relevant to sentencing convicted criminals. It is clearly relevant. Sometimes it reduces punishment and, regretfully, sometimes it increases it. The latter is a hard argument to make and requires a lot of time. It comes out of an effort, parsimoniously, to use imprisonment as a sanction. And finally, there is no need for special institutions for the criminally insane. By whatever name they are called, they are always doubly stigmatizing, deeply denigrating institutions that seem to combine the worst of both worlds.

Before speaking further about each of these four areas, there is one final general comment. I would ask that you do not assume that the principle advocated here would be more punitive than our present practices; the contrary is the case. Certainly, the principle being offered need not be a stimulus to any greater severity. Operationally, it is difficult to see how much worse could be done in relation to our mentally ill criminals. The principle recommended is not reformist in the sense that it is shaped to respond to present squalor, cruelty, or failures of social protection. It represents a struggle toward a principle that is accepted in the treatment of all mental illness: invoke the patient's responsibility for his own cure to the limit of his capacity.

Looking first at the triability question—the competency question—it may be best to consider it in terms of well-known cases. It seems harsh and heartless to advocate the trial of the mentally ill, useless and possibly unconstitutional, but this is not necessarily so. Every committee that has struggled seriously with this matter has come to the conclusion that in certain cases the facts of an allegation against a mentally abnormal person must be found. Did he or did he not do whatever is alleged against him? The report of the English Butler Committee on Mentally Abnormal Offenders came to this conclusion, as did the federal Mental Health Law Revision Committee. State after state makes uneasy legislative compromises. The Theon Jackson and the Donald Lang cases are examples.

When Jackson was twenty-seven, supporting himself reasonably well in an Indiana community, he was arrested for two purse snatchings. The record is not clear whether any violence at all accompanied these crimes—

whoever committed them—but the violence was certainly limited to purse snatching. Jackson was a deaf-mute with virtually no capacity to communicate, being unable to read, write, or to use sign language. He was found unfit to plead. Under the then applicable law in Indiana, he was, as a consequence, committed to an institution for the criminally insane since the state's school for the deaf would not accept the mentally retarded deaf. Psychiatric testimony was presented to the court that Jackson was unlikely ever to become competent to stand trial. That prognosis became a life sentence for the allegation of two purse snatchings. Prior to the charge Jackson was free, civil commitment not having been pursued against or for him. Then came the charge, followed by the incompetency plea, and he was now indeterminantly caged, the safeguards of both the criminal law and the mental health law having been mixed into a farrago. The manifest injustice of that result led the Supreme Court to overturn the continued commitment of Jackson on grounds of denial, both of equal protection and of due process: equal protection because he lacked protections accorded civilly committed patients; and due process because the duration of the commitment bore no reasonable relation to the purpose for which he had been committed, that is, to make him competent to stand trial. It is a step forward, but a very hesitant one and of unclear direction. It puts too much weight on civil commitment, and it does not adequately protect either the community or those like Jackson.

Before developing that argument further, the Donald Lang case should be mentioned. As a result of the Jackson decision, all states were obliged to consider the continued commitment of those held as incompetent to stand trial. One such person was Lang, who had been committed to the Illinois Department of Mental Health in 1966 pursuant to being found incompetent to stand trial on a murder charge. After a tavern pickup and killing of a lady of mercenary virtue, the state alleged that Lang committed the killing and had substantial evidence to support that charge. In 1972 the Jackson decision compelled the termination of Lang's commitment. The state's evidence had withered in the interim, Lang was released, and he was not charged with the 1966 crime. Six months later a murder of starkly similar pattern was committed, Lang being related to it. The Illinois courts are now struggling with what to do in the matter. The latest juridical exercise was a decision of considerable opacity by the Supreme Court of Illinois that, under its recent legislation, the finding of incompetency to stand trial is equivalent to a civil commitment as mentally ill, or as retarded and being a danger to others, which astonished those who had recommended the legislation and who had drafted the legislation as well as the legislators who had voted on it.

Like it or not the issue in these cases has to be decided somewhere because it is central to civil commitment and to mental responsibility. If the issue is finessed or there is a pretense to finesse, the accused in either case will be locked up, putting a great deal of weight on the civil commitment power. In what forum will Lang, Jackson, or all the others, who though mentally abnormal have to be tried, receive the greater protection? Obviously, in the criminal law forum. The facts will be better found there than in the civil commitment hearing, where it has been a personal observation for many years that the facts tend swiftly to be assumed. Evidence about mental illness is often very seriously and very well considered. But when it is central to find the fact of the event as the only substantial basis for the prediction of dangerousness, as it often is, then it seems reasonably clear that it is desirable to have a hearing to find those facts.

Does that mean that society should not have special arrangements to provide sensibly for the mentally ill who have to be tried? No, not at all. One can provide continuances and delays to reach the optimal standard of triability. It is not necessary to take to trial many of those cases that are inconsequential, but only those where there is a social necessity in fact finding, either for the sake of the accused or of the community. There should be special rules of court, corroboration, or standards of proof, and certainly special rules concerning new evidence that may be produced at any time. That line of argument appealed to the Mental Health Law Revision Committee, but it has not yet been accepted in any state.

However, compromises have been developed in many states, and foreign countries also have gradually introduced special factual hearings to find the underlying facts of a case. In this area, misguided benevolence has not achieved beneficence; it has achieved inefficiency, and we would be much wiser, when it is necessary, to do our best to find the facts in these matters at the level of a criminal trial. Would it be constitutional? I believe so. There is no Supreme Court decision to the contrary; there are, however, some dicta casting doubt on it. I think that the Supreme Court would be very receptive to my offered line of argument.

The same principle, in a different form, can be applied to the question of responsibility. Mental illness must be relevant to guilt, to the presence or absence of the *mens rea* of the crime. That is almost a truism and really does not need much defense. If a certain mental condition is necessary for a conviction, then absent that mental condition there can be no conviction no mattter what the reason, be it deafness, blindness, or mental illness. On the *mens rea* question there is obviously the irreducible minimum of the defense of insanity, that because of such illness the accused lacked the required mental state for the crime.

The question is, is there a need to go further? Is there gain in doing so? If there is no sincerity in the defense of insanity, except in only a very few sensational cases, then there is no gain. The presence of psychopathology in the context of crime is not found at murder trials where the distinguished psychiatrists are testifying but in the city courts. Here, if a defense of insanity were mentioned, the only person thought to be insane would be the defense counsel. In the broad sweep of case law and practice, society does not have a special defense of insanity to a criminal charge. We have it only in a few fancy cases, a few murders, to support our own moralism.

Nor do we deal with the people found not guilty on the grounds of insanity as if they were innocent. In Illinois they have just now legislated that before a person so found may be released the prosecutor and the trial judge must be notified so that they can veto a release. How can one look at that and not see the hypocrisy? Society does not adhere to its decisions of "not guilty on the grounds of insanity"; it never does. Instead, we make all sorts of other expedient accommodations to handle the matter.

There are difficulties in relation to crimes of recklessness, and there are difficulties in relation to extreme abnormalities. The Butler Committee accepts the first argument—the *mens rea* argument—as the general answer but leaves a very small category of severe mental illness or severe subnormality which they think unwise to hold responsible. But that is only in the most extreme cases, those in which there is no advantage to be served in finding the lack of responsibility. I would be very happy with that compromise, and there is a movement generally in that direction.

In this context, I would like to draw upon two more topics. First, if the Federal Criminal Code goes through, we have to draft sentencing guidelines. One of the requirements of the federal statute, in the form in which it has passed the Senate, is that "the Court in determining the particular sentence to be imposed shall consider the need for the sentencing imposed to provide the defendant with needed medical care." The court is thus directed, as a statutory matter in imposing sentence, to consider the convicted person's need for medical care, including psychiatric care. The legislation establishes a sentencing commission to provide guidelines and policy statements to assist the federal courts to bring order out of the present chaos of federal sentencing. In Section 194 it states that in establishing these guidelines the sentencing commission is directed to consider the defendant in terms of his "mental and emotional condition to the extent that such condition mitigates the defendant's culpability or to the extent that such condition is otherwise plainly relevant." In other words, the commission sought to press toward situations in which there was a higher base expectancy rate of future crime, as a result of the mental condition, than there otherwise would be. It is possible that this raises very difficult problems of justice, problems on which little has been written. However, it seems that there exists here a legislative mandate to take into account mental illness in a fashion that can both mitigate and aggravate punishment.

Second, society tends to impute lesser moral fault when mental illness or social adversity is a factor in the commitment of a crime. Just as social adversity may lead us to mitigate sentence, so mental illness may lead us to mitigate sentence. However sometimes social adversity leads us to aggravate sentence. If in doubt, consider the life of any young man who lives in an impoverished area, is unemployed, comes from a broken home, is vocationally and educationally ill equipped, and has been a gang member. There was not much choice in that entire pattern of lifestyle, but assuredly it will increase the sentence imposed because his base expectancy rate of further criminal behavior is clearly high. Likewise, as new information is gradually developed, it seems that some categories of mental abnormality are associated with greater risks of dangerousness and violence.

The question of special institutions is the fourth and final situation involving confusion between the state's two separate powers. Over the years different categories of inmates have been put in various psychiatric prison wards or in security sections of mental hospitals. However, after extensive work on the defense of insanity, some work on competency, and on drafting sentencing guidelines for mentally ill criminals, it seems that my integrating principle of bringing together both the criminal law power and the mental health power of the state within a single institution should be possible.

One such place is the Butner Prison in North Carolina. When it suddenly became vacant, prison authorities suggested trying my principle. Butner is a prison for repetitively violent offenders who have at least three convictions, two priors, one of which must be for a crime of personal violence. They also must be eighteen to thirty-five with one to three years to serve. However, included in the prison are 150 prisoners who are psychotic. In other words, there is a small and very adequate mental hospital within the ordinary prison. This was not planned; it just happened. The hospital is well staffed because of the available psychiatric facilities in the area. These inmates have separate living accommodations from the other prisoners and the drugs prescribed are carefully watched. However, these mentally ill prisoners work with and eat with the other prisoners as well as attend educational programs and participate on recreational teams with them.

In sum, it seems that there is little to be gained by establishing special facilities. In our good intentions to provide such institutions, it only serves to doubly stigmatize those who are convicted as both criminal and mentally ill.

Does Guilt Require Sanity?
Constitutional Considerations*

WILLIAM K. CARROLL

Discussions that weigh the pros and cons of abolishing the insanity defense frequently ignore or lightly dismiss constitutional considerations. The recent report to the governor[1] by a New York State task force commissioned to make an in-depth study of the defense of insanity advised the governor that no constitutional impediment exists should the legislature choose to abolish the defense.[2] The task force cited language in a 1968 United States Supreme Court case in support of the thesis that the states enjoy considerable freedom in defining the necessary elements of statutory defenses.[3] However, the implications of the case cited for the insanity defense are far from clear.[4] The constitutional issues involved in the direct or indirect elimination of the defense of insanity are worthy of more serious consideration. An outline of that constitutional discussion is suggested here.

It is important first to clarify precisely what is being proposed when abolition of the insanity defense is discussed. Often several quite different proposals become entangled in the discussion. This frequently results in false agreement or disagreement. Proposals to abolish the insanity defense have at times meant such diverse things as:

A. A proposal to eliminate the condition of mental disease or defect as a matter relevant to guilt. The mental disability would be considered at the

---

*The original version of this paper was prepared for delivery at the conference entitled "Psychiatry and the Law: Reaching for a Consensus," held in Chicago on 12–13 October 1979 under the sponsorship of the University of Chicago Medical Center Department of Psychiatry and the Institute of Social and Behavioral Pathology.

[1] A Report to Governor Hugh L. Carey on the Insanity Defense in New York, 17 February 1978.

[2] Ibid., p. 131.

[3] The state has "wide freedom to determine the extent to which moral culpability should be a prerequisite to conviction of a crime." The language quoted is from Powell v. Texas, 392 U.S. 514 at 545. Justice Black in his concurring opinion states his philosophy that criminal law, as a social tool intended to serve many social purposes, may be exercised with sensitivity to but cannot be constrained by considerations of culpability and blameworthiness when these interfere with appropriate social goals (pp. 544–46). The issue here is what limits there may be to such a sweeping utilitarian doctrine.

[4] LaFave-Scott, *Criminal Law* (1972), pp. 165–68.

dispositional stage only, after conviction. Further, expert opinion testimony would not be allowed on the issue of the presence of the mental state, or *mens rea*, required for the crime.

B. A proposal to eliminate the condition of mental disease or defect as an issue in itself relevant to guilt. Expert testimony would be received if it went to the issue of whether or not the defendant had the required *mens rea*, here understood narrowly as the knowledge or intent required for the crime. Such a specific conscious state could readily be present in a severely delusional individual, an acute psychotic.[5] The psychosis would be irrelevant if the minimal knowledge or intent were present.

C. A proposal to eliminate "insanity" (whatever the legal test) as a separate defense distinct from a claim that the defendant lacked the knowledge or intent required for the statutorily defined offense. Expert testimony, however, is admissible to show the existence of a mental disease or defect insofar as it reflects on the necessary knowledge or intent.

D. A proposal to eliminate insanity (wherever the legal test) as a separate defense distinct from lack of *mens rea*. *Mens rea* however is understood here more broadly than as simple knowledge or intent. Expert testimony of mental disability would be admissible on the issue of whether, in view of this disability, the defendant was capable of such evil disposition that he may justly be held responsible and blameworthy for the harmful behavior. *Mens rea* is here a moral category rather than a narrowly defined conscious state such as knowledge or intent. Where the statute defines the mental element of the defense as knowledge or intent, these are to be read as implying sufficiently *sane* intent or knowledge that it would be just and fair to subject the accused to criminal sanctions.[6]

As is evident, these proposals are conceptually quite different. All eliminate insanity as an independent ground for acquittal, unrelated to the elements that go to make up the offense. Insanity as an independent defense is viewed in these proposals as one might view a running of the statute of limitations or a claim of double jeopardy. These are reasons for avoiding conviction based on social policy. They do not expressly negate some element necessary for the crime charged to exist. Proposals B, C and D, however, would allow during the case expert testimony on the state of mind necessary for the crime to exist in chief. Proposal A would allow no expert testimony on this issue.

Criminal offenses are composed of two elements: the prohibited act or omission (*actus reus*) and the accompanying criminal state of mind (*mens rea*). Proposals B and C understand this state of mind narrowly as knowledge

---

[5]Norval Morris provides an example in "Psychiatry and the Dangerous Criminal," *Southern California Law Review* 41 (1968): 520.

[6]For the many ways in which *mens rea* is understood in Anglo-American legal literature, see Fletcher, *Rethinking Criminal Law* (Boston, 1978), p. 395.

or intent. Proposal B would restrict the scope of the expert's testimony to the issue of whether or not the defendant had this minimal knowledge or intent. The mental disease or defect of the defendant at the time of the offense would be irrelevant. Proposal C would allow the expert to give evidence on mental disease or defect insofar as the expert was prepared to represent that this condition negated the knowledge or intent required by the statute defining the offense. In all probability it would be difficult in practice to distinguish the testimony offered in proposal B from that offered in C—or for that matter, to distinguish the testimony offered in either from what would be offered, for the most part, in a traditional independent insanity defense. There would be a difference in focus, however.[7]

Proposal D understands the required criminal state of mind as something more than what the unadorned words "knowledge" and "intent" convey. Drawing on the Latin meaning and common-law understanding of *mens rea* as guilty mental disposition, it understands these words to mean blameworthy knowledge and intent.[8] This in turn requires that it be sane knowledge or intent. Consequently, it allows expert testimony on the general mental/emotional state of the defendant so that the finder of fact may determine if the defendant, despite his minimal knowledge or intent, should be held criminally blameworthy for his conduct. Testimony offered on this issue would hardly be distinguishable from the testimony of an expert testifying in the usual insanity defense stage of a trial. However, the expert would not marshal his findings and opinions to respond to a legal insanity test question. He would merely describe the pathology and its relation to the offensive conduct. The jury would not be asked to find if the defendant was sane at the time of the offense. They would be asked rather to find if, in view of all the testimony they have heard, the defendant possessed the necessary *mens rea*, that is a sufficiently blameworthy state of mind, to justify holding him criminally responsible. Such a finding would involve a social/moral judgment on the quality of the knowledge or intent and the community's sense of justice.

If the proposal is to abolish mental disability as an independent defense, there are no insurmountable constitutional objections apparent. No constitutional provision would seem to require that insanity be retained as an independent defense, if that is what it has been.[9] On the other hand, if the proposal

---

[7]In each case, in order to set the frame for their opinion, the experts undoubtedly in practice will be allowed to explain the underlying pathology and the evidence for it. However, in the context of the traditional insanity test, the expert would direct attention to the defendant's tenuous hold on reality and his ability to control his conduct. Where the only question is a narrow conscious state, such as knowledge and intent, the expert must be prepared to relate his findings to the questions: Was the defendant aware it was his wife's neck he was squeezing? Was it his immediate objective to squeeze it until she died?

[8]See also Fletcher, *Rethinking Criminal Law*, pp. 395ff.

[9]Constitutional due process would seem not to demand this procedure so long as mental disability is considered somewhere in the process of finding criminal guilt.

is to disallow evidence of mental disability on the issue of guilt at all stages of the proceedings, a serious constitutional issue arises. There is also a constitutional issue if the proposal is to remove mental disability as an independent defense and further to allow evidence of it solely on the issue of the mental element of the offense charged where that element is so narrowly construed as to eliminate what has traditionally been regarded as an implied and substantive element of *mens rea*, namely a sufficiently balanced mental state to render the knower culpable. The practical effect of such a move would be to disallow evidence on factors always considered relevant to guilt, to a fair and just finding that conduct has been criminal in nature.

To date there have been only two legislative attempts statutorily to abolish evidence of insanity as admissible evidence on the issue of guilt. The first attempt was made by the state of Washington in 1909. The next year the Washington Supreme Court struck the statute down as violating substantive due process.[10] The statutory scheme provided for consideration of the disordered mental state at the dispositional stage but not on the issue of guilt. The particular statute involved read:

> It shall be no defense to a person charged with the commission of a crime that at the time of its commission he was unable, by reason of his insanity, idiocy or imbecility, to comprehend the nature and quality of the act committed, or to understanding that it was wrong; or that he was afflicted with a morbid propensity to commit prohibited acts; *nor shall any testimony or other proof thereof be admitted in evidence*. [Emphasis added.][11]

The case involved a charge of attempted murder, a shooting. The trial court refused evidence of insanity on the authority of the statute.

The Washington Supreme Court found the statute violated the unarticulated "law of the land" and thereby substantive due process.[12] It reasoned that sanity is always an implied and substantive element of an offense, as much as is the prohibited act, even if not expressed. The legislature cannot constitutionally eliminate this intrinsic element by narrowly defining the physical act and the mental state which constitute an offense.[13] Sanity is required for blameworthiness and is inherent to guilt.[14]

At the same time the court acknowledged the concerns of the legislature: perceived abuse of the insanity defense, the need for a solid basis for the court to exercise adequate restraint on violence-prone individuals. It also acknowledged that the statutory scheme evidenced legislative intent to deal therapeutically with the convicted insane rather than punitively. Nevertheless it opined:

---

[10]State v. Strasburg, 110 P.1020 (1910).
[11]1909 Criminal Code, Section 7. Cited in opinion at 1021.
[12]*Strasburg* at 1023.
[13]Ibid. at 1024.
[14]Ibid. at 1025.

> The status and condition in the eyes of the world and under the law, of one convicted of crime, is vastly different from that of one simply adjudged insane. . . . As long as this is the spirit of our laws, though it may be much mellowed in the treatment of the convicted, as compared with former times, the constitutional rights here invoked must be given full force and effect when an accused person is put upon trial to determine the question of his guilt of crime.[15]

The court suggested that the better remedy for perceived abuses of the insanity defense was to develop better ways to help the jury determine the mental capacity of the accused. "The remedy is to be sought by correcting false notions, and not by destroying the safeguards of private liberty."[16]

One justice concurred in the result but not in the theory espoused by the majority. The dissenter espoused a legal-positivist view by stating, "It is not the duty of the state to inquire into the moral guilt or innocence of those whom it adjudges guilty of crime, as it derives its power to determine guilt or innocence only as it finds its law violated and its commandments broken by the individual for whose act there is in law no justification."[17]

This dissent would seem to be at the heart of the current debate: is moral blameworthiness an implied and intrinsic element of criminality, or at least of true crimes,[18] so that a conviction cannot stand constitutionally without this element being shown? Sanity will always be relevant to blameworthiness.

The issue might also be expressed as: Does substantive due process require that the *mens rea* of all true crimes include by implication blameworthiness? *Strasburg* supports the affirmative.

---

[15]Ibid.

[16]Ibid. at 1028.

[17]Ibid. at 1028.

[18]Criminal law theory has traditionally distinguished between *malum in se* offenses and *malum prohibitum* offenses. The former are seen as deeds "evil in their very nature" which stigmatize the perpetrator as evil to the extent of the offense. A *malum prohibitum* offense, on the other hand, is viewed as an offense created by statute for the convenience of the community. It is not a violation of the intrinsic relations between persons in community. It is a violation of some regulatory scheme, rather arbitrarily chosen, such as parking regulations, to facilitate community business. The violator of these latter violations is a law breaker but is not stigmatized as evil or criminal. His offense is not a true crime. Consequently there is no need to find the violator of these statutes morally blameworthy. He may be found guilty and reasonably sanctioned merely on evidence he performed the prohibited act, although a requirement that it be a voluntary act can lead to complexities. The view of legal positivism that all criminal offenses are the creations of legislative policy and designed to achieve useful social purposes finds this distinction between *malum in se* offenses and *malum prohibitum* ones meaningless. The constitutional discussion undertaken here can be viewed as an inquiry into the limits of such a utilitarian view of criminal justice. There clearly is today an impetus in Anglo-American law to expand the spectrum of offenses not requiring a showing of moral culpability. For a succinct discussion of this continuing tension between legal positivism and the view that criminal conduct has an intrinsic structure that identifies it independently of legislative action see Fletcher, *Rethinking Criminal Law*, chap. 6.

The other state court case striking down a statute which eliminated insanity as a defense is the 1931 Mississippi case *Sinclair* v. *State*.[19] Actually the statute abolished the defense only in murder indictments. The *Sinclair* court found the statute unconstitutional on grounds of substantive due process and equal protection.[20] The court used language that antedates the language of the Model Penal Code for the mental element of the offense, speaking of malice and malice aforethought.[21] The court's language and analogies suggest that it saw insanity as going to an essential element of the offense charged and not as an extrinsic, policy defense. Insanity was likened by the court to the defense of infancy which, since the early fourteenth century, has been based on the theory that children under seven are not capable of criminal malice, *mens rea*.[22] Evidence therefore could not be excluded constitutionally on a material issue of fact going to the existence of an essential element of the offense charged. The court's opinion appeals to the traditions of western civilization and can be read to imply that culpability and blameworthiness must be read into "malice aforethought." The language of modern statutes that have replaced "malice" with "intent and knowledge" nowhere declares an intent to alter the traditional understanding of *mens rea*.[23] Blameworthiness and sanity would seem to remain as essential elements of *mens rea*, whatever the language used.

More recently some state supreme courts have addressed the issue by striking down their state's bifurcation statutes. Bifurcation is the procedure whereby the evidence on insanity is received in a hearing different than that in which evidence of the offense is heard. The theory is that in this way the defendant is free to introduce, at the separate sanity hearing, evidence of his insanity that he might have been reluctant to offer in the trial of the offense since it implicates him in the crime. (It often results in allowing the prosecution to offer otherwise excludable evidence as well.) Courts have struck down the statutes requiring the bifurcation procedure on the theory that evidence of insanity cannot be withheld from the jury hearing evidence on the issue of whether the offense has been committed, since sanity is an essential element of the offense itself. These courts hold that a defendant cannot be guilty of

---

[19]132 So. 581 (1931). Two years later the Colorado Supreme Court struck down parts of that state's statutory scheme for implementing the insanity defense, Ingles v. People, 22 P.2d 1109 (Colo. 1933). In so doing it relied on the philosophy of *Strasburg* and *Sinclair*. However, it is not exactly on point since Colorado had not abolished the defense but had disallowed evidence of mental disability on the *mens rea* element unless the defense had been specially pleaded.

[20]Ibid. at 584 and 586.

[21]Ibid. at 584. The drafters of the Model Penal Code adopted the nonnormative language of knowledge, intent, purpose; most states have followed this lead.

[22]*Sinclair*, supra at 583; see also LaFave-Scott, *Criminal Law*, p. 351.

[23]For a discussion of the feasibility of truly value-free language in the criminal justice system, see Fletcher, *Rethinking Criminal Law*, chap. 6. The Model Penal Code eschews normative language.

an offense "but insane." Thus the supreme court of Florida, following Wyoming and Arizona, recently found sanity an implied element of any *mens rea:* "The court concluded that the sanity of an accused is an integral part (element) of a determination of guilt and the state must prove beyond a reasonable doubt each element of the crime charged."[24]

The United States Supreme Court has not directly considered the question but its decisions on the issue of burden of proof in insanity cases are relevant to the discussion. However, it has repeatedly stated that a procedure violates due process if "it offends some principle of justice so rooted in the traditions and conscience of our people as to be ranked fundamental."[25] The Court subsequently said that it is a fundamental principle that the prosecution must prove beyond a reasonable doubt every element necessary to constitute the crime charged.[26] Already in 1875 in *United States* v. *Davis*, the Court held that the definition of murder includes the fact of adequate mental capacity as an implied element of the *mens rea* required to constitute the offense of murder.[27] Therefore the burden of proving the defendant's sanity was placed on the prosecution once the issue was raised. This decision was given in the context of a federal prosecution but the majority of states came to follow the rule. The State of Oregon, however, continued to place the burden of proof on the defendant and it was a heavy burden. The defendant had to prove beyond a reasonable doubt that he was not sane at the time of the offense. The constitutionality of the Oregon procedure was challenged in 1952 in *Leland* v. *Oregon*.[28] In *Leland* the U.S. Supreme Court said that the holding in *Davis* had established no constitutional doctrine binding on the state courts but only a rule for the federal courts.[29]

The Court proceeded to find no constitutional defect in the Oregon procedure that required the prosecution to prove "all the necessary elements of guilt" but appeared to make sanity not one of those included elements.[30] For the jurors "were to consider separately the issue of legal sanity per se—an issue set apart from the crime charged."[31] The defendant had the burden of proving beyond a reasonable doubt the lack of sanity. Justice Felix Frankfurter strongly dissented in *Leland*, insisting that culpability and sanity are elements, in combination with others, that convert a homicide into the crime of murder.[32] As essential elements of the offense, they must be proved by the prosecution.

---

[24]State ex rel. Boyd v. Green, 355 So. 2d 789, et 793 (Fed. 1978).
[25]Speiser v. Randall, 357 U.S. 513, 523 (1958); Leland v. Oregon, 343 U.S. 790, 798 (1952); Snyder v. Massachusetts, 391 U.S. 97, 105 (1934).
[26]In re Winship, 397 U.S. 358, 361 (1970).
[27]Davis v. United States, 160 U.S. 469, 491 (1895).
[28]343 U.S. 790 (1952).
[29]Ibid. at 797.
[30]Ibid. at 795.
[31]Ibid.
[32]Ibid. at 804.

More recently, in *Mullaney* v. *Wilbur*,[33] the Court seemed to sidestep *Leland* and to reaffirm *Davis* as a constitutional rule binding state courts that the degree of culpability is an element of the offense charged and therefore the burden of persuasion is on the prosecution to prove the absence of a mitigating circumstance which would reduce culpability. However, in a 1977 decision, *Patterson* v. *New York*,[34] where the issue was whether a new New York murder statute that made emotional distress a factor mitigating murder could place the burden of proving affirmatively such condition on the defendant, the Court said that *Mullaney* should not be read as effectively overruling *Leland*. The Court affirmed the *Mullaney* principle that the prosecution must prove every ingredient of the offense charged but held that in the instant case a mind free of emotional distress was not an element of the offense of murder in New York, because the New York statute did not make it an element. Justice Lewis Powell strongly dissented, observing that to identify the elements of murder one had "need for careful and discriminating review of history" rather than a quick glance at the wording of a statute. The state cannot simply eliminate the elements of murder by definition.[35]

The constitutionality of abolishing the insanity defense or of prohibiting the admission of evidence of mental disability that goes to lack of blameworthiness but not necessarily to intent or knowledge, narrowly defined, apparently will turn on the constitutionality of allowing legislatures to define the mental element of true crimes so as to exclude the requirement of culpability and blameworthiness. This, in turn, depends on whether to do so "offends some principle of justice so rooted in the traditions and conscience of our people as to be ranked fundamental."[36]

---

[33]421 U.S. 685 (1975).

[34]432 U.S. 197 (1977).

[35]The trilogy of *Winship, Mullaney,* and *Patterson* has stirred vigorous debate on the constitutionality of presumptions and the shifting of elements of offenses to the status of affirmative defenses. See Nesson, "Rationality, Presumptions and Judicial Comment," *Harvard Law Review* 94 (1981): 1574.

[36]See note 25 above.

Psychiatric Credibility in the Patricia Hearst Case*

RICHARD ARENS

Heiress to millions, the product of a privileged upper-class upbringing, Patricia Hearst was kidnapped by a quasi-revolutionary group, the Symbionese Liberation Army (SLA), sixteen days before her twentieth birthday. Kept incommunicado for seventy days, subjected to threats, sensory deprivations, assaults, and indignities, she turned up with those captors as an apparent accomplice at the robbery of the Hibernia Bank in San Francisco. As stated in the indictment,

> On or about April 15, 1974, in the city and County of San Francisco, State and Northern District of California, Patricia Campbell Hearst, defendant herein and others not named in this indictment, did by force and violence and by intimidation take from the person and presence of employees of the Hibernia Bank, Sunset Office, money in the sum of approximately $10,690 belonging to and in the care, custody, control, management, and possession of the aforesaid bank. . . .

The prosecution's case rested upon the theory that Patricia Hearst, albeit an unwilling prisoner at the commencement of her captivity, became a willing convert to the revolutionary dialectic of her captors and evolved into a willing conspirator and accomplice in the perpetration of the robbery. Evidence was presented to show that long after the termination of Patricia's physical confinement she manifested her adherence to her former captors by making revolutionary propaganda broadcasts for the SLA, both before and after the Hibernia Bank robbery; failing to make any effort to escape; being entrusted with firearms outside the control of her captors; and providing covering fire to a member of the group whose arrest was sought for shoplifting at Mel's Sporting Goods Store, significantly after the Hibernia Bank robbery with which she was charged. As summed up by prosecuting counsel,

*The original version of this paper was prepared for delivery at the conference entitled "Psychiatry and the Law: Reaching for a Consensus," held in Chicago on 12–13 October 1979 under the sponsorship of the University of Chicago Medical Center Department of Psychiatry and the Institute of Social and Behavioral Pathology.

195

. . . . The most crucial segment of circumstantial evidence in this entire case, ladies and gentlemen, I suggest to you, is the events at Mel's Sporting Goods Store and the following day and night in Los Angeles on May 16 and 17 of 1974. Why? Well, first of all, I suggest that it is reasonable to believe that a person who is in fear of being killed by her captors does not, when confronted with an opportunity to escape from the captors, fire weapons in the direction of other persons in order to free the captors, and does not fail to escape, given an opportunity to escape, or at least an opportunity to get word to somebody other than the captors. Those are two very important reasonable inferences that can be drawn from the events in Los Angeles of May 16 and 17, one month after this robbery, ladies and gentlemen, which bear upon her intent at the time of the robbery of the Hibernia Bank one month earlier. There is no question but what this event happened. The defendant testified:

Q. When you saw the struggle with Bill Harris on the ground, what did you do?
A. I picked up his gun and started firing.
Q. Did you fire at anything in particular?
A. Well, I was trying to fire like up at the top of the building.
Q. Did you think about doing that at all before you picked up that weapon and started firing?
A. No. It was just like a reaction. I mean it happened so fast.
Q. Did you consider the possibilities of anybody being hit?
A. Yes.
Q. Did you make any effort, that you can recall, to avoid that happening?
A. Well, I tried to shoot at the top of the building.
Q. When you pressed the trigger of the automatic weapon, tell us what happened.
A. I pulled the trigger and the gun, just like it jumped out of my hand, and I saw a bullet strike like the divider. It looked like it was hitting in the bushes on the little divider there, and so I had to pick it up again, because I only had it, like, like in my right hand, I had to get it up again and fire it again.

In cross-examination she was asked:

Q. What did happen?
A. I saw them over there and I just grabbed the automatic weapon and started firing, and it fell out of my hands and I picked it up again and kept firing until the magazine was empty, and then picked up the other gun and kept firing.
Q. Well, didn't you testify the other day that it was a reflex action that caused you to do that?
A. That is what it was like. It just happened so fast, I did not even think about it.

The defense conceded the factual transaction of the robbery but claimed the legal excuse of duress for the bank robbery and the different but duress-like defense of psychological coercion for the balance of her behavior. All of her postbank robbery behavior was seen by the defense as symptomatic of traumatic neurosis and devoid of voluntary participation and hence legal guilt. It was designed moreover to explain such phenomena as providing covering fire at Mel's Sporting Goods Store, the defendant's clenched-fist salute, and her self-identification as an "urban guerrilla."

The insanity defense was explicitly rejected. What then was the theory of the defense? Having explicitly and unambiguously rejected insanity, the legal shorthand for exculpatory mental illness, the defense's theory was twofold. First, Patricia claimed to be the victim of duress or coercion at the time of the bank robbery. The defense was that her action was involuntary. Yet, in the contemplation of the law, duress, coercion, or necessity, however liberally interpreted, must meet a test characterized by reasonableness of perceptions on the part of the accused: "In order to excuse a criminal act on the ground of coercion, compulsion or necessity, one must have acted under a *well-grounded apprehension* of immediate and impending death or of immediate serious bodily harm." (Emphasis added)[1] Moreover, the defense lacked even a single witness on duress in its conventional sense, not counting Patty's own testimony disastrously disrupted by her Fifth Amendment claims.

Second, it was claimed simultaneously that the custodial treatment meted out to Patricia by her kidnappers had made her suffer sensory distortions, pathological dependence, and erroneous perceptions which, however, stood foursquare against a jury acceptance that her action proceeded from a well-grounded apprehension of immediate and impending death or immediate serious bodily harm, and well-grounded to any ordinary jury would mean rational, reality-oriented, and untainted by pathological fear. In a word, the defense had presented the jury with two theories which, dealt with as they are in terms of pedestrian courtroom perceptions and not of Freudian analysis, appear to be irreconcilable, barring the working of magic by the defense psychiatrists. And the defense psychiatrists—superlative as witnesses and scientists—lacked magical power.

The defense was appropriately informed that otherwise loyal air force officers, who had made propaganda broadcasts for the enemy during the Korean War, were not prosecuted upon repatriation on the assumption, which was never formulated in a legal opinion, that their action was the product of intolerable psychological group pressures by the enemy. The defense also should have been informed that army records showed repeated prosecutions

---

[1]United States v. Fleming, 7 USCMA 543, 23 CMR 7, 22 (1957). See also Gillars v. United States, 182F 2d 962, 978–980 (D.C. Cir., 1950); and LaFave and Scott, *Handbook on Criminal Law* 377 (1972).

of U.S. personnel who had claimed to have collapsed under the psychological pressure of the enemy and had engaged in radio broadcasts against their country. Reliance upon the theory that American servicemen guilty of such acts should be spared punishment because of their ability to adhere to the right had been "so impaired or diminished by harassment, deprivation, degradation or physical impairment" was adjudged as of no legal merit and the defense of a "partial impairment of the accused's judgment" likewise rejected as not relevant to guilt or innocence.[2]

In a court-martial proceeding with early overtones of the Hearst defense, the diagnosis propounded by defense psychiatrists of a mental disorder identified as induced political psychosis, or induced paranoia, was rejected, and the conviction affirmed upon appeal.[3] The judge advocate's view, as emerging from the Korean War cases, in fact appeared to reject all but the insanity defense in cases in which mental responsibility in its conventional sense was at issue. As phrased in the court-martial proceeding of *United States* v. *Fleming*, "to constitute lack of mental responsibility, the impairment must not only be the result of mental defect, disease, or derangement but must also completely deprive the accused of his ability to distinguish right from wrong or to adhere to the right. . . ."[4] Thus, in the Hearst trial the election by the defense of the seemingly contradictory defenses of duress and the unprecedented psychological coercion defense, plus the rejection of the insanity defense, set the stage for what appeared to be a needlessly hazardous courtroom scenario.

The only defense assertion standing a significant possibility of acceptance might have proceeded along the following lines: Patricia Hearst had suffered an abduction and other traumatic events which, in their totality, induced a mental disease sufficiently critical as to deprive her completely of the ability to adhere to the right. While the psychiatric testimony was not geared to meet such a detailed test, it nonetheless came close to it and, if adequately prepared for in the planning stage, could have achieved such a result, perhaps under the nomenclature of dissociative reaction.

The heart of the case was the psychiatric testimony. The defense had no case if the jury did not believe that Patricia was the victim of duress and psychological coercion. Yet the matter was complicated by the fact that on the one hand the defense relied on the traditional conception of duress, gauged by the reasonableness of the perception of the imminence of life-threatening danger, which was sought to be avoided by the perpetration of a noncapital crime by the defendant. On the other hand, the defense sought to persuade

---

[2]United States v. Fleming, see note 1 above.

[3]United States v. Batchelor, CM 377832 (1954); affirmed 7 USCMA 354, 22 CMR 144 (1956).

[4]United States v. Fleming, 23 CMR 7, 21 (1957).

the jury that the defendant's perceptions and sensations had been critically impaired but not sufficiently so as to raise the issue of exculpatory mental illness, which as noted was repudiated by defense counsel.

The prosecution had no case if the jury did not believe the two government experts—Doctors Fort and Kozol—notwithstanding such acts by Patricia as providing covering fire and identifying herself as an urban guerrilla which, taken in isolation, seemed to point to voluntary adherence to the conspiratorial scheme, if the defense experts were believed, even to the point of creating a reasonable doubt, as to the defendant's freedom of choice as a consequence of mental illness that had been induced by her abduction. The mental illness emerged at least inferentially from the psychiatric testimony, which deserves detailed analysis even in the absence of the insanity defense.

Three extraordinarily prestigious psychiatrists, each with maximal experience in the assessment of psychological coercion of prisoners of war, testified for the defense. Board certification constituted the most elementary qualification common to each. In the order in which they appeared on the witness stand, they were:

Doctor Louis Jolyon West, qualified on *voir dire* as professor of psychiatry and chairman of the Department of Psychiatry at the University of California, Los Angeles. With specific bearing on the case in which he had been called to testify, West worked with the U.S. military during the Korean War to learn the causes of captured air force pilots' "confessions" in China. Another phase of his work for the military had focused on training pilots to resist coercive persuasion in captivity in future conflicts. Author of *Prisoners of War*, he continued his studies on coercive persuasion after terminating his work with the military. West characterized the method of coercive persuasion as DDD—debility, dependence, and dread. Court appointed, he first met the defendant on 30 September 1975 and examined her again on other occasions. He also had interviewed the Hearst family and the defendant's boyfriend before her kidnapping; he had carefully examined the bank film (automatically activated to record robbery), the SLA tapes (including the defendant's alleged propaganda broadcasts), and various other documents. He had examined the psychological tests administered to the defendant by Singer and had otherwise conferred with her. His opinion was founded on the totality of the data he had thus obtained.

In his interviews West described Patty Hearst's responses in some detail. To him, they resembled unmistakably the "survivor syndrome" he had seen in air force pilots. A striking feature was weeping and loss of memory when questioned about the past. Her IQ score had registered a loss of twenty points from what it was before the kidnapping (from 130 to 109). Testing had indicated no attempt to give a false impression; a trained examiner would pick up any such attempt. Significantly, however, West was not permitted to play a taped interview that he regarded as characteristic of Patty Hearst, in which he had elicited the story of her kidnapping and incarceration only with the greatest difficulties. Her narrative was marked by convulsive weeping and patchy recall of the most serious of her vicissitudes at the hands of her captors.

Sketching in the defendant's history prior to the kidnapping, West saw Patricia's background as rendering her significantly more vulnerable to subsequent events; she had had great freedom in her former life. Upon her kidnapping she was confined in a closet, dependent upon the whim of her captors for so much as toilet privileges. She had not been political at all. Upon her kidnapping she was deluged with accusatory political dogma. In brief, she suffered "fear, pain, physical immobilization, isolation, sleep loss and sensory distortion." She was blindfolded and confined in a small closet for fifty-seven days. In this state of helplessness she was sexually molested and raped. Inevitably she regressed. She became pathologically dependent on her captors, suffered severe weight loss and disruption of bodily functions, and experienced great pain from bruises inflicted upon her hands as a result of having them tied behind her back. Furthermore, she was often threatened with death. Dissociation and regression occurred, causing her to become increasingly suggestible. It was in this state that Patricia Hearst was persuaded to take on the role of Tania, SLA member and revolutionary propagandist. Her assumption was that it was either that or be killed. West saw this as a classic example of coercive persuasion in which debility, dependency, and dread all had been inflicted upon the victim with predictable results.

In this state of mind Patty thought she would be killed by the SLA during the bank robbery if she did not play her part punctiliously as prescribed by her captors. The robbery itself "sealed her fate," followed as it was by the attorney general's statement to the public that she was a common criminal now. The SLA continued to drill her to the point of cadaver obedience, which resulted in her providing covering fire to protect her abductors who were threatened with arrest during their subsequent robbery of Mel's Sporting Goods Store, an action that she thought was expected of her and upon which she thought her survival depended. When finally arrested Patty was a person "without an identity." In West's opinion, she tried for several days to cling to her SLA role, especially as long as Emily Harris (one of the kidnappers) was with her, which is ample explanation for the clenched-fist salute and the urban guerrilla signature.

West concluded his testimony on direct examination by diagnosing Patricia Hearst as a victim of traumatic neurosis, acute and chronic, declaring her present condition as considerably improved. The acceptance of his hypothesis, however, was predicated on the inevitability of the pathological disorientation brought about by the process he described. Such disorientation would be consistent with an insanity defense, which had been repudiated by defense counsel. It was not consistent with the classic rule of duress, previously set forth. Its acceptance, under the circumstances of the case, hinged exclusively upon judicial recognition of coercive persuasion as a full-fledged defense in a case of first impression.

Cross-examination strengthened aspects of West's testimony. Asked as to the SLA tapes, he replied with obvious confidence. He had indeed examined them and concluded that they highlighted the classic end product of psychological coercion. His handling of the cross-examiner rises to the level of model expert testimony, responsive both to the legal and psychological demands of the courtroom and to a level of more sustained and hard-hitting persuasiveness than his testimony on direct:

Q. Doctor, have you examined the tapes, the SLA tapes in this case?

A. You bet I have.

Q. And have you examined what is known as the "Tania interview," that is, Plaintiff's Exhibit No. 93 in this case?

A. Yes, I read that too.

Q. And don't you, in fact, find in both the tapes and the Tania interview her expression of a desire to be considered as an individual and her resentment for not having been considered as an individual previously? Do you or do you not?

A. I certainly don't. I don't find anything of the sort.

Q. You don't find any of those words? You don't remember any of those words in either the tapes or the Tania interview, Plaintiff's Exhibit No. 93?

A. I find the Tania interview and the tapes to be unmitigated propaganda.

Q. How do you know?

A. That's how I find them.

Q. How do you know that?

A. You asked me what my impression is. I would compare them with the propaganda broadcasts that were made by the American Prisoners of War and the statements they signed and the petitions that were circulated all over the world. And some of the phrases are so reminiscent that it sounds like they were copied out of the same book. And those were books that I assure you did not enter into the formation of Patricia Hearst's personality up to the time of her kidnapping, because we checked that pretty carefully.

Q. Doctor, you don't find it significant that one of the characteristics that you just isolated, her desire and search to become an individual and be considered as such, you don't find any similarity of expression between that pre-kidnapping sentiment and what you find here in the Tania interview documents?

A. Not a bit. What she was experiencing was the normal desire of a young person, nineteen years old, to be differentiated and become an individual and her own person. And what's in here is the crassest perversion of the idea of individuality, where a small group of individuals goes around and kills other individuals in order to achieve their political goals. That is not individualism. That is terrorism. And there is nothing in her background to prepare her for that.

On cross-examination West was assailed as lacking in extensive courtroom experience, a matter of monumental irrelevance to his qualifications, and as defense-oriented in his general approach.

Striking at his credibility more seriously, however, was the juxtaposition on cross-examination of a letter that West had sent the Hearsts, along with the admission that he had mentioned defense strategy to Patty Hearst in the course of a psychiatric interview. The following is the text of his letter, as read into the record:

Dear Mr. Hearst: This letter is to express sympathy—sympathy for you and your family, concern for your daughter, Patricia, and the hope that her future may not be so blighted as recent events would seem to threaten. Enclosed are a couple of reprints on the subject of so-called quotes brainwashing end quotes. From them, you can see that considerable work from medical and psychiatric stand—viewpoint has been reported concerning the extent to which single-minded captors can profoundly influence individuals who come under their control. There's much that could be elaborated on the subject; but, at this time, I would make the following points: One, there is a high degree of likelihood that a person whose behavior has been grossly distorted under conditions of captivity or in the highly charged emotional climate of a cohesive small group setting may return to a relatively normal state of mind and behavior. This can occur in a short period of time if appropriate rehabilitation procedures are carried out.

Two, there are historical precedents for special legal consideration for such a victim. Perhaps the most dramatic was provided by the United States Air Force in its rehabilitative rather than punitive treatment of fliers who gave false confessions of germ warfare while in communist captivity during the Korean War. It is true that the Navy had jurisdiction over and prosecuted Colonel Schwable, see enclosure. However, more than half of the Air Force officers who were subjected to the quote full treatment end quote by their communist captors gave false confessions of germ warfare. Furthermore, this behavior was not induced by physical torture, hypnotism, stupifying drugs or conditioning techniques. Instead, socialization and group pressure together with subtler forms of debilitation such as sleep loss sufficed. Technically, the behavior of these men could have been classified as treason. However, they were not held culpable and in fact were not even tried by courts martial for such an offense, primarily because of the circumstances and conditions under which their behavior had been influenced.

If Patricia can be protected from physical harm and returned to her family, she stands a good chance of being restored to a mentally healthy and socially responsible state. Furthermore, in spite of the charges that have been filed against her, I believe powerful medical and legal arguments can be mobilized for her defense. With every good wish, Sincerely Yours.

In turn, based upon West's assessment of the competency of the defendant to stand trial, this strategy for the defense was elicited:

MR. BANCROFT: Q. Now, do you recall having a conversation with the defendant at the beginning of the interview in which you talked with her about the defense strategy in this case?

A. I do remember something about that. I was trying to ascertain whether she really was able to cooperate with her counsel since that was an important factor of why I was examining her, not for a trial, but to ascertain whether she could understand and could cooperate with her counsel.

Q. Do you remember talking to her about a particular defense to this case, a particular kind of defense to this case.

A. Yes, I think I do.

Q. Do you recall telling the defendant shortly after Mr. Johnson left the room that, 'He explained to me something about the strategy they planned for the defense, which was the only one I ever saw?' Do you remember using those words to the defendant?

A. I might have said something like that.

Q. Do you recall the defendant inquiring of you, after your statement to her about having been informed of something of the strategy for the defense in this case, that she inquired of you 'Which is?' asked you the question 'Which is?' and that you then responded, 'Which is to emphasize the involuntary and violent way in which you were dragged out of a relatively normal life with a forcible and terrifying sort of indoctrination that you got, and the tremendous pressure of threats in the beginning to make you subservient and compliant with the leadership of this group so that they would be able to keep control of you. I think myself that is the best explanation for what happened. I haven't heard anything to make me think otherwise. Doesn't that sound logical to you?' Do you recall telling the defendant in that conversation words to that effect?

A. Asking her, yes.

Q. Do you not think, Doctor, that in your subsequent interviews with the defendant when she was forthcoming with information that she just might have picked up from that conversation that you just had with her what kind of information you were looking for?

A. Mr. Bancroft, there wasn't a thing I said in that sentence that wasn't extracted from what the patient already said to Dr. Singer, Lundy and Pollack. I was trying to understand whether she comprehended it in order to ascertain—in order to do my job for the Court, which was to tell whether she was capable, intelligently and rationally, to cooperate with her counsel in order to prepare for a trial.[5]

---

[5]It is elementary case law that in the assessment of competency it "is not enough . . . to find that the defendant is oriented to time and place and has some recollection of events. . . .

Redirect examination in turn was designed to show the voluntary disclosure of the letter to the court before trial and indeed before the appointment of West as an expert witness. It was also used to point out that in mentioning defense strategy West was complying with defense counsel's request and indeed the mandate of the court as appointed witness to sift the competency of the defendant to stand trial with particular care. Such procedural niceties however are likely to have escaped the jury, which had the theme of prejudgment by a defense expert mercilessly pounded home to it in the closing argument of the prosecution:

Now, Dr. West specifically testified that he was—had a celebrated lack of knowledge about forensic psychiatry. Again, I mention this as an illustration of the fact that the defense psychiatrists, including Dr. West, were not skilled in the art of evaluating persons charged with a criminal offense. As a matter of fact, I believe the record shows that in twenty-five years of his academic career he testified in only four criminal cases. And we might add, that in each of those criminal cases, his opinion was favorable to the defendant. And during the time Dr. West was on the stand we heard some rather remarkable testimony. We heard that Dr. West had written a letter to Mr. and Mrs. Hearst on June 3, 1974, long before the apprehension on September 18, 1975. And that letter was read into the record, ladies and gentlemen. And I would like to read you at Page 2200 of the transcript the last two paragraphs of that letter written before Dr. West ever saw Patricia Hearst, or indeed before she came to official attention. 'If Patricia can be protected from physical harm and returned to her family, she stands a good chance of being restored to a mentally healthy and socially responsible state. Furthermore, in spite of the charges that have been filed against her, I believe powerful medical and legal arguments can be mobilized for her defense. With every good wish, Sincerely Yours.' Doesn't that show, ladies and gentlemen, a preconceived notion that Dr. West had about this defendant? Presumably, all he knew about her was what he read in the newspapers, and he had already concluded in June of 1974 that 'Powerful medical and legal arguments can be mobilized for her defense,' and that she could be 'restored to a mentally healthy and socially responsible state.' Restored from what? He had already made his diagnosis, ladies and gentlemen, in June of 1974. I think you have to consider that in evaluating Dr. West's testimony in this case.

Further, Dr. West did fare, it seems to us, to be a witness in this case by exceeding the charter he had been given by this Court. You will

---

The test must be whether . . . [the defendant] has sufficient present ability to consult with his lawyer with a reasonable degree of rational understanding—and whether he has a rational as well as factual understanding of the proceeding against him." Dusky v. United States, 362 U.S. 402 (1960). The better judicial view moreover requires competency examinations to explore the issue of exculpatory mental illness as well. Winn v. United States, 270 F.2d 326 (D.C. Cir. 1959); Calloway v. United States, 270 F.2d 334 (D.C. Cir. 1959).

recall he was originally appointed to determine the defendant's mental state at the time of her apprehension, at the time he examined her, whether she was competent to proceed with the trial, that is, whether she was able to know the nature of the charges against her and cooperate with her attorney in providing a defense. That was all he was asked to do. He went on and he advised the Court, yes, she was competent—or, no, she wasn't—I forget what he said in that regard—went on and said she wandered around in a confused state for a great deal of this time, and that she wasn't, in terms he used, in effect a brainwashed victim. Now, I mention that because it seems to us that he went beyond the charter the Court appointed him for. And I think one has to consider that with respect to what his motivations may have been when he turned in that report. Is it any surprise that, in his October fourth interview with the defendant, less than a third of the way through his interview, that he tells the very subject that he is examining, and from whom he is allegedly trying to—or whom he is allegedly trying to diagnose, without himself influencing her responses, 'He, referring to Al Johnson, explained to me something about the strategy they plan for your defense, which was the only one I ever saw.' And is it any surprise that Dr. West then proceeds to lay out for the defendant, with his rather undisguised Good Housekeeping Seal of Approval, 'which is to emphasize the involuntary and violent way in which you were dragged out of a relatively normal life with a forcible and terrifying sort of indoctrination that you got, and the tremendous pressure of threats in the beginning to make you subservient and compliant'—'and compliant with the leadership of this group so that they would be able to keep control of you. I think myself that is the best explanation of what happened. I haven't heard anything to make me think otherwise.' Then later we learn that he put this proposition to Miss Hearst: 'You are relatively suggestible. I would say if sensitized, easily deceived, especially if dependent on someone. You were so successfully coerced.'

What he has done, you see, ladies and gentlemen, was to have laid out a road map for the term concerning brainwashing and mind control that he later gave in this case. He laid out that road map to the defendant when he was examining her. One has only to question whether he was asking the witness—whether he was evaluating the defendant or whether he was telling the defendant.

West's credentials and expertise in the area of coercive persuasion were impressive. His comparison of the techniques used in inducing POWs to "confess" false war crimes to the techniques used by the SLA to induce Patricia to make similarly phrased confessions was effective as read or heard by any rational observer. The symptoms of POWs—anxiety, depression, apathy—were sufficiently similar to those observed in the case at bar to be credible and compellingly persuasive. Additionally, in his evocation of the violent and brutal change in her life and the suffering she underwent at the hands of her captors, West, at this stage of his testimony, could be viewed as arousing significant sympathy for the defendant. Directed at an insanity defense, based upon his demonstration of the total extinction of the defendant's judgment and ability to adhere to the right, his testimony would not have been rationally refutable in my judgment. Alas, the choice of the defense was not his.

The second witness for the defense was Doctor Martin Theodore Orne from the University of Pennsylvania. A psychiatrist as well as a psychologist, he had had significant experience as an air force consultant in preparing service personnel to resist coercive persuasion. Orne testified on direct examination that there was no truly effective way to resist the continuing inroads of coercive persuasion. His work with the air force, therefore, was to strengthen the resistance of the individual to the point of a few extra days. He had seen experienced officers break down easily in simulated training programs.

Orne had been contacted by the defense in this trial. Before agreeing to testify, however, he wanted to make sure Patricia was not simulating. He had known Singer as a psychological expert and so he had first discussed the psychological tests with her; he had subsequently interviewed Patricia to determine whether she was simulating. The patient was still troubled at the time and could not talk about such traumatic events as her incarceration in a closet. She did not pick up on cues. Her condition was graphically and movingly portrayed:

> Q. Are you able to tell us based on your recollection of your first visit what condition you found her in especially with respect to the condition that had been described of an earlier day?
>
> A. I found that she was still quite troubled, quite—had a good deal of difficulty with memory and there I was particularly concerned, memory for what, because again of my concern for simulation. And, I wanted to distinguish between two major hypotheses before kind of going any further. And so, I went after kind of what it was that she didn't remember and was surprised, for example, to find that there were segments of time before she was kidnapped that were just gone for no apparent obvious reasons. And, there was what Dr. West actually called a patchy amnesia, though at the time I didn't call it that. I was just struck with amnesias for various periods of time which didn't make any sense from the point of view of being self-serving.
>
> Q. Did you, in that first interview, make efforts to determine for yourself whether anybody had been assisting her in concocting a story that would be helpful?
>
> A. Well, I was concerned about that, but I didn't ask her. Instead, I tried to use the kind of procedures which we found effective in some of our laboratory studies and that is to try to, in an interview, imply subtly what might be good answers which, typically, someone trying to play a role would pick up on because they would make sense, and found really very much to my surprise that this girl felt she was very troubled and would be trying to relate the events that had transpired, especially things about the closet. It was just impossible for her to talk about the closet, but there was no, in no way she just didn't pick up on cues. It's

really quite remarkable. Normally, I would be very upset at having heard, for example, Dr. West's comment, you know, that, as to her, the nature of her defense, for example. The thing is that this, Miss Hearst really simply didn't lie or—that's not so strange.

Patricia cooperated with all interviews although in intense anguish, evidenced by heavy weeping over many answers. Orne saw her as a person who responded to individuals rather than ideas. The SLA tapes, however, were in striking contrast. They represented the verbiage of someone who thinks primarily in terms of abstractions and not individuals. Orne had found no evidence that Patricia felt political hostility toward her parents. He thought that even if such hostility existed she would not have expressed it as she had done on the tapes. He was struck by the difference in style of the syntax on tape compared with Patricia's normal speech patterns, characterized as they were by a deceptively simple upper-class word use. Propaganda tapes attributed to Patricia on the other hand were seen by the witness as characteristic of the style of Chinese propaganda broadcasts at the time of the Korean War.

Cross-examination left Orne's testimony essentially unimpaired. Like West, he was assailed as an academician, devoid of meaningful forensic experience. The balance of his cross-examination seemed restricted to attempting to score points by eliciting admissions that the defendant had made some "self-serving" statements in the course of her psychiatric interviews and that the inference should be drawn that such interviews were suspect. The integrity of Orne's testimony stayed intact:

> Q. Is there anything else you want to tell us, Doctor Orne? My question was, so you have it in mind, what cues did you give to the defendant that would have elicited answers with respect to the events at issue that were inconsistent—that would have been inconsistent with the narration to Dr. West by the defendant? That was my question.
>
> A. I looked for a variety of examples, and I looked for ways, by the way in which I asked her about what happened to her, about the way she was treated, which would have facilitated openings.
>
> Q. Did you find any inconsistencies?
>
> A. I found no substantive inconsistencies that I could put my finger on. As I testified earlier, this surprised me.
>
> Q. Didn't that indicate to you, Doctor, at all that the defendant might be telling you the same story she had told Dr. West, having previously been led to believe that that was a believable story?
>
> A. It's entirely possible, but for that she would have had to be not only a superb actress, but she would have had to have an incredibly good memory, neither of which I saw evidence for.
>
> Q. You heard Dr. West's testimony that her recounting to him was less than complete. He attributed that to certain reasons. So it wouldn't have taken an awful lot of effort, would it, to make essentially the same recounting?
>
> A. Well, I believe it's the sort of thing which people find very

difficult. In a laboratory when we ask somebody to simulate a simple role with two people, kind of one after the other, they have great trouble keeping it stable.

Q. There wasn't a whole lot of detail, was there, in the recounting given to Dr. West?

A. There was a good deal of detail. There was many, many hours of interviewing, apparently.

Q. What kind of detail would you have expected to see some difference in the recounting where you did not see any difference?

A. In the quality of embroidery. When you give somebody an ample opportunity to expand on something, which would be making yourself look less bad—I mean, it's terribly important for all of us to look good.

Q. Because there was no, as you put it, increased embroidery, you therefore viewed that as an indication that the defendant was not simulating?

A. No. That was one of—

Q. One.

A. Of a large number of things.

Q. And another thing that you looked at to indicate the defendant wasn't simulating was that she was forthcoming with details that she had not previously told Doctor West?

A. That there seemed to be some increased recall, yes.

Q. Well, if when she tells you an additional fact, that doesn't indicate to you that she's simulating and when she tells you the same facts and that doesn't indicate that she's simulating, what kind of factual accounting would have indicated that she was simulating?

A. If the facts that she tells me—if, for example, on the situation with Mr. Wolfe, she had simply played it for what it was worth and that she didn't do, she didn't play it for any small part of what it was worth.

Q. Well, that depends upon what it really was worth, doesn't it, Doctor?

A. Yes.

Perhaps the most damaging part of the cross-examination elicited the admission that Orne had not inquired about the defendant's activities between September 1974 and September 1975, a period following the bank robbery and marked, it was claimed by the prosecution, with opportunities for escape and with dramatic episodes of adherence to the "cause":

I was interested in having her recounting the most . . . significant events. I had a limited period of time with Miss Hearst, not because of her but because of myself. I was here for a three-day period. I found it very difficult in terms of—on me difficult to interview Miss Hearst because she was so much suffering. And, I found it uncomfortable and so, I felt it was only possible to interview her for so much time and I focused on the issues which struck me as most crucial.

Moreover, Orne's presentation had highlighted the inconsistency of the two legal defenses rigidly maintained by counsel throughout the case. He had pictured Patricia's disturbance far too convincingly to support the "well-founded apprehension of death," and he too had laid the foundation for an insanity defense, whatever its formulation, if it had been elected by the defense.

The last defense witness, Doctor Robert Jay Lifton, professor of psychiatry at Yale, spoke from a wealth of experience unmatched by any witness at the trial. He had worked with returning POWs in 1953 and conducted research on Chinese Communist thought reform in 1954 and 1955 by interviewing people in Hong Kong who had been in Chinese prisons, interviewing them again three and one-half years later. He also had studied coercive persuasion in U.S. religious cults. In addition to numerous other authoritative treatises, Lifton was the author of two books based upon his studies of Chinese thought reform. He testified that he had first been contacted by Stephen Weed before Patricia's arrest. Weed had wanted his opinion as to whether she might have undergone the same experiences as those of Chinese prisoners described in Lifton's works. He told Weed no definite answer was possible until details of Patricia's experience were available, but that the tapes indicated some coercive process.

Lifton described coercive persuasion, in a setting of imprisonment, as comprising common features: 1) complete control of communication to the victim; 2) threats, assaults upon identity, and humiliation; 3) manipulation of the victim's guilt by showing his responsibility for his own plight; 4) a self-betrayal confession process; 5) leniency, relief of pressure, which in turn opens a path for survival; and 6) a program of thought reform presented for the prisoner to learn in his quest for survival.[6] Lifton further described common symptoms that persisted after the victim's release: 1) a last show of compliance to former captors; 2) extreme confusion and anxiety; 3) bodily fears and complaints; and 4) improvement over time.

Patty Hearst's treatment by her captors was lucidly shown to be substantially identical with the model form of coercive persuasion outlined by Lifton:

> . . . when kidnapped and taken to an apartment, she felt herself in an environment that was totally controlled and, more than that, an environment that had achieved total knowledge or omniscience over her, her family, her life. I would emphasize the importance of that total control, especially during the early months, the early phases, because, as I said earlier, the sense of being totally controlled by one's captors extends later on and has a lot to do with why she was eventually so terrified by the Harrises and why she had so much difficulty in extricating herself from them and getting in touch with her friends or her family. As far as

---

[6]For further elaboration of Lifton's theoretical model see R. J. Lifton, *Thought Reform and the Psychology of Totalism* (1961).

the second principle, the assaults upon the self, or identity, they were direct and immediate for Patricia Hearst. She was put through a process of forcible interrogation, but if you compare her experience with the one I just described for a Chinese prison, it was both similar and different. It was similar in that she was also dehumanized, living in a closet; the second closet, I understand, was twenty inches by five and a half feet or something like that. It's a very small area in which to exist. She told me, and I quote her now, 'I felt like a thing in the closet.' That's just a very simple expression of total dehumanization under those assaults.

Now, in some ways, one could say some of the people I interviewed in Hong Kong underwent much worse experiences than Patricia Hearst. Some have had their backs broken or they received disabling injuries, some had long periods of sleep deprivation or interrogation. On the other hand, her experience was much worse than those people I interviewed. Nobody I interviewed was alone in a closet for sixty days, fifty-seven days, whatever it was. People at least existed in bigger cells and, after awhile with other people. Nobody, among the people who went through thought reform as I studied it in Hong Kong, had been blindfolded for fifty-seven days. In those ways, she experienced very, very vividly and in a way that was absolutely crucial for everything that happened to her those assaults upon the self in that process of dehumanization, and of course, she was told, 'You are a criminal. You are an enemy of the people. . . .'

Now, in terms of guilt and blame, she was said to be, by them, totally responsible for her plight. Now, the questions come up did she feel guilt because she was a Hearst? Well, sure. She did feel guilt. She felt a little bit uneasy about being a Hearst as has come out, but you know, she also felt the guilt that you and I would have felt if we were in that closet being accused in that way because all of us have a store of guilt. That is to do, as I said before, with transgressions, disobediences that we have all had as a part of growing up, conflicts with parents who were, after all, our first trainers, and the sense of conscience and guilt which we have which can then be immobilized and used for malignant or destructive or negative purposes, and that's why there is also a sense of guilt, and I am speaking of psychological guilt. I mean the psychological capacity to experience one as bad or wrong and that is a more important basic kind of a human guilt they could draw upon than the guilt of being a Hearst or anything else. And that's why everybody who gets into that process is susceptible to that kind of manipulation of guilt.

In terms of the extraction of the confession, she told me—and incidentally, she is only coming to understand a little bit of this, she hasn't really fully understood at all what's happened to her and she is now beginning to have some sense just in a very beginning way some of these things—she told me that she began to confess to everything and she began to tell them all kinds of things that weren't true. It was the typical response that I mentioned before of a captive trying desperately to satisfy one's captors when they would not be satisfied. And she made her confessions in the form of the tapes, the propaganda tapes that were released with all the canned language that's characteristic of thought reform, and struggling to find the right phrases when they let her use her own phrases, say, the first when they began to provide the phrases for her, struggling to make them as realistic or as convincing as possible. Self-betrayal or the fourth pattern I mentioned, well, the tapes themselves, especially dehumanization of her family under that coercion, are the beginning of a self-betrayal. It's fundamental, you attack your family. It's done routinely in coercive persuasion. 'Pig Hearsts,' referring to her father as Adolph in words supplied to her and the self-betrayal process was well underway early on in her captivity. The ultimate act of self-betrayal is the coerced bank robbery. Once she did that and was in that bank robbery, she could be convinced in a very understandable way that she had no chance to return, that she had burned her bridges. That's what self-betrayal is in everyday language. It's the forcing of the victim to burn his bridges. And of course the process was enhanced by the unfortunate statement by the then Attorney General that she was 'A common criminal,' or something to that effect. But the bank robbery, as she was coerced into doing, in my judgment, was the ultimate act of self-betrayal. . . .

After that, the embrace of the new role and here I would distinguish between compliance and ideological or political conversion. By and large, what she underwent was the process of absolute compliance, but in my judgment, and I questioned her closely about this, it's a subject that I've worked on and am much interested in, virtually no ideological conversion and very limited ideological influence. But the compliance was absolute. She was at a psychological state where she would do anything that was required of her or that she perceived to be required of her.

Cross-examination again harped on the academic preoccupation of Lifton, his relative inexperience in forensic matters as a witness (he admitted never having interviewed fugitives in felony cases nor working in any assessment of criminal responsibility before this case), and his alleged defense orientation (Lifton admitted testifying for the defense in the trial of the Camden 28 and conducting "rap sessions" with Vietnam veterans).

The attack upon Lifton took on a primitive and crudely aggressive note, one thoroughly familiar to defense lawyers. Accused of championing a lack of objectivity in advocacy research, he was asked if he had not endorsed "an empathetic relationship" with the subject studied. He replied, appropriately for the classroom but perhaps without the elaboration called for by the courtroom arena, that "that was a fundamental principle of psychiatric work." His harassment at the hands of the prosecutor became so pronounced as to prod Lifton into the only careless response in his testimony—his endorsement as a doctor of the views of Circuit Judge Bazelon in matters of courtroom testimony, a view that however appropriate may have cost Lifton some jury sympathy for touching matters outside his medical expertise.[7] Beyond that

[7]For example, see Durham v. United States, 214 F.2d 862, 876 (D.C. Cir. 1954); Carter v. United States, 252 F.2d 608, 616–617 (D.C. Cir. 1957). The classic case in which Judge

his testimony appeared weakened, however slightly, by the fact that although his examinations were intensive (extending over fifteen hours of interviews), he had entered the case barely a month before trial and was thus shown to be reconstructing the scenario of the defendant's ordeal at some distance in time.

The testimony of all the psychiatric experts for the defense saw the propaganda tapes of the SLA broadcasts as part of an enforced process of self-betrayal, thus constituting some of the most damaging evidence against the defendant. As expressed by Lifton, some of these tapes, made by Patricia Hearst barely two weeks before the Hibernia Bank robbery and which appeared without further analysis to reflect her free and enthusiastic conversion to the cause, were "the imposed burning of bridges through not only self-denunciation but denunciation of family, friends, and former associates . . . with most of the words provided by her captors."[8]

Significantly, only one defense expert was capable of detailed scientific demonstration that the style, word use, and idea content of the propaganda broadcasts were grotesquely at variance from those communications characteristic of Patricia Hearst both before and after her abduction. Only that same expert, by reason of her training and experience in psycholinguistics, over and above that in general clinical psychology, could demonstrate that the long pauses and the type of inflection used and relied on by the broadcaster were more suggestive of responses to coercion than free choice. But that expert—Margaret Thaler Singer—was not allowed to testify before the jury. Her testimony, offered in evidence outside the hearing of the jury, was rejected by the Court as without precedent and not relevant to the issue of intent.

As offered in the Hearst trial, Singer's testimony clearly buttressed the necessary legal contention of continuing psychological coercion (a matter in no way inconsistent with the probably more productive claim of exculpatory mental illness, not expounded in the case, though the two are obviously not mutually exclusive).[9] The problem was not one of Singer's testimonial credibility but one of the adequacy of the legal support given her presentation by defense counsel. Thus, defense counsel was unable to cite more than one

---

Bazelon secured a court majority to warn against the use of "conclusory labels" and endorse the use of expert "explanation of the disease and its dynamics," in expanding the theme of the Carter case, was Washington v. United States, 390 F.2d 4444 (D.C. Cir. 1967).

All the defense witnesses were eloquent in the exposition of both the legal and scientific aspects of the Bazelonian approach as they testified. An analysis of the Hearst case and the psychiatric testimony for the defense seems to vindicate the Durham view of Bazelonian jurisprudence significantly after its demise. One might go further and say that the defense psychiatrists almost won the case with little assistance from legal counsel.

[8]R. J. Lifton, "On the Hearst Trial," *New York Times*, 16 April 1978.

[9]See Arens and Meadow, "Psycholinguistics and the Confession Dilemma," *Columbia Law Review* 56 (1956): 19.

case in which such testimony was received. Other cases in which psycholinguistics had been endorsed as a vital tool of fact-finding were not brought to the attention of the Court.[10] Nor was defense counsel prepared to claim that the testimony of Singer bore on the defendant's intent, that is, the freedom or lack of freedom with which Patricia had acted during the critical periods and hence vital to any assessment of duress or coercion as a defense.

After the exclusion of Singer's testimony, moreover, defense counsel did not recall Orne who had worked closely with Singer and who could have qualified as a psycholinguist on his own authority and might well have furnished much of her excluded testimony on his own. Psychiatrists without significant psycholinguistic backgrounds had previously secured the admissibility of their testimony on psycholinguistic issues in the federal courts.[11]

Why, then, the verdict of guilty? The repudiation of the insanity defense, in which the idiosyncratic vulnerability of Patricia Hearst to group pressure could have been validly and cogently explored as legally relevant and indeed compelling, lies at the heart of the guilty verdict. The jury faced two logically and psychologically irreconcilable claims to sustain the defense as presented by James Bailey. The theory of duress, founded on the well-grounded apprehension of the reasonable person making a sound judgment that the perpetration of a noncapital crime is the only means of escaping the imminent and direct threat of death or serious bodily injury, crumbled irreversibly as the defense presented the case of the traumatized Patricia retreating into the fantasy land of Tania, the urban guerrilla, under the theory of coercive persuasion.

Despite this asymmetry in defense theory, the jury seems to have come within an inch of acquittal as a sympathy verdict, unpersuaded by the legal argument but clearly moved by the suffering of the young girl so convincingly portrayed by the defense psychiatrists. In the light of the overwhelmingly persuasive expert testimony of Doctors West, Orne, and Lifton, any positive effects enjoyed by the prosecution "psychiatric" testimony is in part attributable to the fact that no legal effort was made to secure the exclusion of all of Fort's testimony as that of an individual who, by his own admission, lacked the requisite psychiatric qualifications to assess intent or state of mind, and of so much of Kozol's testimony as represented the celebrated "doctor's version of a legal opinion." The case cried for rebuttal testimony in which the inane assertions that anyone with protracted exposure to criminal defendants, for example, a social worker or a journalist, could testify upon the exquisitely difficult issue of *mens rea*, would be authoritatively repudiated

---

[10]See State v. Thompson, 338P. 2d 319, 323–324 (Wash. S. Ct., 1959); State v. Gallagher, 97 Ariz. 1, 397P. 2d 241, 245 (1964); United States v. Haygood, Criminal Action No. 748–60 (D.D.C. 1960). See also Arens and Meadow, "Psycholinguistics and the Confession Dilemma."

[11]For example, see United States v. Haygood.

by leaders of the American behavioral sciences not connected with the case. What would have happened if the president of the American Psychiatric Association had been subpoenaed to testify as to the methodology and plausibility of the Fort-Kozol work product, as exemplified by the transcript of their testimony?

However, these are afterthoughts. Kozol and Fort's testimony remained unrebutted. The government gloried in their testimony and attempted to persuade the jury that it had been exposed to the best in forensic methodology when Fort and Kozol testified and the worst when it heard the defense experts. Browning's closing statement is worth partial quotation, as it is characteristic of the virulence and crudity of prosecution oratory in many cases in which a psychiatric issue is raised. As he put it,

> I want to ask you to bear in mind—and I am speaking generally with respect to psychiatric testimony now that the doctors who were called by the defense in this case had basically no experience in examining persons who are charged with criminal offenses, as were Doctors Fort and Kozol. You will recall the defense, I think everyone of them referred to the defendant as "patient." Most of these Doctors who were not trained in evaluating persons charged with criminal offenses tend to accept everything that the person tells you. . . . Secondly, I think it is clear that most of the psychiatric experts called by the defense, if not all three of them, are basically literary people. In other words, they are academicians, they are not forensic psychiatrists. They are apt to find in any subject whom they examine a varying degree of the particular malady or the particular psychiatric problem that is found in that branch of psychiatry that they happen to specialize in, that they teach and write about . . . these people . . . are not well-founded in the evaluations of persons charged with criminal offenses. . . .

It is essential to observe at this stage that no request was made by the defense for a judicial instruction to the jury that courtroom experience was wholly irrelevant to the persuasiveness of the expert. And who can say that this omission was a matter of small consequence?

The question must be raised as to whether, given the tempestuous prosecutorial appeal to convict in the name of love of country and the plain unvarnished facts of the case as against the defense presentation of a complex and unusual ordeal, the jury was not faced with a uniquely unendurable assault on its own sensibilities. Compelling and unceasing horror—and this is a tale of it—may have been beyond the psychological power of the jury to sift, analyze, and understand, particularly when a courtroom was transformed into an arena by the one-sided reliance of the prosecution on the worst features of the adversarial process.

Beyond this, however, the emotional acceptance of a defense, founded on the assumption of the collapse of intellectual and emotional resistance under the intensive pressure of a group viewed instinctively as "the enemy," required the capacity on the part of the fact-finders to say of Patricia Hearst's submission to such pressure: "There, but for the grace of God, go I." Such empathy, inhibited by the disturbing need to contemplate the frailty of one's own mind under such circumstances,[12] was further rendered difficult in a trial as negatively charged against the defendant as the instant and litigated in the shadow of the attorney general's prejudgment that "she is just a common criminal."

In conclusion, however, the defense did not founder on a lack of psychiatric credibility but on the internal and legally created conflicts in the twin theories on which the defense chose to rest.

---

[12]Would anxieties obstructive of the defense of coercive persuasion have proved equally obstructive of the insanity defense as here outlined and suggested? As seen through the experience of this trial lawyer, the answer is that the juror's anxieties over recognizing the potential frailty of his own mind would no doubt have been troublesome but in no sense prohibitive of the successful assertion of an insanity defense. For in asserting the insanity of the defendant, the defense will have seriously reduced the juror's anxieties, which reached peak intensity at the sight of a "normal" defendant—like the juror—with the difference that notwithstanding such substantially identical normalcy with the jurors, she (Miss Hearst) reacted to the stress involved by severely delinquent behavior. See Lifton, "On the Hearst Trial."

An insanity defense, in contrast, is predicated upon the assumption of an "abnormal" defendant, shielded by exculpatory mental illness (which the jurors are less likely to view as something to which they themselves may fall victim) under traditional doctrine. Significantly, this doctrine would be presented, unclouded by logical conflict between rules, as exemplified by those of duress and psychological coercion, and acquittal would be facilitated by the gulf that the stereotype of the insane invites between juror and defendant. The consequent avoidance of the agonizing decision making by the individual juror of whether he could or would have resisted the pressures to which Miss Hearst had succumbed would have been avoided to a greater extent. The method may be criticized as lacking in a methodology calculated to distill the truth at all relevant levels. But this unfortunately is not what our courts are for. See J. Frank, *Courts on Trial* (1950). The criticism would have evaporated with the acquittal of the maiden in distress, followed none too slowly by her restoration to normal civic freedom.

The Psychiatrist in the Legal Process:
Caught in the Seamless Web*

JOEL F. HENNING

Much, but by no means all, of the public scorn heaped upon lawyers and the courts is systemic. In other words, lawyers are suspect by definition. Their arguments are based on advocacy rather than personal conviction. They are thought to be amoral technicians on behalf of their clients. Lawyers are sanctioned in the conduct of their clients' affairs to do things that would not be appropriate in another context: defend the "guilty" or exploit legal process to disinherit deserving children and conceal important facts, as in the notorious case of the lawyers in upstate New York who concealed knowledge of a woman's death from her father. Lawyers open tax loopholes, defend dangerous and unsafe products, and even assist Nazis in delivering their inflammatory and poisonous propaganda to Jewish survivors of Hitler's atrocities. On cross-examination, they ruthlessly rend the expert testimony of psychiatrists in the course of trials in which the rules often seem to prohibit encountering the essential facts. And, unfortunately for lawyers seeking to be loved, they cannot shirk such responsibilities. In many instances to do so would violate the Code of Professional Responsibility.

Doctors, on the other hand, have it relatively easy. Lawyers defend the guilty; doctors cure the sick. Lawyers create and sustain conflict; doctors ease the body's pain and soothe the troubled mind. Lawyers learn their craft from books and are taught to be amoral advocates of everyone's cause, while doctors learn their craft at the patient's bedside and are taught to relate intimately to his or her needs.

These superficial comparisons between the two professions will be extended within this analysis. Particular emphasis is placed on the psychiatrist's role in the legal process and the problems attendant upon this role. Finally, a pragmatic proposal is offered for mitigating these problems by establishing a variable scale of psychiatric involvement in the judicial process, which inversely correlate to the moral gravity of the acts at issue.

---

*The original version of this paper was prepared for delivery at the conference entitled "Psychiatry and the Law: Reaching for a Consensus," held in Chicago on 12–13 October 1979 under the sponsorship of the University of Chicago Medical Center Department of Psychiatry and the Institute of Social and Behavioral Pathology.

Law and psychiatry are both systems dealing with truth seeking and deviance. Both have similar objectives: to establish the truth in order to restore order, to temper behavior so that it is consistent with social order. Both may attempt rehabilitation, and they need each other when that rehabilitation is to be attempted in involuntary circumstances. Both systems deal with individuals, but it could be said that law deals with the relationship of the individual with his external world and psychiatry with the individual's internal world. One could almost say that the two systems reflect the dual nature of our Judeo-Christian concept of God—as father (psychiatrist) and as king (law maker and law enforcer). The problem is that these authority systems occasionally can be in conflict. Most importantly, there are certain kinds of deviant behavior that the public does not allow the father to handle but insists on elevating them to matters for official state action.

The law depends on accurate and precise verbalization of direct evidence. From its experts, who are the only witnesses allowed to testify beyond the facts of a matter as known personally to them, the law is desperate for precise formulations of cognitive capability: who is responsible for criminal acts, who is competent to stand trial, marry, raise children, and bequeath property. Yet the rules of evidence restrict the extent to which psychiatrists can describe in depth the individuality of the patient. As the late Professor Karl Llewelyn said, "the actual trial of fact must be before a tribunal artificially sterilized of the facts, under a procedure which rigidly eliminates a great deal of evidence. . . ."

One of the principal tensions that psychiatrists feel in the legal process is their inability to express "negative capability," a term used by Keats, if not invented by him. In a letter to his brothers George and Tom in December 1817, he described negative capability as "when man is capable of being in uncertainties, mysteries, doubts, without any irritable reaching after fact and reason." In the psychiatric context, negative capability involves the ability of the psychiatrist to contemplate with equanimity questions to which there may be no answers, at least no precise answers of the kind that are admissible in court.

Mystery has no place in court. Psychiatrists are respected not only for being scientists but also for acknowledging the limits of their science and yielding to the unknowable. In a letter to Arnold Zweig in 1932, Freud said "the only things we can be sure of are our feelings of the moment!" Freud talked about two realities, the "inner" and the "outer." The sole aim of psychoanalysis, he stated, "is the enhanced harmony of the ego, which is expected successfully to mediate between the claims of the instinctual life (the 'id') and those of the external world; thus between inner and outer reality." Unfortunately, the law cannot deal with inner reality. It cannot see it, quantify it, or evaluate it. Negative capability, inner reality—these qualities do not stand up well under hostile cross-examination. Nor can the public always understand the place of inner reality in determining guilt or innocence of the mentally diseased.

These tensions are the inevitable result of conflicts between the objectives of our judicial system—to establish fault and apply a remedy—and psychiatry—to identify symptoms and relieve them. And yet, in practice, the conflicts seem to be resolved to a surprising extent. A person found guilty of a crime or acquitted by reason of mental illness is likely to find himself in a large public institution with little privacy, inadequate psychiatric care, and inadequate access to legal services in the protection of his remaining rights. Professor David Levine of the University of Chicago collected data recently from a large public mental hospital in the United States.[1] He discovered that 70 percent of the patients were there mainly because they had committed acts that would be deemed illegal if the element of criminal "intent" could have been proven. He also found a significant correlation between how much time the patient spent in that hospital and how much would have been spent in prison. Incidentally, he collected similar data from a large mental hospital in Great Britain, which showed the same association between time spent involuntarily in the hospital and the degree of criminality.

Most importantly to this discussion, Levine discovered that a person's attitudes toward mental illness are part of a general orientation to social issues rather than a narrow function of his concept of mental illness. That is, the public will tolerate psychiatric interventions in the justice system so long as they do not result in significant deviations from the public conception of justice. For example, if a murderer, acquitted by reason of mental disease or defect, spends as much or more time involuntarily committed to a mental institution than in prison, the public is content.

Two interesting trends should be reviewed before returning to the tension created by psychiatric interventions in the public perception of justice. The first involves enlargement of the narrow, cognitive exceptions from criminal liability set out in the classic McNaughtan rules. Under the Durham rule[2] and other modern formulations, including the Model Penal Code of the American Law Institute,[3] psychiatric evidence of emotional as well as cognitive disturbances is admissible in many jurisdictions. Under these modern formulations, psychiatric witnesses play a larger and, at least arguably, more realistic role in informing the court about the mental and emotional state of the defendant. The theory of diminished responsibility, adopted by a number of jurisdictions,[4]

---

[1]David Levine, "Crime, Mental Illness, and Political Dissent," in *Law, Justice and the Individual in Society*, ed. Tapp and Levine (New York: Holt, Rinehart & Winston, 1977), pp. 224–38.

[2]Durham v. U.S., 214 F.2d 862 (D.C. Cir. 1954).

[3]ALI Model Penal Code, sec. 402(1), official draft (1962).

[4]For example, People v. Goedecke, 65 Cal Id 850, 423 P.2d 777 (1967).

also broadens the involvement of the psychiatrist in criminal matters by allowing testimony with regard to abnormal mental conditions that may not constitute legal insanity but may suggest that a lesser degree of the crime at issue was in fact committed.

Second, the courts and legislatures in many jurisdictions seem to be recognizing the right or responsibility of the psychiatrist to participate more broadly in such proceedings. At the same time they are also recognizing the due process rights of prisoners and patients. Thus, Levine's data may soon be obsolete in that involuntary commitment of the defendant held legally insane now requires a full-blown hearing with due process afforded, as in the case of any other person.[5] Once committed involuntarily, a person no longer may be held unless actual treatment is provided.[6] And the patient is entitled to release in many jurisdictions when he no longer exhibits the symptoms that led initially to commitment.[7]

These trends are not inconsistent. Expert testimony now can inform the courts on a deeper and more subtle range of psychiatric issues concerning the appropriate disposition of criminal cases. Regardless of whether the defendant ends up in prison or in a hospital, it is appropriate to demand that the state provide the remedy ordered by the court. The problem is that the system does not appear to be working, and perhaps it cannot work universally with regard to all "perpetrators," as the police now call their prisoners.

Events in California, New York, and Illinois suggest that liberalizing the traditional constraints on psychiatric involvement in certain cases may cause an across-the-board return to the McNaughtan era. In California, where evidence of diminished mental capacity can be introduced to establish the absence of criminal intent, former City Supervisor Dan White was tried for first-degree murder of the mayor and a city supervisor. He was convicted of "voluntary manslaughter," with the jury having heard evidence that included the so-called "Twinkie Defense," psychiatric testimony suggesting that White's inordinate consumption of sugary junk food led to an imbalanced mental condition. A riot followed in which considerable damage to persons and property resulted, and two bills were promptly introduced into the state legislature that would substantially reduce use of the diminished capacity defense and restore the McNaughtan test.

In New York on Thanksgiving Day 1976, policeman Robert Torsney shot a youngster at point-blank range at an east New York housing project. The shooting was apparently unprovoked and occurred when the boy was on his way home after walking his grandmother to a bus stop. Indicted for murder, Torsney was acquitted in fall 1977 by reason of insanity. He was committed the same day but released after a hearing in which he was held to be "symptom

---

[5]Jackson v. Indiana, 405 U.S. 715 (1972).
[6]O'Connor v. Donaldson, U.S. Supt. (1975).
[7]For example, Jackson v. Indiana.

Psychiatry and the Supreme Court*

ALAN A. STONE

Among the nightmarish paintings of the fifteenth-century Dutch artist Hieronymus Bosch is one called "The Ship of Fools." It portrays a strange assortment of people in peculiar attitudes who appear oblivious to their perilous situation as they seemingly drift out to sea. Bosch's iconography has never been fully understood or interpreted, but it is generally accepted that he intended, at least at one level, to depict the medieval version of civil commitment: expel the insane from the community. There are many who would assert that twentieth-century American practices have improved very little on the medieval metaphor "ship of fools," and there is doubtless some truth in that assertion. Bosch was not the only one to memorialize the ship of fools. In the late fifteenth century it had become a favorite subject of art and literature. Why? Michel Foucault writes in his remarkable book *Madness and Civilization*[1] that for Bosch and other artists of that time the ship of fools had become a profound and significant symbol.

The religious imagination of Europe had inspired in many the conviction that the world would come to an end in 1500. Stark symbols of death evoking the apocalyptic end of man had been a dominant theme in art until, according to Foucault, they succumbed to the ironic symbol of madness: "It is the tide of madness, its secret invasion, that shows that the world is near its final catastrophe; it is man's insanity that invokes and makes necessary the world's end."

Foucault's interpretation may or may not be valid, but it is clear that throughout the centuries madness and the fate of the mad have served as an amplifying mirror in which the artist or the social critic has seen a vision of the human condition and the ailments of the entire society. Consider Shakespeare's *King Lear*, Dostoevski's *The Possessed*, and Balzac's *Louis Lambert*. In present-day literature Ken Kesey's *One Flew Over the Cuckoo's Nest* is meant to describe as much about the world today as it does about state mental

---

*The original version of this paper was prepared for delivery at the conference entitled "Psychiatry and the Law: Reaching for a Consensus," held in Chicago on 12–13 October 1979 under the sponsorship of the University of Chicago Medical Center Department of Psychiatry and the Institute of Social and Behavioral Pathology.

[1] Michel Foucault, *Madness and Civilization: A History of Insanity in the Age of Reason*, trans. Richard Howard (1965; reprint ed., New York: Vintage Books, 1973).

hospitals. Each artist and social critic who depicts madness and madhouses brings to the task his own ideology. Foucault sees the insane asylums populated by the "underclass of society." Thomas Szasz finds there the victims of the "psychiatric inquisition." For R. D. Laing and similar visionaries of the 1960s, it seemed that the world was insane and only those in the madhouses had fully realized it. But most important is the ideology of the legal activists who consider mental illness a "suspect classification" and those stigmatized as mentally ill an oppressed minority. The struggle for their rights is the last major battleground of the Civil Rights Movement for these activist lawyers, and the statutes authorizing involuntary confinement of the mentally ill are the legal instrument that implements our modern version of the medieval practice of the ship of fools.

Although the distinctive aspects of the ideologies of Foucault, Szasz, and the civil rights lawyers have only been touched upon, the ship of fools conveys their common theme. For all of them, to be labeled mentally ill is to be unfairly stigmatized, to be involuntarily confined is to be removed from society and abandoned, to be treated involuntarily is to be mistreated. The motivating vision inspiring much of the constitutional litigation on behalf of mental patients has been stigma, abandonment, mistreatment, the patient as a victim. One has only to recall the titles of texts cited as authority in this litigation to confront this vision: *Prisoners of Psychiatry, The Manufacture of Madness, On Being Sane in Insane Places, The Myth of Mental Illness, The Right To Be Different.* Where there are victims there must be persecutors, and as these titles suggest the finger of guilt has been pointed at psychiatry.

This ideological history that portrays the patient as a victim of psychiatry is as crucial as any theory of due process or equal protection to our understanding of the cases that have made their way into the Supreme Court. The cases discussed here, which reflect the relationship between psychiatry and the Supreme Court, are *O'Connor* v. *Donaldson*,[2] *Addington* v. *Texas*,[3] and *Parham* v. *J. L. & J. R.*, which was consolidated with *Bartley* v. *Kremens*.[4] All involve patients who, their lawyers claimed, were the victims of psychiatry, and they invoked the Constitution and the Bill of Rights on their behalf.

Several cases which deal with mentally ill or disabled persons who also face criminal charges have been decided in the past decade by the Supreme Court. Those cases will not be discussed, but one, the most important, deserves comment. *Jackson* v. *Indiana*[5] dealt with the confinement of a deaf-mute with the intelligence of a child. Charged with the crime of handbag snatching and found incompetent to stand trial, the defendant was indefinitely confined. The

---

[2]O'Connor v. Donaldson, 422 U.S. 563 (1975).

[3]Addington v. Texas, 441 U.S. 418 (1979).

[4]Parham v. J. R., 442 U.S. 584 (1979); Bartley v. Kremens, 402 F. Supp. 1039 (E. D. Pa. 1977).

[5]Jackson v. Indiana, 406 U.S. 715 (1972).

Supreme Court rejected such indeterminate confinement, ruling that there must be some reasonable relationship between the purpose for commitment and the length of commitment. In deciding this case, the Court used the occasion to comment on the legal situation of the mentally ill: "The states have traditionally exercised broad power to commit persons found to be mentally ill. The substantive limitations on the exercise of this power and the procedures for involving it vary drastically among the states." After briefly describing these variations, the Court further commented: "Considering the number of persons affected, it is perhaps remarkable that the substantive constitutional limitations on this power have not been more frequently litigated."

Many read these words as suggesting that the Supreme Court was ready and perhaps eager to examine the constitutional implications of confining the mentally ill. More particularly, the Court was willing to consider the criteria justifying involuntary confinement and the safeguards available to patients. In the following years, however, the Supreme Court has consistently avoided the difficult questions it identified in Jackson, and the three cases to be discussed were decided in ways that demonstrate that the U.S. Supreme Court intends to do nothing that would drastically alter the fate of the mentally ill. To evaluate what the Court has and has not done, it is necessary to establish some standard of judgment. Two standards are offered: one, that of a group to be called the civil libertarians, and the other my own. In describing these two standards, it is also hoped to expose the policy considerations that are crucial to any rational reform at the juncture between law and psychiatry.

Consider first the civil libertarian perspective. Historically, the justifications for civil commitment have been based on two overlapping but distinguishable rationales: helping people and protecting society. The first, often referred to as *parens patriae* (the state in the role of parent), allows the state to intervene in the lives of its citizens, to help those who cannot help themselves. The liberals reject this *parens patriae* justification, taking as their rallying cry John Stuart Mill's famous line: "The only purpose for which power can be rightfully exercised over any member of a civilized community against his will is to prevent harm to others." Ironically, in the very next paragraph of his famous essay "On Liberty" Mill wrote: "It is perhaps hardly necessary to say that this doctrine is meant to apply only to human beings in the maturity of their faculties." As the entire essay makes clear, he meant to exclude the insane as a group not in the maturity of their faculties. But in order to exclude the insane they first have to be identified, and this contemporary civil libertarians have claimed psychiatrists are incompetent to do.

In making this claim civil libertarians rely on radical critics of psychiatry: Szasz, "there is no such thing as mental illness"; Rosenhan, "psychiatrists are incompetent to distinguish between those who are and are not insane"; Dershowitz, "psychiatry is too vague to be the basis of any legal decision affecting liberty." This criticism of psychiatric expertise is summed up in the title of a paper written by Bruce Ennis, one of the leading litigating attorneys in this area: "Psychiatry and the Presumption of Expertise: Flipping Coins in the Courtroom."[6] Disenchantment with the performance of psychiatrists in the courtroom has become epidemic among enlightened lawyers and judges. This group includes those like Judge David Bazelon who only ten years ago was enthusiastically welcoming psychiatrists into the courtroom to help solve law's most intractable problems.

The new mood of criticism of the psychiatrist's capacity to identify the mentally ill has made its way into the lower federal court decisions, which increasingly speak about psychiatric incompetence and reject or restrict the *parens patriae* justification for civil commitment. Reviewing those decisions and concurring with them, one federal judge noted that along with his concern about personal freedom "a close second consideration has been that the diagnosis of mental illness leaves too much to subjective choice by less than neutral individuals." If in fact the courts are convinced that psychiatric diagnoses are nothing more than subjective choices by less than neutral observers, then they have no recourse but to abolish all civil commitment. The problem goes deeper than whether mental illness is a suspect classification. If courts, with the help of psychiatric testimony, cannot distinguish even those who are psychotic from the rest of the citizenry, then mental illness is a nonclassification, and the law has no legitimate or rational basis for treating them differently than any other person.

Instead, the constitutional decisions inspired by the civil libertarian perspective have looked to another traditional justification for civil commitment, one that is derived from the police power of the state and allows intervention only to protect society. All important federal decisions have accepted this perspective, at least to some extent, and have emphasized dangerous acts as the important objective standard to be met in civil commitment, while they have deemphasized the unreliable standard of mental illness and the benefits of psychiatric treatment. Although the judicial rhetoric, for example in such sweeping decisions as *Lessard* v. *Schmidt*, echoes libertarian arguments and emphasizes dangerousness to others, some aspect of the *parens patriae* rationale has been retained in every recent decision. All of these decisions and recent legislation have contained language that permits the *parens patriae* confinement of suicidal patients and those who cannot survive outside the hospital.

The result of these developments, however, is to curtail decisively the role of illness, the need for treatment, and the psychiatrist's opinion in involuntary confinement, which must now be based on such objective legal criteria as "did he hit someone?" In addition to these objective standards, civil libertarians have insisted that the alleged patient be provided all procedural

---

[6]Bruce J. Ennis and Thomas R. Litwack, "Psychiatry and the Presumption of Expertise: Flipping Coins in the Courtroom," *California Law Review* 62 (1974): 693.

safeguards that are available to a criminal defendant. The goal of these reforms is to make civil commitment as close to a criminal trial as possible. Although I agree that loss of liberty must be controlled by law and not by psychiatrists, what is the purpose of this loss and is the civil libertarian approach a sensible method for achieving this purpose? I think not, and there are so many problems with this libertarian approach: 1) The vast majority of those with serious mental illness are not dangerous and do not commit dangerous acts. 2) Empirical evidence makes it clear that the vast majority of those who continue to be hospitalized under the libertarian standard are in fact confined because they fit the *parens patriae* justification and not because they are dangerous to others. 3) If society were to confine only those who are dangerous, it would be selecting a spectrum of patients for involuntary hospitalization that psychiatrists have demonstrated no capacity to help. 4) A critical mass of such dangerous and violent people who cannot be treated would destroy the therapeutic milieu of the hospital. They will make it impossible for other patients, including those who voluntarily enter our public mental health facilities, to receive good treatment or even feel safe. 5) There is no empirical evidence or theoretical reason to expect that society will be significantly protected from dangerous persons, which is the only purpose acknowledged by the civil libertarians. 6) Finally, if libertarian reforms were all in place and society confined only dangerous people who have committed no crime and who cannot be treated, we will have created what is nothing more than a system of preventive detention. That would be ironic since preventive detention always has been anathema to civil libertarians.

Nonetheless, this civil libertarian perspective on civil commitment offers criteria by which the Supreme Court's decisions can be evaluated: 1) Will the Court reject or at least downplay the *parens patriae* justification for civil commitment? 2) Will the Court limit the role of the psychiatrist? 3) Will it emphasize dangerous acts rather than the status of mental illness and need for treatment? 4) How far will the Supreme Court go in providing the procedural safeguards of a criminal trial, such as the right to zealous counsel; the right to notice and hearing within forty-eight hours; the right to remain silent when interviewed by a psychiatrist; notice of the charges justifying confinement; notice of the right to a jury trial; the right to cross-examine doctors, relatives, and others who testify against the patient; and proof beyond a reasonable doubt that the patient is mentally ill and has committed a dangerous act? A fifth criterion also needed to be mentioned. The civil libertarians have argued, and the view has prevailed in the lower courts, that to be involuntarily confined as mentally ill is to be stigmatized. Thus, alleged patients must be protected not only from loss of liberty but also from the stigma of psychiatric hospitalization. The libertarian can ask: How seriously does the Court take the problem of stigma?

Turning to my own standards for judging the Court's decisions, I believe that civil commitment and, indeed, every intersection of law and psychiatry has been abused in the United States. My intention is not to justify the past nor to exculpate psychiatry but rather to suggest a new approach. First it must be made clear that the abuses of the past will never be remedied until society remedies the shocking failures of the public facilities designed to care for the mentally ill, the mentally retarded, and the aged. Civil commitment could be abolished tomorrow and the vast majority of the mentally disabled would be no better off. The question, therefore, is can some approach to civil commitment be developed that will provide due process safeguards and guarantee that patients receive good treatment? I think there is, but in direct contradiction to the civil libertarians the only way is by making *parens patriae* the sole justification for involuntary confinement. The great abuses of the past have occurred not because the *parens patriae* approach is inherently wrong but because it was invoked by the state and by psychiatrists when they had neither the capacity nor the will to do what was good for patients. Because many of us are afraid of the mentally ill, society has fallen into the false assumption that most mentally ill persons are dangerous and most dangerous persons are mentally ill. The assumption is false, and a great deal of harm has been caused by embodying this false assumption in the dual justifications of civil commitment, that is, helping people and protecting society. Protecting society is the responsibility of the criminal justice system. Psychiatry has very little to contribute to that effort; it can neither offer scientific predictions about who is dangerous, rehabilitate the vast majority of dangerous people, nor solve the intractable problems of violence in our society.

It is therefore absurd that psychiatric considerations, the medical model, or availability of treatment be the dominant reasons in the disposition of dangerous people. Civil commitment should be stripped of its police power function. If those charged with the responsibility for law enforcement believe that a person is dangerous or has done something dangerous, then that person should be relegated to the criminal process; if such people need psychiatric treatment, it should be provided in the prisons. My approach to civil commitment is predicated on three considerations. First, does the state really know what is good for the mentally ill person? If not, it has no basis for interfering in that person's life. Second, does the state in reality have the resources to do what it knows to be good? If not, it has no basis for interfering in that person's life. Third, even if the state knows what is right and has the capacity to do it, does the person to be coerced lack the capacity, the competence, to make his or her own decisions? Only when these questions can be answered in the affirmative is benevolent coercion by the state morally acceptable.

To implement my approach, there are specific standards that I believe to be more objective than those offered by the civil libertarians and that would provide most of the procedural safeguards demanded by civil libertarians. My system is no less radical; indeed, it may be more radical in the reform it requires. The court would decide five questions:

1) Does the psychiatrist make a convincing diagnosis of severe illness?

2) Is the patient suffering?

3) Is effective treatment available and how long will it take?

4) Is the patient's objection to the proposed treatment irrational and indicative of incompetence?

5) Does the patient or his attorney have any objection to the specifically proposed treatment? If the patient does have an objection, which the court finds tenable, and no alternatives can be found, the patient should not be confined.

These questions could be addressed at a hearing with counsel within a few days of initial confinement. The basic test that this approach asks the court to consider is whether this person, if not mentally ill, would be willing to give up a specified amount of freedom for the treatment being offered. In other words, a patient might be committable to one institution but not to another. In some states it might mean that no one could be civilly committed. Every commitment would be limited to the time agreed upon by the court, and extension would require a new hearing.

The impression received from reading recent decisions affecting the mentally ill and from Justice Fortas's Gault decision,[7] which dealt with the due process rights of juveniles, is that behind the constitutional ratiocination is a painful perception of an appalling reality. These judges recognize that many of our mental hospitals and juvenile facilities are destructive and degrading rather than constructive and rehabilitating. Knowing all this they respond by adding procedural hurdles that make it slightly more difficult for patients and juveniles to be admitted. This makes little sense. If a hospital is incapable of providing adequate treatment, then no one should be admitted no matter how much due process the court gives them. In addition, the only reason for sending a person to a hospital is because he needs treatment, and therefore psychiatric considerations, the medical model, and the availability of treatment are crucial elements in the decision to involuntarily confine.

My approach offers three simple criteria to evaluate the Supreme Court's decisions. First, does the Court accept the *parens patriae* justification for civil commitment? Second, does the Court concern itself with whether the patient needs treatment and the hospital is able to provide it? Third, does the Court recognize that the symptoms of mental illness are what stigmatize and not the diagnostic and treatment efforts of psychiatrists?

With these standards in mind let us consider the Supreme Court cases. The first is *Donaldson* v. *O'Connor*. For fifteen years Kenneth Donaldson was a patient in the Florida State Hospital at Chattahoochee. He was diagnosed as a chronic paranoid. Doctor O'Connor was the superintendent of that institution, which during most of the time Donaldson was a patient had a

---

[7]In re Gault, 387 U.S. 1 (1967).

ratio of one doctor per every one thousand patients. More than a dozen times Donaldson had applied to various state and federal courts for his release from involuntary confinement, and each time the courts had rejected his plea. Finally he turned for assistance to Morton Birnbaum, a physician and a lawyer who is the father of the right to treatment litigation that seeks to improve the quality of care in mental hospitals. Birnbaum initiated a right to treatment suit. Eventually Ennis of the Mental Health Law Project took over the case. During this period O'Connor suffered a coronary and resigned, and the new superintendent discharged Donaldson. Donaldson never had been dangerous, had refused medication, and during the fifteen years of his hospitalization never had received anything I would call treatment. Neither the *parens patriae* nor the police power rationale for civil commitment was justified in his case. He should not have been confined either by my standards or by civil libertarian standards. No doubt the same might be said for most of the patients at that hospital and at most of the large state hospitals in that era. After Donaldson's discharge and with Ennis's legal input the lawsuit took a different direction. It became a 1983 suit for damages under the Civil Rights Act, and O'Connor was to pay for Donaldson's loss of constitutional rights.

It was not clear as the case progressed from the Fifth Circuit to the Supreme Court of what constitutional right O'Connor had wantonly, maliciously, or callously deprived Donaldson. If O'Connor had violated Donaldson's right to be treated, then Donaldson had such a constitutional right and so did every other involuntary patient in the country. That was the thrust of the Fifth Circuit's decision. But the Supreme Court took a much narrower view of the case. It decided that only those patients who were not dangerous to themselves or to others and who could survive outside the hospital and were not getting treatment within the hospital had a right to be discharged. This was a unanimous Court, and it was saying that if Donaldson had been dangerous he had no right to be discharged; if he had been unable to care for himself he had no right to be discharged; and if he were receiving treatment he had no right to be discharged. Only when there is absolutely no possible justification for confinement has a patient the right to be discharged. Lest there be no mistakes about the decision, Justice Burger wrote a concurring opinion in which he scathingly criticized the Fifth Circuit's reasoning in holding that there was a constitutional right to treatment. Although the decision was hailed as a great triumph for civil libertarians, this was only accomplished by misleading and misquoting. In fact, by my criteria or by civil libertarian criteria there was relatively little to applaud in this timid decision. What it amounted to was that the Court challenged none of the standards for involuntary confinement. The one cautious step it took was to set limits on purely custodial care, and this at a time when in most states massive deinstitutionalization of custodial patients was already well under way.

The second case to come before the Supreme Court was *Addington* v. *Texas*. Rumor had it that the Court now regretted the call for constitutional litigation it had set out in *Jackson* v. *Indiana*. *Addington* had been selected because it presented the narrowest possible issue, and there seemed to be substance in these rumors since the Supreme Court had refused to consider a number of cases that posed the civil libertarian issues already described. *Addington* was ridiculous, one of these rare instances where the narrow preoccupations of lawyers really do obscure and hinder rather than clarify and resolve conflicts in human affairs.

Addington had been involuntarily confined after a week-long jury trial in Texas. The length of this trial testifies to the new due process safeguards available to alleged patients. *Ex parte* hearings that took five minutes have become jury trials that take five days. Texas has a particularly convoluted statute on civil commitment, one that is very hard to understand. But *Addington* did not challenge the convoluted statute. The Supreme Court was asked to decide only what the state's burden of proof should be in applying the statute to Addington. Must the state prove beyond a reasonable doubt that Addington meet the statutory requirement, or only by clear and convincing evidence, or by the least difficult criterion by a preponderance of the evidence? In other words, the Supreme Court was going to decide what the standard of proof was to be without deciding what was to be proved.

It was quite clear by listening to the oral arguments in this case that several of the judges, based on their questioning, did not believe psychiatrists could prove anything beyond a reasonable doubt. This supposed incompetence suggests to libertarians that society tighten its legal standards and get rid of psychiatrists, but for the Supreme Court it seems the inadequacy of psychiatry made it necessary to pick not the least but a lesser burden of proof: clear and convincing evidence. This case was a major disappointment to the civil libertarians. Loss of liberty and stigma of hospitalization, they believe, requires the most stringent standard—proof beyond a reasonable doubt, the criminal standard as a safeguard for alleged patients. To the question how far will the Supreme Court go in providing procedural safeguards, the answer *Addington* gave was not very far. The civil libertarians took comfort from the fact that most states already had mandated beyond a reasonable doubt, thus *Addington* would do little harm.

From my perspective the actual decision gave no positive satisfaction, only the feeling that disaster had been avoided. It had been a concern that the Court, by adopting the beyond-the-reasonable-doubt standard, would be telling the states to buy the entire criminal law approach that the civil libertarians were pushing, an approach that ignores the patient's needs. But there was something from which to take comfort. The language and ideas submitted to the Court from the American Psychiatric Association's (APA) amicus brief had made their way into the decision. There was at least dicta, which recognized the *parens patriae* rationale and discussed civil commitment as a medical decision concerning hospital admission. The psychiatrist as persecutor had no role in the decision.

The final decision involves two cases dealing with the admission of minors to mental health facilities: *J. L. & J. R.* v. *Parham* and *Bartley* v. *Kremens*. Adults can be voluntary or involuntary patients. Children, if they meet the state's standards, can be involuntary, but how can a child who does not have the legal capacity to consent be a voluntary patient? The traditional answer has been that the parents or someone standing in *loco parentis* can consent for the child. The plaintiffs in *Parham* and *Kremens* challenged the constitutionality of this practice of substituted consent. The lower court in *Bartley* v. *Kremens* agreed with the plaintiffs and ruled that the child was to be provided a variety of procedural safeguards, including his own lawyer, to contest his admission in a preliminary and then a full hearing. Once again the Court failed even to consider, never mind define, what it was that would be decided at these hearings. The Court cited Rosenhan's "On Being Sane in Insane Places,"[8] talked about the stigma of being labeled mentally ill, commented on the inadequacies of psychiatric diagnoses, and then ordered procedural safeguards without even stating what was to be decided.

The civil libertarians considered the lower court decision a significant victory. First, the Court adopted procedural safeguards; second, it emphasized that this was necessary because of the ambiguity of psychiatric diagnosis and decision making; third, it took the power out of parental and psychiatric hands and placed it in the legal process; fourth, it emphasized the stigma of psychiatric intervention; and, finally, it transformed a totally unregulated and abused practice into one controlled by due process. From my perspective, however, the lower court's ruling was preposterous. It failed to address the reasons that would justify admission to a hospital, thus giving hearing officers and judges absolutely no guidance as to what they were to decide. But most importantly, the crucial issue had once more been ignored. After a child receives all his due process safeguards, is he then allowed to be admitted to a disgraceful facility that has no capacity to properly treat him and that in turn may worsen his condition?

Perhaps the most startling element in the oral argument in *Bartley* v. *Kremens* was Chief Justice Burger's question to the lawyer representing the children: Is too much due process like too much insulin? When the decision was finally published, the civil libertarians had been dealt a serious setback. Although agreeing that some due process was in order in such cases, the majority in effect suggested that all required due process could be met by an independent and periodic review by another psychiatrist on the hospital staff. Furthermore, the chief justice, speaking for the majority, said that judges, after adversarial hearings, are no better at making decisions than medical experts. Then quoting from the APA's brief in the previous *Addington* case, Burger emphasized that stigma arises from the symptoms of mental illness and not from the treatment. Despite Burger's acceptance of this idea and

---

[8]D. L. Rosenham,, "On Being Sane in Insane Places," *Science* 179 (January 1973): 250–58.

despite his resistance to the temptation to scapegoat psychiatry, this was not a good decision by the Court. It gave psychiatrists no guidance. It neither said anything about the treatment needs of children nor about the serious shortcomings of the institutions to which they are being sent in most states throughout this country.

The Supreme Court has failed not only by civil libertarian criteria but also by my own, although by other sets of criteria what the Court has done may in fact be correct. One can sense in Chief Justice Burger's opinions and hear explicitly in his speeches that he believes that the courts cannot solve all human conflicts. He wants the law to stop its seemingly endless expansion into human affairs. His opinions at the juncture between law and psychiatry speak to this effort to limit the compass of law. Although not in agreement with Burger's choice of where to restrict the law, I sympathize with his general sentiment. There is another sense, however, in which what the Supreme Court has done is profoundly correct. The civil libertarians do not have all the answers, nor do psychiatrists. Almost every state is in ferment, changing its laws and learning what happens to patients under new legal and psychiatric approaches. It is my belief that psychiatrists can and will acccommodate to due process constraints, and that civil libertarians and the mental health bar will eventually realize that the needs of patients must be met.

Over the past two decades the mental hospital census has been reduced by more than one-half million patients, and most of that resulted without new laws on civil commitment. During this great period of adjustment and adaptation, it would have been a grave mistake for the Supreme Court to have attempted to give final answers. As it is, those who work at the juncture between law and psychiatry can continue to struggle along, trying to improve on the medieval practices depicted by Bosch's "The Ship of Fools."

Nothing Fails Like a Little Success*

SIMON DINITZ

The liberal-reformist impulse in criminology and corrections institutionalized a century ago in the 1870 Declaration of Principles in Cincinnati by what is now the American Correctional Association, and nourished by the New Penology which surfaced under that glorious title around 1935, is now utterly spent. Intellectually, the reformist impulse was made respectable by the victory of positivism over classicism, by empiricism over speculative philosophy, by the clinical over the legal perspective, by causal ambiguity over legal certainty, and by elevating the actor over his act. On the policy level this liberal-reformist impulse focused, to the exclusion of nearly all else, on humanizing the prisons and jails and on rehabilitating the inmates. To these lofty ends the new penologists, a mixed bag of crusty prison wardens and otherworldly academic types, supported by a cast of moral entrepreneurs, humanists, clergy, concerned laity, and cause-oriented persons of all descriptions, changed the system in big and little ways—from the creation of the juvenile court system and the implementation of probation and parole, to the elimination of mail censorship and the introduction of small amenities into the drab and unstimulating lives of the incarcerated. A full recital of these changes would be long and impressive. The list, in recent years, includes the revision of state penal codes and the medieval conceptions they harbored, bringing legal and due process procedures into the prison milieu, using volunteers in probation and throughout the system, former inmates as agents of reform, the abolition of corporal and, for a few years, capital punishment, and the development of a great variety of ineffective prevention programs. This truncated list hardly does justice to the silent and often unpublicized changes wrought in the last century.

As in any debate or political campaign the incumbent points with pride, the challenger views with alarm. Despite the improvements, any reasonable review might fairly conclude that the correctional systems, both juvenile and adult, are probably in poorer shape today than in the heady period of New Penology, usually dated 1935–50. Giving the reformer the edge, they are

---

*This slightly revised version of Simon Dinitz's "Nothing Fails Like a Little Success" is reprinted from *Criminology* 16, no. 2 (August 1978): 225–38. By permission of the publisher, Sage Publications Inc.

only marginally better. One must ask, however, whether they would be tolerable at all were it not for the New Penology and the quiet but persistent agitation for reform. That the same failure to alter the system systematically prevails in nearly every other aspect of the health, education, and welfare complex is little consolation. Ideas, and the practices that flow from them, are rooted in the material and organizational climate of the times. Such is the present climate that reform, in the traditional sense, has run its course. The question is, "why?"

First, the liberal-reformist impulse was hacked to death by its own modest successes no less than by the upheavals of the civil rights, antiwar, urban, and student revolts that shook American society to its very foundations in the twenty years after the *Brown* v. *Board of Education* decision of the Supreme Court in 1954. For the moment, at least, the evolutionary impulse in criminology, like a spent candle, flickers ever so tenuously. The liberal impulse, to push the flickering candle metaphor, is almost but not quite burned out. Neither the radical rhetoric, devoid of solid scholarship, nor the neoclassical resurgence, an exercise in sterile syllogisms, has or will destroy it, although both flanks of this movement have already achieved noteworthy and necessary changes. Critical criminology has again called attention to the systemic rather than individual nature of our problems; neoclassicism to the need for redress of the social defense-offender treatment balance. The radical view surfaced, quite obviously, in response to the inequities of a social system that produces some winners and all too many losers; neoclassicism resurfaced as a response to this radical challenge and to the increasingly justifiable paranoia about crime in the streets committed by these socially processed losers.

Second, the liberal-reformist impulse was a response to the technological revolution that destroyed the old social order—the "cake of custom" so cherished by Sumner, the *Gemeinschaft* of Tonnies, and the social integration of Durkheim. This reformist impulse flowered as masses of rootless and uprooted people, immigrants and migrants, seeking to reconstruct their lives, descended on our cities and towns. When private philanthropy proved inadequate, to say nothing of being patronizing, the preconditions existed for the institutionalization of this reformist ideal in education, in health, in employment, and in criminal justice.

Third, dissatisfaction with the prevailing social order received yet another jolt—the ascendancy of Freudian, neo-Freudian, and pseudo-Freudian doctrines as the explanatory framework for the massive personal disorganization and pathology during much of this century. Overlooking, for the moment at least, the cool reception accorded Freudian dogma for several decades after the introduction of psychoanalysis to a stunned and unbelieving medical profession, this psychoanalytic perspective, coupled with the decay of traditional social institutions, may be said to constitute the basis of the rehabilitation and reform ethic.

Fourth, the postindustrial society gave rise to our quasi-welfare state—the Swedenization of America—incorporating just about every element of Norman Thomas's Socialist platform planks via the New, Fair, Square, and other Deals and Frontiers except, of course, for public ownership of the means and fruits of production. The social welfare tradition is now deeply embedded in American life. The Fabian views have been translated into conventional policies and practices and, more to the point, into the conventional wisdom of the social and policy scientist. In corrections I can think of no recommendation in the 1870 Declaration of Principles that is not now in place. Such is the fickle nature of the health, education, and welfare industry in this country (and HEW is one of the largest of our enterprises) that many of the glories attained by the liberal-reformist tradition—indeterminate sentences, educational, psychological, and classification services, various elaborations of psychotherapeutic intervention, the special handling of juveniles—are now under fire; some, like the parole system, are in the process of being dismantled in favor of mandatory sentences. Yesterday's humaneness is today's patronization of the defenseless. The historic fight for the right to treatment has become today's struggle for the right to be left alone. Yesteryear's belief in rehabilitation has been thoroughly undercut by the reintroduction of the three horsemen of penal history—punishment, deterrence, and incapacitation.

In short, the string has run out on the reformist position. Ameliorative efforts have alleviated some of the grosser inequities of the criminal justice system. Piecemeal efforts at reform have been just that—successful in minor ways. Most correctional reformers, like most old New Dealers, are older and possibly wiser. They are also more pessimistic, discouraged, and disenchanted by their failure to create a more just, fair, and humane system. The questions now are not whether we fight the new death penalty laws in the states in which they have been enacted, replace the megaprisons, whether we abolish parole, and how we recruit, train, and pay for better staff. These are still open questions, to be sure, but all seem unimportant to that gallant and exhausted band of aging dreamers. The central issue now has little to do with nostrums and panaceas. The current concern is whether the criminal justice system is to function as the ultimate repository for the social misfits and the déclassé whose labor and existence are redundant in our postindustrial world. If it is to be the ultimate warehouse, then no amount of conjugal visiting, work, educational and home furloughs, fixed net sentences, lowered age of adulthood (16, 14), or other reforms in the prison or in the subsystems of law enforcement, prosecution, and courts will promote the return of such superfluous persons to the mainstream of American life.

As an academic and a reformer with bona fide credentials for swimming against the current, I think the time has come to give up on our earlier claims and face the ultimate temporal reality: unless drastic alterations occur in postmodern society, the health, welfare, and educational sectors will fail to reform, to educate, and to provide the decent health services that many Western

European societies seem so much better able to furnish. The dilemma is this: either we lower our expectations and accept social inequality, stratification, and deprivation in our social system, or we recast present society radically and dramatically. The neoclassicists argue the inevitability of the former, the critical criminologists the latter. Neither group knows its history any too well. Both extremes will soon depart the scene, much like other historical oddities. In the meantime, a frustrated and fearful public looks to its experts for guidance—experts too honest, too committed, or too discouraged to offer all but the most prosaic recommendations for reshaping the prison and the system of which it is so much a part. Improving the lot of inmates is no small matter, of course. But the many recommendations for reform are not going to alter fundamentally a system that has a dearth of options.

THE FALL AND RISE OF THEORIES

In the absence of a verified body of knowledge, criminology has consisted of one etiological and correctional bandwagon after another. Most such theories, chiefly the organic, have mercifully departed the scene quietly after a rapid rise and slow burnout. I refer, by way of illustration, to the Dugdale and Goddard abominations stemming from their respective work on the Jukes and Kallikaks: the rise and fall of the EEG fad that produced so many tracings and so little substance; and, most recently, to the tumult and great expectations arising from the discovery of the XYY chromosome and, in a different context, of methadone treatment. Indeed, this faddism may be traced back to the phrenologists, the constitutional inferiority writers, the earlier "juicers" or hormonal researchers, the Lange, Rosanoff heredity as destiny European school, the Glueck type of eclectics, and the various brands of determinists and free willers.

One principle defies refutation in the history of criminological thought. This principle is that any perspective, no matter how outlandish, tends to surface over and over again in the guise and terminology appropriate to its temporal resurrection. Thus, sociobiology is back in the person of Edward O. Wilson. The earlier "juicers" are back; the Pavlovians now parade under the banner of behavior modifiers, and the bell that produced salivation in the dog is now called the reinforcer. The dysgenic and drift theories have been repackaged by Jensen, Shockley, Herrnstein, and their colleagues as well as by highly respected researchers such as Mednick, Kallmann, Christiansen, and others. An in-depth review of this cyclicity of ideas dressed in the newest verbal fashions has been explored by Ysabel Rennie.[1] But Rennie is by no

---

[1]Ysabel Rennie, *The Search for Criminal Man* (Boston: Heath, 1978).

means the first to document the ebb and flow of theories in criminology and, more importantly, their incorporation in penal law and correctional policy.

A second outstanding characteristic of the criminological enterprise is the propensity for modern scholars to forego hard scholarly work in order to assume leadership roles in the intoxicating world of social and ideological movements. Such has too often occurred to the detriment of the scholars and the field. In only a few historical periods was it considered inappropriate for intellectual types to get involved in sociopolitical movements. In these periods scholarly productivity frequently blossomed, in stark contrast to the present when the media consume ideas like prisons consume people.

THE AMERICAN CONTRIBUTION

The Chicago school, the first authentic American view, was a derivation of the Social Gospel movement among white, small town, Protestant reformers responding to the hordes of immigrants and to the accelerating process of urbanization. The Chicagoans wanted to return to the *Gemeinschaft* of the small midwestern or New England communities from which they came. Origins aside, Albion Small, Lester Ward, W. I. Thomas, E. A. Ross, Robert Park, Ernest Burgess, Walter Reckless, E. L. Faris, and many others paved the way for the emergence of nearly all non-Marxist sociological perspectives. Drawing on a variety of European social-political theorists—Weber, Durkheim, Spencer, Tarde—the Chicago school evolved a perspective which, above all, focused on a consensus and integration as the "normal" state of social organization and within this cohesive context, a limited amount of deviant behavior as necessary and functional to the social system.

The Chicagoans' emphasis on cohesion found in these unassimilated millions the naive human resources for Zangwill's unfulfilled and probably unfulfillable dream of the "melting pot," for universal public education, for the emergence of the juvenile court. The Chicagoans pushed social welfare beyond Hull House and the Educational Alliance. They rejected the old country rigidities of class and clan. They placed their bets on social mobility and meritocracy as the basis for progress and the amelioration of social problems. Above all, the Chicago view was optimistic. There were ends to be achieved, problems to be solved, progress to be made. Technology, according to Ogburn, was the genie. It would create an unimagined range of problems (and in this he was surely correct). But this same genie also would provide the solutions. The time discrepancy between the appearance of the technical blockbuster and its containment was dubbed "culture lag"—a concept which, unfortunately, is now out of vogue.

The Chicago school came to focus on social disorganization as the key element in deviance. By social disorganization Shaw and the rest meant the breakdown of the consensual norms and standards: norms had lost their holding power in the ethnic and national ghettos of the largest American cities. This process of the attenuation of earlier norms proved to be the basis for differential association and differential identification, as Sutherland and Glaser were to argue.

Meanwhile, Sellin was dealing with much the same problem of normative disintegration in his justly famous statement on culture conflict and its significance for crime. This position is nowhere more definitively observed than on the current Israeli scene where clashes of religious, cultural, western-nonwestern, modern-traditional groups are not only replicating but also recapitulating the American experience of the period 1890–1940. As in the United States, far from assimilating this diversity and creating a new man, these conflicts threaten the internal fabric of Israeli life.

In sum, the American ethos and cultural universals emphasized optimism, modernism, progress, and consensus. American criminology drank deeply of this intoxicating brew. Conflict only afflicted the old world with its silly national, religious, and ethnic antagonisms. There was nothing inherent in society that a lot of goodwill and a pinch of technical know-how could not set aright.

Similarly, the American ethos rejected the cold-blooded rationality of utilitarianism. Ours was, after all, a compassionate society. An examination of the early textbooks in sociology demonstrates convincingly a preoccupation not with class and ideology but with such social problems as alcoholism, crime, poverty, racial injustice, mental retardation, and prostitution. In short, dependent, disruptive, and deviant people were the problems. Major institutional change was neither necessary nor warranted. This was substantially true in all areas—from the legal and economic to the family and educational institutions. The system was assumed to be fair, but no system is perfect; crime, mental illness, and chronic drunkenness are, after all, perfectly normal no matter what the social organization is like. The prescription: leave the system alone and treat the personal pathologies. Rehabilitate, educate, provide insight. Above all, make it possible for the lowliest and most humble of men and women to climb to the top or, at least, to rise.

In practice, the reformers did improve the facilities and care given the three d's—the dependent, disruptive, and delinquent, if only very modestly. Dix, Beers, and Deutsch took on the mental hospitals; the Wickersham Commission took on crime; Gompers, Hillman, Mitchell, and Lewis the appalling conditions of labor; the Anti-Saloon League, Demon Rum; the Child Savers, the deplorable treatment of delinquent, neglected, and abused children; the police, the courts, and the Federal Bureau of Narcotics, the alleged drug problem. Under the New Deal, alphabet agencies proliferated. The coalition put together by the New Dealers consisted of the underprivileged, populists, academics, ethnics, urban (blue-collar) workers, and some farmers. It survived long enough to move the United States into the age of the quasi-welfare state, a direction that no one has been able to reverse. Indeed, the tension between the warfare and welfare state merely slowed the movement toward the latter. One need not be a prophet to predict national employment, income, health, and housing standards to replace the present chaos in these areas. If nothing else, the accelerating fiscal bankruptcy of our major cities and counties may push federalization of services as different as education and criminal justice. Revenue sharing, contrary to its stated goals, may be the forerunner of various federalization policies. The liberal impulse, spent in criminology-corrections, is still very much a factor in the formulation of policies in other social areas.

Certain events become benchmarks in human affairs. Often these events are so "silent" that their significance becomes evident only in historical perspective. Such an event was the closing of the American frontier in or about 1890. If Frederick Jackson Turner is to be believed, this closing profoundly and irreversibly altered the American dream. It dampened the unbridled optimism of the times, circumscribed future growth, changed migration patterns, and eventually forced the sovereign states to become the sovereign nation. Greeley's prescription, "go west, young man," is now answered by the former governor of Oregon who said, in essence, "stay home, young man."

With all due respect to Turner's thesis, an even more notable landmark in the American experience was the successful structural and, to a lesser degree, interpersonal assimilation of the millions of immigrants who were admitted, if not warmly welcomed, to this country. By the end of World War II the etiology of deviant, disruptive, and dependent conduct could no longer be attributed to social pathology, social disorganization, and culture conflict—shorthand concepts for the acculturation experience and consequences. A profound shift had again occurred in the lay and professional construction of social reality.

It became evident, though usually unsaid, that many of the unassimilated had become the unassimilable. No amount of social intervention could or would melt the "unmeltable" millions in our midst. Behaviorally, and in contradiction to our long-professed and much-admired ethos, a two-tiered social system took shape. Warner and then Hollingshead began to look at the constituent elements of social class; Hunter initiated the search for community elites; Mills for the power elite. The dam had burst, the unthinkable became speakable.

The realization of the existence and persistence of a semipermanent underclass of losers with its own ethic, values, goals, and expectations startled the social science community and fragmented it politically. Old "brain trusters" like Moley, Lawrence, and Sokolsky spread the word in their syndicated columns. Respected political sociologists like Lipset, Nisbet, and the *Commentary* circle of Kristol, Podhoretz ("Your Problem and Mine"), Nathan Glaser,

Moynihan, and peripheral figures like Himmelfarb agitated the intellectual community. The most recent flap was the turnabout of James Coleman on the effects of busing.

A historian might date the origin of the unmeltable assumption to a most influential book—Whyte's *Street Corner Society*. In discussing the divergent paths taken by the street corner and college groups, Whyte became the forerunner of some of the subcultural and limited opportunity themes later pursued by Cohen, Cloward and Ohlin, Wolfgang and Ferracuti, and Liebow. As Walter Miller elaborated, the underclass has internalized a coherent set of values—trouble, toughness, smartness, expressive goals—conducive to deviant conduct. For Miller it is not position discontent or limited opportunity, though both are real, but rather the lifestyle of segments of the underclass that makes street crimes a virtual underclass monopoly.

This more or less permanent underclass, by implication and by whatever empirical research has been mustered, is different from the previous sets of underclass groups in two respects: first, it is different qualitatively, and second, the social system seems indisposed to develop new methods to permit the upward circulation of this underclass. On the first account, the new underclass consists of the socioeconomic failures, some four generations deep now, of previous rural migrations to the city. Included, too, are the remnants of earlier immigrant groups. To these must be added the personally disorganized—alcoholics, drug addicts, and the ambulatory mentally ill. The socially created and processed unmeltables consist of the ghetto blacks and Hispanics and, in some parts of the country, the native Americans. This more or less permanent underclass has no voice and no effective vote. This makes them prime targets for political exploitation. More and more isolated in central cities, cut off from community life by inner belts and by the provincialism inherent in their status, the line between class and caste is fading. Few of the poverty and welfare programs have actually touched this sizable underclass. Nothing on the horizon is likely to be more effective.

On the second count, reformers premised their activities on some variation of the Protestant ethic. They assumed an inherent and universal desire for self-improvement. The will was there, the tools lacking. Provide the tools and upward social mobility must and will follow. Current disillusionment with reform, I contend, is related to the shift in the nature of the values ascribed to the underclass. If one rejects upward social mobility as an unattainable goal and is preoccupied with "getting by," the prescriptions of the reformers seem odd indeed. Education and vocational training offer little to people who already have failed repeatedly in our schools. One can afford the luxury of the latest therapeutic games like primal screams when other needs have been met. Even behavior modification, through either positive reinforcement or aversive conditioning, works more poorly with the underclass group. In short, our individually oriented rehabilitation programs do not and cannot reach the caste-like underclass.

Even more depressing to reformers has been the collapse of consensus on what constitutes a desirable and normative lifestyle. Sinful and immoral conduct gave way to abnormal, pathological, aberrant, criminal, and disorganized behavior in the 1930s, which became deviant in the 1950s and merely variant in the late 1960s and 1970s. Our tolerance has markedly increased for variant lifestyles, however outlandish. We accept as normal that which we only recently abhorred as sinful. We are fearful of being perceived as square and straight—the new outsiders of our time. We can now conclude with Erasmus that when everything is possible nothing is true. If so, what and who stands in need of rehabilitation? Lynd once asked, in a most provocative volume, "education for whom?" The penal reformers face the same problem: "rehabilitation for what?" Many have unfortunately concluded that little or no special education is required to remain a loser, a never-will-be, a permanent outsider with a variant lifestyle. I submit that more than any other development the American acceptance and even celebration of deviance has mortally undercut the zeal of our reformers. How can they expect conformity to ambiguous norms when their own children are frequently part of the increasingly variant family arrangements and unusual sex patterns that are so contrary to our moral legacy? Presently only zealots can be certain of the rectitude of their ways. In a world of competing norms and life patterns, who has the temerity to proclaim the truth—to define, let alone implement, the people-changing ideal?

The failure of rehabilitation has been trumpeted by Lipton, Martinson, and Wilks. Martinson's comment that "nothing works" is a succinct, if unpleasant and overstated, conclusion. Parallel pessimism applies to compensatory and related education programs and to conventional programs dealing with alcoholics and addicts. Other examples abound in all areas of counseling and therapy. The solution, however, is not in polemical Marxist prescriptions or a return to eighteenth-century verities.

For the reform impulse to make a difference once again will require fundamental attention to the needs of the lower-class unmeltables. Those of us who have melted successfully are incapable of understanding the focal concerns of those who have not and cannot do likewise. The programs must be elaborated by the losers. The classic reformer—prosperous, educated, informed, well-meaning—is an anachronism. The world has passed him by. He himself is likely to be anything but a straight. At the very least he is probably unconventional and is as troubled by his "problems of living" as those he seeks to reform.

In summary, I have argued three points:

1) The liberal-reformist movement in corrections has succeeded in implementing most of its ideas and programs. The impulse is spent and most of the reformers are sadly disillusioned that their schemes have created no utopia.

2) The characteristics of the at-risk populations, especially the under-class, are markedly different now than in the past when the Protestant ethic and the inevitability of progress were perceived as being American monopolies. Indeed, the cores of the largest and even some of the middle-sized cities are becoming huge reservations for blacks and other déclassé groups, including the aged and handicapped. If it is true, and I believe Miller is generally correct in his assessment of the differential values of the social classes, then the nature of our problem is qualitatively different than that in the past. We have a new and largely transplanted underclass of unmeltables. We also have an overabundance of self-proclaimed outsiders who refuse to accept many of the conventional standards as personally binding.

3) The approaches with which we felt comfortable in the past—self-improvement, social reintegration, psychological intervention—are con-sequently futile avenues for major reform. Unless and until we develop new conceptions, penal reformers are likely to continue to support recommenda-tions for change that are superficial and largely cosmetic.

Index